For
Jack O'Leary

from one "square"
to another

Esther Milner
1995
_____

The FAILURE
of SUCCESS

The FAILURE
of SUCCESS

The Middle-Class Crisis

(Second Edition)

By

Esther Milner, Ph.D.
*Associate Professor, Brooklyn College
of the City University of New York*

WARREN H. GREEN, INC.
St. Louis, Missouri U.S.A.

Published and Distributed by
WARREN H. GREEN, INC.
10 South Brentwood Blvd.
St. Louis, Missouri 63105, U.S.A.

© 1968 by ESTHER MILNER.

Library of Congress Catalog Card No. 67-27951

Printed in the United States of America
2-A

*to the survival of parenting
as craft and commitment*

Preface to the Second Edition

DURING THE PAST HALF-DECADE, Americans have been discovering that the "silent 50s" were not nearly as protest-free as they seemed at the time to be. Rather, from the point of view of the publishing establishment, editors and reviewers alike, they were the "prudent 50s": better not to incur suspicion by publishing—or reviewing—fundamentally critical analyses of American society. The original edition of *The Failure of Success*, with the sub-title *The American Crisis in Values*, was one of the casualties of the prudent 50s. The circumstances of its writing and publication might well provide an illustrative commentary on that period: the manuscript was begun in the Fall of 1954, essentially completed in early 1956—but not published until late 1959; and, although read by many opinion-leaders, it did not reach the larger, college-student and college-graduate, audience it was addressed to.

The focus of literary and sociological interest has since shifted to the "younger generation"—that is, to those born after 1940; on what grounds can one justify re-publication of a book which centers on the generation born before circa-1935?

The Failure of Success, The Middle-Class Crisis, is being re-published at this time in somewhat revised and updated form because it continues on two scores to be intensely topical. First, it is in at least three ways even more individually and socially relevant than it was in 1955:

> It centers on the age-group—35-40 to 60-65—which includes the present "command generation," otherwise known as the American Establishment.

> The varied patterns of behavior of the younger generation are much more understandable when viewed in light of their parents' values and reactions.

> Probably the quiet-majority of today's college and post-college young people are, despite the mass media cum literary preoccupation with the non-conforming minority, *acting on*—if not quite as fully accepting—*their parents' value-systems and aspirations*.

The Failure of Success continues to be relevant for another, ultimately more important, historical-sociological reason, a reason summarized by Alexander Kendrick (in a personal communication dated Jan. 27, 1967) as follows:

> ". . I wouldn't like to see any up-dating done at the expense of a more fundamental approach, such as you have shown in your book. The questions you raise are still the basic ones, though the varieties of experience which give rise to them have increased. . . For despite all the motion of the past decade, 1967 is still only a phase, just as 1957 was, in what seems to have become a 'permanent' transition period. I think it is the period, rather than the phase, that is the more significant."

Most of the changes in this edition comprise: updating of and additions to the illustrative examples cited, additional references to the younger generation in pertinent contexts, occasional direct reactions to earlier-edition statements, extension of references to psychological and sociological data and concepts. Chapters 4, 6, 9-13, 16 and 17 contain the greatest amounts of additional material. The stance of devil's advocate continues to be deliberately adopted for purposes of clarity; yet it should be noted that qualifying terms have been more carefully chosen and more judiciously used than may be apparent to the casual or over-hasty reader.

As before, this book is explicitly addressed to that—now substantially larger—group of middle-class " 'independents' who are not sure why they are dissatisfied, nor what they should do about it, but who have had sufficient inner stamina to keep up a kind of positive groping in the face of persistent discouragement."

ESTHER MILNER

Preface to the First Edition

THIS SMALL BOOK is addressed to an as yet small but potentially large and influential group in the American middle class. These are the people of all ages who are dissatisfied with the pattern of their lives and with accepted group values, but who have given themselves over neither to the absolutism of scapegoating nor the absolutism of one foreordained, clear-cut path to personal and social "salvation." They constitute a core of emotionally and intellectually uncommitted "independents" who are not sure why they are dissatisfied, nor what they should do about it, but who have had sufficient inner stamina to keep up a kind of positive groping in the face of persistent discouragement.

The discussion to follow is an attempt to analyze the nature and the sources of the dilemma into which the American middle classes have allowed themselves to be maneuvered. The thinking in this discussion makes use of principles and findings accepted by many students of human behavior and society. Yet it should be made explicit at the outset that this analysis is based on the values and the theoretical orientation of *one* such student. It frequently represents a projection beyond what is as yet sociologically or psychologically established and accepted.

This analysis is offered in the belief that to recognize the nature and the dimensions of a problem is the first and essential step towards its positive and constructive solution, personally and socially difficult as this first step may be.

ESTHER MILNER

Acknowledgment

THE QUOTATION in the footnote on page 107 is reprinted from *The Prophet* by Kahlil Gibran, by permission of Alfred A. Knopf, Inc. Copyright 1923 by Kahlil Gibran. Renewal copyright 1951, by Administrators C.T.A. of Kahlil Gibran Estate, and Mary G. Gibran.

Contents

The FAILURE
of SUCCESS

We need to characterize American society of the mid-twentieth century in more psychological terms, for now the problems that concern us must border on the psychiatric. It is one great task of social studies today to describe the larger economic and political situation in terms of its meaning for the inner life and the external career of the individual, and in doing this to *take into account how the individual often becomes falsely conscious and blinded.*

C. WRIGHT MILLS
From the introduction to *White Collar*

PART I

The Touchstone Fallacy
of Our Time

Chapter One

Ourselves: Means or Ends?

At a time when the "pursuit of happiness" has, for most Americans, come to supersede every other of our inalienable rights in personal meaning and priority, we of the American middle classes have come to share a common view of the most effective means of attaining happiness. We have dedicated ourselves to the proposition that the achievement of high occupational and consumer status will convert us into happy, psychologically whole human beings. I call this implicit belief of ours the touchstone fallacy of our time.

The basic theme of this discussion is that our subscription to this fallacy has made a major contribution to the two developments most typical of our times—the increasing abridgment of our inalienable rights as *human* beings, and the growth of social immorality and personal disorganization in our society. It is more than time that we of the American middle classes examine the genesis and the consequences of this belief of ours in the psychological magic of success.[1]

Perhaps the major characteristic of urban middle-class living today is the degree to which we of this population group have lost control over the course of our individual lives and of the collective social life. We have also lost much of that confidence in ourselves and in our destiny which for so long has been our trade-mark as a nation. Explanations of the current state of the individual, social and political *malaise* in which we find ourselves typically takes two forms. Either they blame forces beyond our direct and conscious control, whether these forces are seen as economic or social or unconscious-psychological

---

[1] These paragraphs were also the opening statement of the original version of *The Failure of Success*. It is expressly acknowledged that a steadily increasing number of Americans have become and are becoming aware since 1955, when these words were written, both of the social immorality cum individual devaluation and disorganization of our time *and* of the fallaciousness of the touchstone fallacy. But those who realize that there is a dynamic relationship *between* these two sets of phenomena are still few enough to warrant the retention of the original opening statement in unmodified form.

in nature. Or, from the opposite extreme, critics maintain that we *as individuals* are directly and entirely responsible for our troubles, and that only a widespread "moral re-awakening" in each and every one of us can bring us back to a "state of blessedness."

The former kinds of explanation are comforting because they absolve us of direct responsibility for what is going on in our lives and in the world around us. The most frequently proposed of such explanations is that various economic and technological developments have led to the disruption of an earlier state of social equilibrium, but we have not yet reached the new balance which is presently in process of crystallizing. We are living, in short, in a time of cultural transition, and such transition-points in human society are inevitably marked by an abnormal degree of social and individual disorganization. Corollary explanations stress similarly overriding influences on individual reaction, such as economic trends towards bigger organizational units and greater mechanization of work functions, or the inexorcisable presence of deeply irrational, unconscious psychological forces within the "human animal." The latter type of explanation is intended to— and usually does—arouse our ever-ready guilt-feelings.

In my judgment, neither order of explanation is adequate. The answer is at once more complex than the second and more ascribable to ourselves than the first. I believe that the individual adult is more aware of what is happening to him, and has more control over his own behavior, than the first explanation allows for. We are "acted on" by society from the moment we are born, true, but more of us are able as self-aware adults to "act back" constructively on that society than is acknowledged by any of the "uncontrollable forces" explanations. We of the middle classes make up a major and potentially powerful segment of American society. Rather than taking an active hand in the shaping of our new destiny which is willy-nilly emerging, we have been sitting passively by as political and social beings—in marked contrast with our hyperactivity as economic and recreational beings.

The second type of explanation is a diversionary oversimplification. It chooses to overlook that most of us are *obliged* to be in some way immoral in order to survive in our highly competitive society. It is primarily we ourselves whom we must blame for our current difficulties, yes; but for these two reasons—we have not had enough respect for our own humanity and individuality; and as a group we have defaulted on a number of important social responsibilities, among them the active development of new political, social, economic, and legal forms and practices which the major economic and social changes of particularly the last few decades have made unavoidable.

There is a real irony here. From what is known about American reading habits, it is not the majority in the middle class, to whom the "we" of this analysis is intended to apply, who will read this discussion. It is, rather, a minority who have *already* begun to question the beliefs and living patterns of the majority, who are most likely to do so!

We are to blame because, first, we have not maintained the same high regard for our worth as human beings that the founders of our country expressed so clearly in the preamble to our Constitution. We have lost our conviction that we as growing human beings must be the ultimate value and the ultimate goal of the collective social life. Citizens of all nations which are highly industrialized *or aspire to be* must make this conviction an even more dominant principle of their social and economic life than the golden rule. Indeed, without this belief as a prerequisite to the golden rule, today's perversion of it becomes possible: "Deny thy neighbor as thou deniest thyself."

We Americans particularly, who are strongly committed to large, hierarchical units of economic organization and to the increasing use of labor-saving machines, are in real danger of subverting our constantly emergent humanity—or divinity, as it is also termed—to ends which serve to limit or deprive us of our inherent capacity for humanity and uniqueness. Our belief that human progress is *equivalent* to a combination of ever-increasing technological efficiency and the wider distribution of that technology's consumer-goods products, along with our belief that this definition of progress is the essence of Americanism, together show how thoroughly we have confused means with ends. These beliefs are a major factor in the slow-down, even a reversal, of our social, psychological and moral progress.

The meanings we have come to ascribe to the idea of "freedom" also shows our displacement of emphasis. Originally a political concept in the broadest sense of the term "political," we currently define it in practice in a solely economic sense. Which of two economic definitions of freedom we espouse varies in accordance with that level of the economic hierarchy with which we identify. Freedom for those at the lower end of this hierarchy has come to mean freedom either from want or from economic instability. Freedom at the top of the hierarchy, and for those of us in the middle who identify with this small group, has come to mean freedom from economic regulations and restrictions. All levels consider that our government's only really valid function is to enforce one or the other of these limited, self-interested versions of freedom—versions which are, not at all incidentally, functionally in direct conflict, from the overall-social point of view.

I find it the towering irony of our times that the hostility of the two major antagonists on the world scene originates in their mutual commitment to the same philosophic fallacy, the doctrine of "economic man." Both the United States and the Union of Soviet Socialist Republics espouse social ideals of the highest order, but *in practice,* the leaders and the people of both countries believe that the economic aspects of man's life are not merely of primary but of ultimate importance. Our disagreement lies essentially in our insistence that our own economic system is the better pathway to the goal—but the goal is essentially the same:

> On both sides it is asserted that the only, or at any rate the main, objective of nations should be industrial prosperity. This is implied in the dogma of economic materialism, which forms the basis of both these systems, ostensibly opposed as they are. And as these theories merely reflect the state of public sentiment, industry, which was formerly regarded as one means to a higher end, has become the supreme end for individuals as well as for whole societies. (17)

Although the writer of these words was speaking of what at his time were two economic theories only, his words have proved more prophetic than he could have realized. Émile Durkheim wrote these words in the 1890s, twenty-five years before the formation of the U.S.S.R., and over seventy years before our current international stalemate.[2]

Both the U.S. and Soviet Russia are faced, or are about to be faced, with the same paradox. *How can it be that beliefs which originally captured the imagination and the allegiance of men precisely because of their promise for human emancipation and growth, eventually lead instead to the curtailment, even the denial, of man's present and potential humanity?*

This kind of paradox seems to be a recurrent theme in the history of human institutions and political systems. The earlier role of the

---

[2] The addition of Communist China to this equation has not been overlooked. This analysis cannot be generalized to include the present, first revolutionary generation there; but if and when, as occurred in Russia, successors of the original revolutionary leaders emerge and are able to maintain and consolidate the revolution, similar generalizations will apply. By then, if convergences between the U.S. and the U.S.S.R. continue at their current rate, these two once-at-odds colossi will have to be *grouped together* in comparisons with the Peoples' Republic of China.

Holy Roman Church and its later, Middle Ages, role seem to me to constitute another such paradox. I think the reason for such a cycle is this: ideas and practices that originally won men's allegiance and dedicated effort *because of their promise as a means to the higher end of man's increasing humanity*, became in the course of time and events dissociated from their purpose; became, instead, ends in themselves. When men forget that *any* formula for human advancement, idealized as it has come to be, *is* no more than a means, that it has value only as it relates to its avowed end, men unknowingly institute the psychological conditions for their enslavement, inwardly and politically.

A major result of our commitment to the economic aspects of living as all-important has been a shift in our generalized bases for judging individual worth. In pioneer days (and still in some isolated, sparsely populated, "backward" sections of our country), the bases for judgment were more or less unanimous and were largely centered in the individual—his personality characteristics, values, and socially constructive (or destructive) behaviors. In today's complex, stratified, urban society, the judger's own position in the social or economic scale strongly influences his bases for judging others' worth; and, particularly for the middle class, external, economically based symbols of status have come to play the major role in such judgments.

In smaller urban communities in longer-settled parts of our country, such external bases for judgment are important, but do not entirely supersede the individual himself as a behaving and valuing being. Some of the factors which affect one resident's judgment of a fellow-resident's social status are closely related to income level, such as: the part of town in which the person resides, the kind of house (and grounds) in which he lives, whether he owns or rents it, his amount of education. But more subtle factors also enter in, such as: the church attended, the public and private recreational patterns, the public social behavior, taste in home furnishings, the length of time the individual's family has been resident in the community, the social clique associated with publicly and privately—in short, the individual's social behavior patterns and associations and a whole system of value-attitudes were the final arbiters of social status in pre-Depression Yankee City (69) and post-Depression Jonesville (70). According to standards of judgment employed by middle-class residents of these two small cities, two families with the same yearly income could be placed as much as two full classes apart on the social scale evolved from the data obtained from community informants.

A description of the salient characteristics of the *middle four* of the six social classes derived by W. Lloyd Warner from such smaller-community data (71) reveals the intermingling of economic and individual factors as bases for social status judgment and forms a useful source for later references to these social status groups.

> *Upper-lower (UL):* Income through wages which are sometimes sporadic; employed in the semi-skilled trades, service and low-paid clerical jobs; money is seen as something to be handled carefully; live in marginal areas, but some attempt made at house or apartment maintenance; some formal associations; a high-school education at the most; church allegiance usually close; respect for and attempt to imitate the social patterns and value-attitudes of the next higher class. Often the determining factor affecting which of the two lower classes an individual is placed in hinges on whether or not he strives for middle-class values and behavior and displays "social responsibility." The "respectable working class." (Approximately 35 percent of the population.)

> *Lower-middle (LM):* Regular income from wages, salary, small business; training in skilled trades or lower-paid professions; money is a symbol of status, and actively striven for; live in small, well-kept houses or apartments in clean but monotonous areas; close church allegiance; acceptance of and active following of the external social patterns of the next higher class—"keeping up with the Joneses"—is the dominant value of the socially mobile of this class. (Approximately 35 per cent of the population.)

> *Upper-middle (UM):* High income from salary or fees or large business; trained in the more highly educated professions and managerial positions; live in choice residential areas; houses or apartments large and well kept; self-conscious of their personal reputations, status in and value to the community; extensive formal associations of the help-your-community type; represent to the community the virtues of hard work, private property, high morality and self-discipline; aspirations towards the "cultured life." (Approximately 10 per cent of the population.)

> *Lower-upper (LU):* Level and source of income, as well as value attitudes, similar to the class below, but private property and dividends are also a major source of income; family has resided in the community for at least two generations; large and palatial homes in landscaped grounds; community participation on the charity-board and fund-donation level; sponsors of the cultural activities in the community; highly exclusive association patterns; the "new aristocracy." (Approximately 1½ per cent of the population.)

Indeed, this class-structure—and the differing psychological worlds associated with its various status-levels—are so characteristic of the

American way of life, they have taken precedence over other, more traditional, allegiances such as ethnic and religious and racial identifications. The few religious-sect exceptions to this situation, such as the monolithically orthodox Chassidic Jews for whom the European ghetto-community tradition continues to have more positive than negative associations, are now so few, they tend to "prove" this generalization. For the immigrant-European (and Puerto Rican) "ethnic" and the emigrant-southern Negro alike, to become "assimilated" has meant to become a *middle-class* American. So strong is this identification, those second and third generation ethnics and Negroes who have become middle-class through upward mobility, dissociate themselves, usually with strongly negative feelings, from their fellow-ethnics who are still unassimilated-lower-class, especially *lower* lower-class.[3]

This "reference-group" aspect of middle-class status is by no means limited only to those of recent-ethnic background. Research studies indicate that were a sheerly *subjective* index of social status to be the criterion (e.g., "What social class do you belong to?"), as many as 85% or more of the population of the United States would have to be ranked in the "middle-class"!

Among the large-urban middle classes, however, there has been an almost total shift in the bases for judging the worth of individuals, particularly as applied within the middle class and above. The physical and social conditions of big-city living have led to two distinct categories of social relationships for the individual—his "outer circle" of

---

[3] Neither the "Negro revolt" nor its current leadership disarray can be understood without taking into account the fundamental role of the "social class factor." Civil-rights leaders are almost all middle class. There may be differences among them as to means but not in their basic goals, which are, in essence: (1) full middle-class American social privileges to those Afro-Americans (sic!) who already conform to middle-class occupational and educational and behavioral guide-lines; (2) truly equal opportunity with whites for upward mobility *into* the middle class for those of lower-than-middle-class status. The more thoughtful and altruistic of these leaders have decidedly mixed feelings about the interjection of the commonality of color as a uniting ploy, for very good reason: they are aware that its short-term, group-limited usefulness—the promotion of self-respect and of political awareness, especially among poor Negroes—may work against the longer-term and broader-social interests of this very group, which require political coalition with similarly deprived poor whites for their realization. Governmental "anti-poverty" programs and the vividly TV-transmitted riot-cry of "black power" have been serving to strengthen the already formidable anti-Negro prejudices of economically insecure white persons: they are bitterly resentful of what they consider to be *preferential* treatment of the "shiftless" Negro.

impersonal, casual and, frequently, competitive interpersonal contacts; and his "inner circle" of personally meaningful relationships. This situation, converging with the middle class's commitment as a group to the material aspects of existence as ends rather than as means, has led to our use of immediately discernible factors external to the individual as our basis for judging the worth of persons we meet in our outer circle of social contacts. Where the possibility of developing a more intimate, inner-circle type of relationship is involved, this initial judgment is employed as a screening device.

These external-to-the-individual factors are nearly all economically based, and the ones we tend to place most emphasis on are usually a function of what we ourselves would like to have more of—prestige of occupation (judged more by its money-making reputation and "glamor" than by its usefulness to society),[4] dress, address, speech, general physical appearance, number and monetary cost of possessions, values and taste as a consumer, self-confidence of bearing

---

[4] Although consumer power is basic in judgments of the prestige of an occupation throughout the large-urban social scale, I would say there are additional factors involved in this judgment, which vary from status level to status level. For example, the lower-middle group values consumer power plus an aura of respectability (*i.e.*, professional status); the upper-middle group values consumer power united with concrete evidences of social distance; the "upper" groups take consumer power for granted and stress a combination of social distance and power in the hierarchical sense. Also, in such long and congestedly populated megalopi as New York City, two sub-divisions of the middle class are insufficient to account for the variety of ways of middle-class life. My current guess, based on a fair amount of informal grass-roots observation, is that each of Warner's divisions should be further subdivided into "old" and "new"—i.e., into "old upper-middle" and "new upper-middle," "old lower-middle" and "new lower-middle," *four* middle-class groupings in all. The criteria for "old" and "new" are summarized in this chart:

Index	*Old*	*New*
Parental background:	Parents (especially mother) were born into a middle-class home.	Parents (especially mother) were born into a working-class or lower lower-class home.
Family atmosphere from the child's perspective:	Stable; ethnic tradition seen as positive.	Unstable; much parental "status insecurity."
Child-rearing values and practices:	Directed by long-term goals: (viz. Miller and Swanson's "entrepeneurial" family) (43).	"Other-directed:" (viz. Miller and Swanson's "welfare-bureaucratic" family).

and manner. The last-named has become so closely associated with economic affluence, many a confidence man and petty pretender uses a self-confident "front" as his sole, and usually effective, "stock in trade." Conversely, an unassuming person, lacking other obvious compensatory symbols, is taken to be of little account.

This urban shift to judging personal worth on the basis of symbols external to the individual has resulted in a sharp split between our nationally espoused yardstick and our actual one. Two of our country's enshrined principles are that the individual must be valued and respected *as an end in himself* ("that they are endowed by their Creator with certain inalienable rights"), and that it is the obligation of organized society to help the individual fulfill himself as an individual. Yet, except in intimate friendship groups where we all see ourselves as on much the same status level, we virtually ignore as having primary social value the many other roles, potentialities, capacities, abilities, sensitivities, which make up that highly complex entity, the human individual.

This narrow, externalized basis for judging others'—and our own —worth is contributing directly to a number of serious symptoms of individual dislocation which are as yet relatively localized in very large cities, but which have begun to spread throughout the country:

> individual unhappiness to the point of psychological difficulties among middle-class men and women;
>
> certain patterns of "parental delinquency," acknowledged as the most potent factor contributing to children's emotional difficulties and juvenile delinquency;
>
> the virtual elimination of self-expressive, creative individualism of the kind that made us what we are as a nation and *in the name of which* we continue to cling to beliefs and practices that are serving to destroy it.[5]

These three trends indicate that probably most of us in the middle class have been led by our own values to deny to ourselves the possibility of realizing our unique humanity and individuality, of achieving inner freedom, of attaining happiness. In effect, *we ourselves have discarded the inalienable rights as human beings "guaranteed" us by our Constitution.*

I have just implied that economic and social trends can have major psychological effects on adult individuals—a proposition which many

---

[5] The continuing effectiveness of the national "gun lobby" is an example of the successful exploitation of these beliefs.

behavioral scientists and psychiatrists would dispute. When I claim such a relationship, I am making two assumptions: 1. Social trends and events external to the adult can affect him at deep enough personality levels to prompt psychological distortion, under the following condition—that psychological vulnerability to these particular events is *already* present in the individual, to the extent that they constitute an ego crisis for him. 2. The inner personality functioning of a number of individuals may be sufficiently alike to lead to their reacting similarly in the face of externally common events—to lead, that is, to *group trends in reaction.* Studies on the role of the individual's social environment in his development and on the nature of social class in our society allow me to assume that there are similarities of "inner dynamics" along social-status lines.

These assumptions need to be made explicit because they seem to contradict the fundamental psychiatric principle that the causes of each person's (and each family's) inner difficulties can be discovered only through extensive examination of each individual's unique background of experience. This principle is derived from the circumstance that every individual reacts to his particular cumulative-social-world highly selectively, partly because of his unique constitutional endowments and functioning, and partly because of the unique ways of perceiving, organizing and reacting to his experience that he has built up since birth (this latter, highly individual, process psychologists term "personality").

Am I, in stressing group trends in reaction, ignoring the "individual dimension"? Not at all. Rather, it is a matter of *study perspective* which is involved. So long as the odd personality distortion of a certain type occurs in isolated fashion, we cannot legitimately consider it to be of more than specialized clinical interest. Or if "parental delinquency" were an isolated phenomenon, it would not be valid to speak of it in terms of a definable trend. But when such varied sources as mental health and crime statistics; basic-research studies; case reports of psychologists, psychiatrists, social workers, and court authorities; newspaper reports, popular literature, songs, movies, radio and T.V. programs analyzed as projections of the individual dimension, all combine to reveal that many persons and families are experiencing similar difficulties, *group trends* are showing up. As such, *they acquire general social significance.* Explanations solely in terms of individual neuroses and anxieties or individual-parent delinquency, as if these people existed in a social vacuum, become inadequate under these circumstances.

The extent to which the raising of the following questions has validity is the extent to which our own beliefs have led us to become means rather than ends in today's America.

Do we exist for the greater glory of gadgets and more gadgets, or are gadgets made for our advancement as human beings?

Do we have social value only as consumers towards the end of advancing business and industry, or does business have value to the extent that it contributes to our advancement as growing human beings? (*It may well be that we Americans must learn to ask this question just as surely as citizens of totalitarian states must learn to ask, "Were we made for the State or the State for us?"*)

Are human beings intended to advance the ends of applied science and technology, or does technology exist to advance the ends of our increasing humanity?

Should human beings be expected to adjust to whatever physical and social living and working conditions are available to them, or should our living-working environment be designed to meet the human needs of children, adolescents, mothers and fathers, families, adult men and women, older people?

Should the creativity of our more gifted people be fostered selectively for the advancement of purposes determined by special interests and immediate demands, or should their creativity, as our most precious national resource, be fostered without predetermination and used to promote the greatest long-term good to the greatest number?

In a complex, interdependent society, can the tremendous educative influence of the mass media be considered any less a public responsibility than the public school system?

Why have we of the American middle classes come to have so little regard for our own worth as human and unique beings?

It is the core thesis of this book that our subscription to the touchstone fallacy—the belief that we shall somehow become happy, psychologically whole beings when we have achieved high occupational and consumer status—has played a key role in this development. This cherished delusion of ours has initiated a number of individual and social chain reactions which have led us into this impasse.

Chapter Two

Rome Wasn't Necessarily the Last

THERE IS AN ADDITIONAL REASON for our loss of control over our lives beyond the circumstance that we lack regard for ourselves as worth-while individuals. We ourselves are to blame for our loss of control over our individual and collective life because, second, we have not faced up to the social, political and personal implications of the fundamental economic, technological and social changes which have occurred in our national life, particularly during the last few decades.

Economically, we have shifted from a highly individualistic, free-enterprise pattern to a highly interdependent, corporate pattern. Technologically, we have shifted from emphasis on the development and application of skill on the part of the individual worker, through a period of stress on his skill in operating a single machine or function in an assembly-line framework, to current emphasis on the development of more and more skilled machines that are gradually eliminating not only the "semi-skilled" worker category, but also increasingly more of the non-professional "skilled" worker group. In our living patterns, we have changed from a nation of farm and small-town dwellers to a nation of urbanites and suburbanites. As these changes have occurred, there has been a sharp increase in the specialization and diversification of economic and social functions in our society: not too long ago, typical rural families fed, clothed, educated and entertained themselves; in today's urbanized living, every one of these functions is performed by an army of specialists and must be paid for by the individual wage earner—the family head. A trend to larger and larger, hierarchical units of economic and bureaucratic organization has accompanied these several changes.

But these shifts in the external world have not been accompanied by a corresponding change in our internal picture of social and political reality. We persist in obsolete conceptions of "the good citizen," "the moral person," "the good parent"— and, consequently, in obsolete practices of these fundamental responsibilities. We continue to cling to the old primary spheres of social responsibility—family, employer, occupational group—when the times require an additional, far broader exercise of citizenship, parental and economic functioning. We are not to any real degree:

actively exercising the heavy political responsibility which devolves upon the individual in a complex, self-governing society (the "creative citizen" function);

directly and indirectly helping, not just our own children, but the entire next generation grow up psychologically as well as physically healthy (the "universal parent" function);

assuming moral responsibility for the social effects of our economic and occupational actions.

We have, in sum, lost our sense of "community."

In a simple society where the major functional groups are few and relatively self-sufficient—which was true of our society not too many years ago—a lack of responsibility of one group toward other groups, and towards government as representing organized society, was undesirable, but not necessarily dangerous. But today, when we neglect to practice broader social responsibilities at the very time when increasing occupational and social specialization has made such widespread practice particularly essential, we of the middle classes are contributing directly to the disruption of the two types of reciprocal social relationships which are necessary for the harmonious functioning of any society—those between the individual and his society, and those between the various specialized parts of society. This tattering of the web of mutual social obligations is the key characteristic of the disorganization of our times.

Each specialized part of our society has become so isolated in its special function that it is no longer able to understand, respect, appreciate and accommodate to the other parts' essential social functions. As a result, inter-communication has become negligible, mutual hostilities have developed, and group self-interest first has become the ruling principle. The mass media provide countless examples of the more obvious consequences of this lack of communication and accommodation. On one and the same day in late-January, 1967, it was possible to read in a mass-circulation magazine an article which described in full and consciously humorous detail the gastronomic hazards of a Caribbean luxury cruise during which ten meals a day were served, *and* to hear radio reports describing the strong measures taken by Chicago police against the looting which had erupted in slum-areas in the wake of a paralyzing snow-storm—measures so stringent as to result in the death of at least one young lawbreaker. Perhaps an even more striking example occurred some years back when *Time* magazine featured the president of General Motors as "Man of the Year" the same year that driving fatalities climbed to 38,500.

Instead of accepting the responsibility of making us aware that—and why—this social divisiveness is occurring, our schools and colleges and mass communications media are merely *mirroring* the social fragmentation of our times—and in so doing, are serving not only to reinforce it but to compound and extend it.

Yet people must develop and maintain for themselves a coherent, consistent and personally meaningful picture of the world in order to keep functioning psychologically: how have we—and the members of other complex, technological, rapidly changing societies—been able to do this in the face of so much fragmentation of our daily life experience and so many contradictions in the real world?

We have been able to do this through the development and use of the art of "word-magic" to a degree of refinement beyond any past period of world history.

"Word-magic" is a term I've adopted to stand for two quite different, yet related, contemporary practices. It is used at this point in the sense of a reversal of the process through which each of us, as we grow up, learns (or should learn) to relate adaptively to reality and, in adulthood, to the exigencies of daily living. The psychologically healthy person's words, ideas, meanings, world-picture, show a great deal of correspondence with objective reality, since he typically takes situations and events which occur in the real world into account in his formation of such meanings. The reverse of this process occurs when a person starts from a prefabricated, artificial picture of reality, a picture which has anxiety-reducing and inner-needs-satisfying value —but which is related only incidentally to the real world—and habitually twists external reality to conform to this *a priori*, wish-fulfilling picture through the use of verbal clichés and pat, unchallenge-able formulas. The latter person is not only practicing word-magic on himself, *he is highly susceptible to others' practice of the art on him.*

Certain of our political and social attitudes and practices constitute concrete examples of this definition of word-magic—attitudes and practices which have become much too expensive luxuries for even our wasteful and wealthy country to continue to maintain.

We have a strong tendency to confuse our social ideals, particularly as they are expressed in our sacred national documents, with the ways each of us actually believes and behaves from day to day. Our eagerness to believe that the exception is the rule contributes materially to this confusion. This widespread tendency to assume that our daily personal, social, economic practices are identical with our espoused ideals has led to the further tendency to believe a person is attacking either these documents or the "American way of life" when he has occasion to point objectively to some discrepancy between our national ideals and *the things we actually do.* Both these tendencies combine to make intelligent, objective and constructive discussion of social problems on a wide scale well-nigh impossible.

The practice of our society's leaders and schoolteachers to confuse *what ought to be* or what we wish were so with *what actually is,* has contributed to much confusion, disillusionment and cynicism among our teen-agers, especially among teen-agers of ethnic and social-status groups whom we tacitly discriminate against socially or economically.

Also, we have a tendency to react to certain widely used words much as children react to the threat of a "bogey-man" or the promise of Santa Claus' coming. The "bad word" or the "good word" needs only to be mentioned, and our capacity for rational thought and analysis evaporates. We even become suspicious of the speaker or the writer who uses these words in ways other than those we have come to expect. Take such a currently bad phrase as "social planning:" anything said about it that is not negative or condemning makes most of us conclude that the speaker must be as "bad" and "subversive" as the phrase itself. Or if a writer makes an attempt to analyze objectively such "good" words as "free enterprise" or "enlightened self-interest," he is obviously attacking the sacred idea for which the word stands. Still worse, he is attacking our very selves, because some part of our very vulnerable egos has become attached to this "good" word. By this stage of high-pressure indoctrination, many Americans no longer realize that the indispensable core of the concept of democracy is representative *self*-government, not a "free-enterprise" economic system, nor even a political system of checks and balances.

Our tendency to personalize words and ideas also shows up in our reactions to other nations. When we adopt certain policies, or our representatives say certain things, these policies and these statements are automatically "right" for no other reason than that *our* nation has done them or said them. But when another nation, particularly one which we perceive as hostile to us, does and says exactly the same kind of thing from *their* point of view, what they have done and said is "unprincipled," or "aggressive," or even "aimed at destroying the free way of life."

When such immature thinking is widespread among our population, it becomes easy for anyone who wishes to manipulate us to apply the technique which Hitler used so effectively in the past, which Soviet Russia and Communist China use so frequently with their peoples, and which demagogues on both the "left" and the "right" in our own country have used and still use so freely. Such a person selects the very ideas and means which, if explored, modified and adopted, *might* heal many of our own and our country's ills. He labels these ideas and means as threats to such an emotion-arousing concept as "our sacred national ideals and honor"—and keeps repeating the charge, usually aided and abetted by other sympathetic persons and media. Eventually, the bulk of we the people are led to form a strong emotional bias against the very medicines which might cure our many real afflictions—and the possibility of a rational approach to, analysis of, attempts to solve, urgent social problems recedes into the day before yesterday.

Nor can it be any consolation that citizens of other nations react on as childishly irrational a level to our actions as we do to theirs. Quite the contrary: it is just these childish ways of thinking which adults everywhere must outgrow in the age of the hydrogen bomb. What is most discouraging is that the great educational potential of the various mass media, here and in other countries, is almost uniformly used in the opposite direction: these media do not merely cater to the irrational child in people; most of them actively, and very often deliberately, *foster* such reactions in their citizens. After all, so far as *we* are concerned, such practices do sell more newspapers and sponsors' products, do they not? And, particularly for totalitarian countries, they do keep the publisher or broadcaster in the good graces of his political superiors, do they not?

Our picture of the role of government in our lives is another luxury too expensive for our nation to continue to maintain. It reveals our collective inability to move past a situation which occurred almost two centuries ago. We tend to conceive of the implementing or executive aspects of government as something *inherently* arbitrary, vindictive, destructive of the rights of individuals—and therefore as something to be resented, resisted, rebelled against, "got around," much as some adolescents react to their parents. Government may have had these characteristics at the time of George III, but our departments and agencies of government today—local, state, national—are the means *we* have developed as the instruments for carrying out our collective will. And if they are not as efficient servants, nor as incorruptible and considerate of individual rights as we feel they should be, we have—or should have!—both the power and the means to make them more so.

We do not need psychological evidence concerning the wide range of individual differences of every type in the population to know that some persons are uninformed and socially irresponsible all of the time, that some are so most of the time, that some are so some of the time, and that some are so very seldom. Yet we persist in electing representatives whose political actions seem governed by the unshakable belief that their constituents *en masse* are, by some magical transmutation, dead right all the time. Personal principles and integrity, the courage to maintain them under attack, assumption of responsibility for the enlightenment of the uninformed and irresponsible—all are characteristics of responsible leadership that we consider essential in our leaders only rarely. As for the currently emerging, generally more principled, younger generation of political representatives, they frequently, albeit unintentionally, represent a special section of their constituency. They were/are elected primarily because their own— or their (grand)parental family's—self-made success-story provides a reassuring symbol of the continuing validity of their own aspirations to those of their constituents who actually vote.[1]

There is another series of examples which illustrates our institutionalized recourse to word-magic. These relate to the circumstance that we have become a highly militarized nation, but are unable to accept the national and international implications of this fact. We continue to inveigh against the evils of socialism, yet we use public tax monies to subsidize missile research and production, to maintain our armed forces establishment, and to provide an endless list of social services to veterans of previous wars. We continue to consider ourselves as a moral and principled nation, particularly when compared with godless Soviet Russia, yet it is the fixed policy of *both* our major political parties to pour a large share of our nation's economic and human resources into the development and production of weapons of partial and total destruction—at the same time that national subsidies for research into ways of identifying, slowing down and resolving world-wide pressures contributing to the likelihood of war are non-

---

[1] Such limited representativeness *and* the reasons therefor are also applicable to the elected leadership of most professional groups which are national in scope.

existent. And under which of our country's moral principles shall the rest of the world subsume our current/recent exercise in the use of international power politics?

The release and discussion of information documenting the physical and psychological unreadiness of American soldiers for the war in Korea—and especially for the rigors of captivity—at the time prompted widespread criticism of our methods of child-rearing and of our schools. But so far as I am aware, none of the critics pointed to the anachronism of war itself in the mid-twentieth century and to the inherent contradiction between the kind of child-rearing and education which prepares a man for democratic living and the kind of child-rearing and education which fits a man for organized killing and war-conditions survival.

The economic and social changes which have occurred in our national life are realities no Congressional committee fiat can erase. We of the American middle classes are forever deploring the trend towards an increasing centralization of the planning and governing functions in private pressure groups over which we have no direct control and in national agencies over which we still have some control. So long as we ignore the reality of marked economic and social changes and their implications for our social and political and personal life, we surrender to others *by our own default* the functions of planning and governing.

When the bulk of our population was self-employed on the land or in small business, one man's vote could be assumed with some validity to be equal to every other man's vote. Under such circumstances, widespread exercise of the franchise was enough to ensure the reality of self-government and free political debate. But in a time when fewer than one-fifth of the population controls the livelihood of more than four-fifths of us, and one per cent of employers hire forty-eight per cent of workers (46), mere exercise of the franchise can no longer be considered an adequate discharge of the political and social responsibilities of citizens of a nation which desires not only to remain self-governing, but to retain the "inalienable rights" of the individual.

When we, as the major segment of our society, play a passive rather than active role during this difficult period of transition, we are prolonging it unnecessarily. We are also, by our very inaction, contributing directly to the emergence of a political balance that may represent—may have already represented!—the end of our free society. Ironically enough, while we exercise ourselves over the dangers to our society from without, our own inertia as political and social beings is serving to subvert the American way of life far more effectively than any external threat or internal conspiracy.

Both our inertia in this area and our contrasting hyperactivity as consumers, occupational opportunists and psychological escapists stem, I believe, from an underlying psychological constellation which is widespread particularly among the large-urban middle classes. A major factor in the genesis of this psychological constellation—to be described in Chapter 5—is our continuing subscription to two beliefs which no longer have a foundation in reality. The touchstone fallacy— that high occupational and consumer status will somehow transform us into happy, "whole" beings—is the first of these beliefs. The other is the success myth that a sociologist labeled the "American Dream" some time ago: anyone can succeed if only he tries hard enough. We are so sure of the Dream's promise, we are convinced that if a man *doesn't* succeed after trying and trying, there must be something very wrong with him. Both those who succeed and those who fail tend to react to failure as a personal sin, and therefore as a strictly individual matter. In so believing and so reacting, we are rendered incapable of objective appraisal of the external factors which have entered into our failure (as well as into our success), and as a result, we fail to recognize not only that we are one of many with the same problem, but that *there are common reasons for our common problem.* Our assumption of personal guilt serves to render us incapable of taking intelligent group action in our own behalf.

Most of us subscribe so strongly to the Fallacy and the Dream that these two beliefs can be considered the American middle class's "axioms of life." Yet these two beliefs, developed during and relatively appropriate to an earlier period of our history, no longer have a realistic base because of irrevocably changed social and economic conditions. Persistence of values and practices rendered inappropriate and even socially dangerous by changed economic, social, physical conditions, have in the past led to the decline and fall of once powerful societies—and may be leading to that of ours. Here is reason enough for examination of the touchstone fallacy and its effects.

Chapter Three

The Touchstone Fallacy of Our Time

THE TOUCHSTONE FALLACY exemplifies a carry-over of the most primitive kind of thinking into our own time. The line of progression is a direct one—from the savage who believed a wax image of him *was* himself and succumbed slowly to the pins stuck into the wax doll's heart; to the Middle Ages "scientist" who searched for the Philosopher's Stone so that, at its touch, base metals would be transmuted to gold; to us modern Americans, who believe that some simply spelled out, easily followed formula, such as the acquisition of some particular set of possessions, or achievement of a certain occupational status, or carefully regular attendance at church, or the reading of a particular book—or the most recent, new-generation recipe, the imbibing of LSD—will automatically and *painlessly* transform us into adequate, psychologically whole beings.

The kind of primitive thinking which the touchstone fallacy represents is typical of, and thoroughly normal for, young children, because of their more limited stage of mental development and life experience. But it is by no means confined to children and primitive peoples. Our entire advertising industry could not exist in its present form were it not for this childishness or primitiveness in us: our belief in a material touchstone renders us as manipulable by our modern "hexers" as were and are our most primitive counterparts by theirs. It leads us to the acquisition of the "consumer drug habit": having been made psychologically vulnerable to material possessions by inadequate parental responsive-nurturance during infancy and early childhood, we are led, in an economy committed to the principle of constant expansion, into a compulsive need for more and more of the latest gadgets and items of conspicuous consumption.

A one-time president of one of our major radio and TV networks showed thorough familiarity with this compulsion of ours when he said that the advertising pressures of our time are well justified socially, for this reason: consumer goods provide the incentives that keep us working harder than do workers in other countries, where the variety and quantity of consumer goods is not as great as ours (72). This gentleman has since been replaced in his position by other reasonable facsimiles, but it is doubtful whether there has been any change in the advertising industry's self-justifying philosophy which he so candidly spoke for. The deliberate manipulation of people through their infantile irrationalities and vulnerabilities has evidently become a basic instrument of national business policy.

From the teen-ager, whose touchstone (lacking better examples from his elders) is the wearing of certain clothes in a certain way or driving a sports car or frequenting the "right" cultural activities or smoking "pot," to the hard-working middle-class adult, whose touchstone is acquisition of a certain job status plus a certain type of home in a certain suburb or "exurb" plus a certain group of friends, the fallacy is the same—that with our performance of some relatively simple, external-to-ourselves ritual/incantation, our anxieties, self-hatred, guilt feelings, and loneliness will evaporate, and in their place will come a capacity to feel deeply, positively, and in tune with all the world! We've developed gadgets that have given us everything else we've ever consciously wanted or been induced to want: *why not a gadget that can take the place of the tremendously difficult, deeply experienced, frequently painful and uncomforming, life-long process of self-emergence, self-discovery, self-development?*

But let me not be, perhaps, misunderstood. I am *not* saying that there is anything *inherently* wrong in any of the activities or possessions I have enumerated or might have enumerated. What I am saying is that when their doing or their acquisition are considered supreme values *in themselves,* we have an example of the operation of the type of thinking that I call "the touchstone fallacy."

This tendency of all men everywhere to do substitutive thinking is one of the roots of the touchstone fallacy. Another of its roots is more particular; it is embedded in the rich soil of our nation's history.

The concept of the inalienable rights of every human being developed out of the reaction of the American Revolution's leaders against the Old World's system of allocating rights and privileges according to birth and prestige. In the New World, everyone was to have the right to live on a human level, to personal freedom, and to the opportunity to pursue happiness—for no other reason than that he was a human being. Man was to be an end in himself!

This concept remains the American *ideal.* But a number of developments have considerably narrowed this ideal in practice. The individual's right to the "pursuit of happiness," appreciated to be a highly complex and emergent goal by its cultivated originators, came to be equated early in our history with his right to amass as much money, property and personal prestige as he was able to gather through his own efforts. And it became the American Dream that *anyone* can "get ahead," if only he tries hard enough.

But the spell of this Dream was as powerful as it was in early America not for the obvious material rewards it promised. Religious doctrine of the time implied that attainment of material success was *concrete evidence* of God's special blessing for hard work, virtue and self-denial (73) — a belief admirably adapted to the rigors of pioneering, incidentally. But cause and effect came to be somehow reversed: success in itself came to be seen as the touchstone which would transform its possessors into happy beings, full of "God's grace." *Like the child's vision of Christmas, it was the psychological rewards implied in the Dream which made its spell so potent.*

Advancing industrialization and our advertising industry have combined to make the equation still more simple for most Americans: after two generations of steadily intensifying advertising-copy indoctrination, we have come to see "progress" and "the good life" and "happiness" as *automatically* coincident with the development and the acquisition of purchasable commodities and services—in today's terms, the latest gadgets, personal services, commercial recreation, a "tastefully" designed and furnished home, the conspicuous consumption of leisure.[1] Indeed, it is only when *this* version of the pursuit of happiness shows any sign of being abridged from any source that we become vocal politically: our remaining inalienable rights do not seem to have remotely comparable personal meaning to us.

Probably this narrowed interpretation of our inalienable rights came about precisely because this nation was born in revolt against a social system that parceled out prestige and worldly goods according to birth. We tend to overlook that it drew to its shores not only those persecuted for their political and religious beliefs, but also successive waves of immigrants who were primarily representative of the groups in their Old World homelands with "lesser privilege." To these underprivileged groups, a lack of political rights was far less driving

---

[1] The unremitting brainwashing which undergirds our economic way of life has proved so effective, many of our "privileged" young people have not abandoned the kind of thinking which makes the touchstone fallacy possible. Rather, on finding that their parents' touchstone is meaningless for them, they have turned to an even more instant and magical touchstone: the so-called "mind-expanding" drugs.

a factor in their emigration than their hunger and their cold. The possibility of earning, owning and spending, with no restriction except their own industry, encompassed their wildest dreams of happiness. Their background made them ripe for the kind of thinking represented by the touchstone fallacy—thinking that substitutes the symbol for a thing or a means to a goal for the thing or the goal *itself*.

The belief that possessions and economic status are equivalent to happiness, and the belief that both are attainable through hard work and thrift (and later, education, also), together resulted in that pattern of economic striving so typical of the upward-mobile first-generation American ethnic family and the already-middle-class small entrepreneur. Ownership of property and an independent business were the old avenues to secure and expanding middle-class status. So long as the population was relatively sparse, and economic, natural resources and geographic frontiers remained relatively open and available, enough strivers achieved enough success *in their own lifetimes* to sustain the potency of the Dream—and therefore to establish and to vindicate an economic system of free enterprise.

These earlier generations of self-made men, whose values still dominate American life, overlooked an important distinction. It was not the possessions and status they achieved, usually just before they died, that brought them satisfaction. It was, rather, their accomplishment of life-long personal goals of deep psychological importance to them.

But the frontiers have been closing at the same time that our population has been expanding. As these changes have occurred, two parallel occupational trends have also developed. First, more and more people, proportionally, have come not only to work for others rather than for themselves, but for progressively fewer and fewer others—which means that some small, individual businesses became big, and that big businesses are getting steadily bigger.

C. Wright Mills has estimated the proportion of total employed who were self-employed in the early 1800s to have been four-fifths, in 1870 one-third, in 1940 one-fifth. He further estimated that many of the "other-employed" four-fifths earn their livings by working for the two or three percent who as of 1940 owned forty or fifty per cent of the private property in the United States. "Among these workers are members of the new middle class, white collar people on salary" (as opposed to the old middle class, the small property, including the small-business owners) (46). More recently, Miller has analyzed trends in self-employed vs. salaried among those in the top five per cent in income in the United States (44, pp. 129-131), and shows a marked acceleration towards "other-employment" among this leadership group since 1940; viz:

Self-employed: in 1950, 42%; in 1960, 26%.
Salaried: in 1950, 28%; in 1960, 48%.

The most marked decrease in the self-employed category during this period was among small-business owners: from twenty-three to thirteen per cent; the most marked increase in the salaried category was among managers: from eighteen to thirty per cent. Except for some of our newer immigrant groups and those American Negroes who acquire a skill or go on beyond high school, actual opportunity for upward occupational and status mobility has decreased with each generation. For those *already* in the middle class, horizontal mobility to different occupations at much the same status levels has become more typical (60).

But second, and in seeming contradiction, there has at the same time been a general upgrading of the occupational hierarchy and a flattening and broadening in its middle regions, along with general income upgrading and a somewhat broader distribution of the national wealth. This second trend, among a people who have come to define freedom in exclusively consumer/economic terms, has tended to obscure effectively the personal, social *and* political implications of the trend towards "other-employment." Apparently the spell of a comfortable physical standard of living is as Lethe-like today as it was in the time of the Hebrew prophets.

Even this second trend is turning out to be a transitory, short-lived state of affairs. The rapid spread of the second industrial/technological revolution of automation and cybernation is presaging a major modification in the occupational pyramid: in addition to the few owners of these sophisticated machines, there will be a small, over-worked group of professional, managerial and technical workers at the top, a medium-sized group of service workers underneath them, and a large mass of machine-displaced, permanently unemployed persons forming the base.

For the great majority in the middle class, the promise of the Dream is no longer being fulfilled: success in the old sense is being attained by proportionately fewer and fewer of us. And for those who do succeed, to do so necessitates the output of more and more effort. Yet we continue as a group to dream the old Dream and to believe in the magically transforming powers of its attainment. The proportional numbers striving for success have, if anything, increased. For those strivers already in the middle class, higher social status is as important as higher income—at a time when high-status occupations are almost the only relatively sure means for such upward mobility. The status problem confronting us as individuals depends on whether we are in the lower reaches of the middle class trying to reach the higher, or whether we have already accomplished that jump. If we are in the former, much larger group, we find that entry into high-status occupations is dependent either on spending long years in formal or informal preparation, or in finding favor in the eyes of a complex supervisory hierarchy—or, increasingly frequently, both. If we are in the latter, much more "select" group, we must maintain the occupational status we have won with so much effort, in the face of constant, unremitting competition from our peers and of pressure from below.

In either case, our success is dependent less on factors within our control than on factors outside our control—economic trends, the labor market, admission to the "right" college, getting "a break." Contrary to the (significantly) popular song of a while back, it takes a lot more than "heart" to "open any door" (1).

The conflict between our aspirations and the difficulty we have in realizing them has had a major psychological result for us as individuals. The economic aspects of our life have become psychologically most crucial to us: most of us in the middle class are thoroughly ego-involved in our occupational and consumer status. Particularly for the middle-class male, *the stakes to be won through his striving have become very high. The stakes have become his very self-respect,* his right to look himself, his family, his relatives and neighbors in the eye, his ability to keep on living with himself with any degree of inner comfort, even the privilege of seeing himself as adequately masculine. Our feelings of self-worth are dependent upon our reaching goals external to ourselves and largely outside of our immediate control—a highly precarious inner state of affairs. Small wonder that we are uninterested in activities and responsibilities which we do not see as directly related to our status struggle—or which do not give us some surcease from the constant high tension within us and around us.

It is not so much "civilization" which is the cause of our tensions, a statement frequently made in connection with the higher and earlier incidence of heart disease in the United States. It is far more the personal effects of our continuing to cling to values and beliefs which have become divorced from reality.

In order to demonstrate how characteristically middle class is our tendency towards ego-involvement in our economic roles, let me sketch in the effects of our culture's material emphases on other-than-middle-class population groups. It is a traditional blind spot of middle-class Americans to believe that America and middle-class values and way of life are synonymous—a blind-spot that severely limits communication among the various population groups and causes both ourselves and our numerous non-middle-class neighbors no end of difficulty in many facets of community and national functioning. One of the more serious results of this state of affairs is exemplified in a frequent occurrence in our urban public school systems: the nice, young, over-protected middle-class teacher is affected with sometimes traumatic intensity when she assumes that her slum-reared charges have a background of values and experiences similar to her own, and tries to get them to absorb her middle-class version of public education.

Members of the "slum culture," usually economically sub-marginal, typically aspire to an immediate minimum of physical sustenance and consumer capacity. Here are the deprived in every area of living except in that privilege so over-romanticized by us inhibited middle-class persons—the privilege of free, spontaneous and direct emotional expression. Here are the perpetual children of our society who are easily and constantly overstimulated by the material displays of our shops and advertising media and who do not have the "built-in" defenses against direct expression of their aggressive feelings that the middle-class person does.[2]

The hard-working, respectable "little blue collar" and service groups with marginal earnings and economic security typically settle for the immediate practical goal of gaining sure guarantees of economic security for themselves; but their goals for their children frequently coincide with those of middle-class parents. From this group, particularly those of minority-group background who identify strongly with the middle-class, has been and will be coming our white-collar people of the future, including the majority of our schoolteachers, who will continue to pass on the Dream *and* the Fallacy to our nation's children.

---

[2] The "violent summer" of 1967 provides a concrete example of this generalization. When we of the middle class get so angry we're afraid we'll lose control, or when we get so frustrated we develop an ulcer or a heart-attack, we have enough sophistication *and* money to go to either a psychotherapist or a "regular" M.D. But ghetto adolescents are too unsophisticated, too poor—and much more direct: some of them expressed precisely the same feelings directly-physically.

At a time when some Americans are beginning to question our long-held belief that material possessions and personal "success" are the touchstones to inner "grace," faith in the Dream and in the Fallacy continues to beat most strongly in the hearts of new Americans and our society's native-born equivalents, the lower-class American Negro. Perhaps this circumstance helps to explain why the psychological re-action against their adopted or native land can be so strong for the more idealistic and sensitive members of these groups when the Dream is not fulfilled for them quickly and in full measure. Perhaps, too, it helps explain why second- and third-generation Americans who have attained some measure of security and status frequently become "super-duper" Americans.

Some of our best liberal intellectuals and labor leaders are also continuing in the grip of the old spell. In still stressing the unique and penultimate importance of economic security, they are showing they do not recognize that the old Dream is no longer psychologically and *historically* valid. They seem to continue to believe that we shall *automatically* achieve our inalienable right of happiness when we have dependable means for the acquisition of material goods and comforts. They continue to see what is at best a means to, or rather, a pre-condition of, the goal as the goal itself. When union leaders demand a guaranteed annual wage and civil-rights leaders call for a negative income tax or universal basic income, they are expending their ef-forts on much too limited a goal. Its accomplishment while our people generally continue to believe that economic security is a goal of life *sufficient in itself* may well result in even more widespread apathy than we have at present—the kind of apathy that stems from having no goals at all, not even an inadequate one.

I am not advocating here that we do not strive for economic se-curity for all levels in our country; on the contrary, I am very much in favor, for reasons beyond those usually given, of basic levels of economic security for all. What I *am* advocating is that we move ahead on a number of parallel tracks at the same time in our thinking and planning, with only one of these tracks economic security pro-grams. I shall elaborate further on this point in later chapters.

Chapter Four

The Middle-Class Ego Struggle
Has Deep Roots

Neither historical events, nor economic trends, nor even a general tendency towards irrationality in men's thinking can *in themselves* explain why the middle-class status struggle has become the middle-class ego struggle. For us to be so ego-involved in our economic roles, experiences prior to adulthood must have made us psychologically vulnerable to these roles. A complex psychological process has occurred and needs to be accounted for.

A psychological explanation requires reference to the *triple role of the family for the child*. The family's universal *social* role is an outgrowth of its basic *biological* role of caring for the completely helpless human infant and child: transmitting to the new arrival the group culture into which the human infant is born, in such a way as to transform the helpless, unconforming, amoral infant into the independently functioning, moral member of his group.

At birth, the human infant is functionally a mammal; his humanity is present only as biological potential. He becomes a human being—as his social group defines the term—through the prolonged, interrelated processes of maturation and of cultural learning or "socialization." The latter complex and largely unknowing process begins with the child's inevitably emotionally toned interaction with the already formed personalities of his mother, father and other family members. Thus his family also plays a highly important *psychological* role for the individual. From the infant's and child's point of view, the interaction between parent and child is very often negative in emotional effect, for two core reasons: his caretakers have already been shaped as behaving and valuing beings by *their* culturally defined experiences; and, as adults, they do not usually recognize the implications for their baby of the great difference between their own and their child's level of development.

[32]

These early experiences of children with family members, both positive and negative in emotional tone, constitute the first and psychologically most fundamental building-blocks in their personality make-up—Freud's basic and now generally undisputed contribution to our understanding of the individual. The values and practices of the general culture and sub-cultures of which our parental family was a part reached us, was experienced by us, not abstractly during our infancy and early childhood, but very concretely, *in the ways in which they influenced the behavior of the family members with whom we interacted constantly and directly.* Although the fundamental psychological role of these early family-centered experiences is universal, their characteristics and their effects on the child have been found to differ along social-status lines in complex societies such as ours.

The American family does not function in a social vacuum, contrary to the impression given by many discussions of juvenile delinquency and childhood behavior problems. In our complex society, the family—and the individual—functions less within a general American culture than within a social-class *sub-culture.* So far as a general culture exists, it is differently interpreted by members of the different social strata. Their recreational behavior is different, their sexual behavior is different, their religious behavior is different, their drinking behavior is different, their picture of the role of education in their lives is different, their political attitudes are different, their level of anxiety and how they express it is different—to mention only some of the differences in behavior found to exist on a group basis. Individual deviations from general patterns are, of course, always present. Social trends affect and are experienced in different ways by members of the different social levels.

Further, and most important from the point of view of personality development, families of the different status levels have been found to have measurably different child-rearing values, objectives and practices, again on a group basis (14, 16, 18)[1]. This finding, along with others, means that American children tend to have common life experiences within a social-class context, since individual variations in parent-child and extra-family relationships ordinarily function *within* this context. Most of us adults now in the middle class, whether we grew up in a "respectable working-class" family or in a more economically stable lower-middle family had surprisingly many experi-

---

[1] Although continuing studies since the 1940s show that changes have occurred and are occurring in these values and practices and therefore in the differences between the status levels (10, 19, 62), differences continue to be evident (9).

ences in common—a great number of which we have preferred to forget, usually with success.

But before I dig up these far from decomposed childhood skeletons, let me present a psychological yardstick for evaluating this background. Let me review the kinds of experiences, from infancy through adolescence, which are believed to develop in the growing individual a continuing broad capacity to learn and to grow, emotionally, socially, and intellectually.

The child's very first experiences with another person, ordinarily his mother, occur at a developmental stage which is dominated by our species' mammalian inheritance—a stage when he has no words for his experience, no objective understanding of what is happening to him, and no defense mechanisms to protect him from their impact. He senses any affectional and physical deprivation at, literally, the gut-level; as a direct threat to his very existence. Here is the reason that these early experiences tend to have such a fundamental and lasting emotional carry-over. Even if he has the most loving and responsive of caretakers, the infant and young child cannot, because of his physical and mental limitations and complete dependence on others, escape experiencing some degree of "existence anxiety"—strong and pervasive feelings of helplessness, fear, threat. The infant's "existence anxiety" is to be distinguished from the "cosmic anxiety" of the adult, which is equally as natural and unavoidable, but which stems from a very different set of developmental and environmental factors (47).

Because of the baby's direct physical contact with his mother at this stage, it is her actual gut-level reactions to him that he senses, not her assumed or verbalized reactions. For optimal effects on his later development, the responsiveness of her physical care to his urgent needs, and the positive emotional quality of his first human relationship should result in these psychological carryovers: a readiness for new experience, a tendency to go towards rather than away from people, a picture of himself as an adequate and important being, a level of anxiety low enough to be tolerated psychologically.

Such permissive and responsive practices take into knowledgeable account the circumstance that the "mammalian" neurological principle in our species' dual neurogenetic inheritance is dominant over the "human" principle during the early years of human development. But the human principle, which begins to show itself within a very few months after birth, also needs to be catered to—and requires quite a different order of experience, and therefore of parental practices, for *its* optimal development: rather than responsive and consistent catering to a particular infant and child's innately determined patterns of maturation and of physical and emotional needs, which the mammalian principle calls for, firm and consistent imposition of limits on certain categories of behavior *and* the provision of a richly stimulating environment are necessary for the development and eventual functional dominance of the human principle (48).

At first impression, these two types of child-rearing approaches may appear to be at direct cross-purposes, as both the "experts" and conscientious parents who attempt to follow their advice often interpret them to be. Not so! Since the degree to which, and when, the human principle becomes stably dominant in behavior is dependent upon how adequately the *developmentally prior* mammalian needs have been met by the babe's caretakers, these two approaches are to be seen, rather, as *complementary*—as requiring the wisely timed and individual-child-attuned catering to *both* principles.

Lest strong anxieties and frustrations accumulate and serve to retard the individual's progress from one developmental stage to the next, the behaviors which his family and social group expect him to learn by the end of each major stage of development—infancy, early childhood, later childhood, pre- and early adolescence, mid-adolescence, later adolescence and early adulthood, mature adulthood, later maturity and old age—should be realistically graded to the physical and mental limitations which his stage of development and his previous opportunities to learn impose on him, and to the pattern of physical, mental and temperamental tendencies with which he is endowed by inheritance.

To insist that a baby be toilet-trained by the age of eight months is to ignore a developmental unreadiness for voluntary bowel and bladder control, and to cause the building up of strong anxieties in him. To expect to convert a dreamy, inwardly attuned pre-adolescent with strong esthetic or intellectual interests into an aggressive, practical "junior businessman" teen-ager is not merely unrealistic, but destructive of his psychological balance and potential for a positive social contribution. To ignore that the behavior of a gifted child can be as atypical of his age group as that of a mentally ill child is to force some gifted children into mental illness. To expect a late-maturing adolescent to be as interested in and aggressive towards the opposite sex as an early maturing friend is to impose unnecessary frustrations on him or her, and may push him into homosexuality. To act as if we and other adults no longer have strong dependency needs, on the mistaken assumption of our culture that we outgrow such needs, is to impose severe and unnecessary emotional strain on ourselves and others.

On the other hand, the quality and scope of the child's early experiences with his physical environment, the emotional quality of his relationship with his parents and other persons in his immediate social environment, and his steadily increasing and dependable control of his emotions, made possible by the maturationally attuned setting of limits by his parents, should continue to promote and expand his earlier positive attitudes to his world and to himself. These learnings contribute to a wide ability to tolerate failure experiences as he experiments with his broadening physical and social environment. Such failure-tolerance tends to encourage in him a receptiveness to physical and social reality as he grows up, and an increasing acceptance of and attentiveness to his emerging inner development of self. By early adolescence, the individual who has had such positive emotional experiences with himself and with his social and physical world has learned to enlist his emotional energies towards the constructive ends of his social, intellectual and inner-personal growth.

So much for the ideal; now for the real. Instead of seeking to minimize experiences which emphasize to the infant and young child how thoroughly helpless and vulnerable he is, middle-class child-rearing practices have tended to do just the opposite—right from the moment of birth. In the interests of efficiency and asepsis, most of our hospitals separate infant and mother, and place the new-born child on a schedule of feeding and handling suited to hospital routine rather than to the babe's unstable pattern of physiological functioning. Many mothers, because of outer social pressures or lack of inner inclination or sheer lack of knowledge, continue this displacement of reference-point during this early period, so crucial for their child's later patterns of emotional reaction and intellectual development. They subordinate close, responsive and *relaxed* contact with their infant to any number of other activities—and usually begin to substitute the practice of word-magic for the *concrete opportunities for experience* they should be providing for their child. Here I have come to my second definition of word-magic.

When a person's goal is a change in some complex behavior or the development of a new behavior-pattern in another person *or* in himself (such as the development of a religious attitude, or consideration for the rights of others, or a changed attitude toward a minority group), and when, instead of providing opportunities for the other person (or himself) to have concrete, gut-level, goal-appropriate experiences, he uses words, words and more words, only, as his teaching method (as: exhortation, repetition of verbal formulas such as the Ten Commandments, threats, factual information, reassurance all is going well) that person, whether adult or child, parent or teacher or pastor or friend or spouse, is practicing word-magic. This child-rearing use of word-magic lays the groundwork for its use by the grown individual and by the general society—as already described in Chapter 2.

The early pattern of handling infants, just described, is only the beginning of a long series of species-inappropriate child-rearing practices. The majority of working-class and lower-middle-class parents in competitive urban settings are influenced by their own values and anxieties to push their children to perform beyond the level that each successive stage of development and their innate pattern of capacities permits. Most of today's parents of children and teen-agers were subjected to strict methods of weaning and toilet-training and to prohibition of such necessary and natural early behaviors as taking pleasure in their bodies, direct aggression, and lack of concern about modesty. These methods and prohibitions have been rated by competent judges as among the most severe in expectation and enforcement of a wide sampling of the world's cultures (74).

Since to the infant and young child, his self is his body, these practices deprived us of experiences which are a primary and essential source of self-development, self-satisfaction, and self-expansion. In so depriving us, they served to weaken, frustrate, and belittle our emerging individual sense of self at the very beginning of its development. The frequent result was that many of us developed reduced readiness for new experience, ambivalent attitudes towards other people and to ourselves, and too high a level of anxiety to be tolerated with ease.

Beyond infancy, from developing bladder control to achieving high marks in school and popularity with other children, many of us were exposed to such parental training techniques as shaming, giving and withholding affection, pointed comparisons with brothers and sisters and other children—all ego-belittling experiences. This constant pushing to achieve and to excel frequently resulted in our undependable or over-restrictive emotional control and in a narrowing ability to experiment with our social and physical environment. By early adolescence, many of us had already developed the confirmed tendency to retreat from and to ignore much of reality and of our inner selves. It was easier on our by-now vulnerable egos to channel our energies ever more narrowly into more intense competition on the one or two things which won us adult recognition and approval, *whether or not we ourselves gained inner satisfaction from these activities.*

As for providing opportunities for us to learn such behaviors as were expected of us at each stage of our development, our parents were typically inconsistent. They, and eventually we ourselves, attached too much negative emotional importance to failure, for one thing. For another, how often were we exhorted by our parents as we approached our mid-teens to be self-controlled, responsible and to take initiative, after they had consistently overprotected us from reality, from the consequences of our own mistakes, from the necessity for us to develop our own dependable inner emotional controls, and from our unavoidably inadequate first efforts to do things on our own!

In some families, this pattern of inconsistency and constant pressure was counterbalanced by affection and support; in some, it was not.

The growing-up experiences just described seem scarcely to warrant a reaction in superlatives. Yet if doing a job thoroughly deserves recognition, then these experiences must be given their just due: they have been amazingly effective in prolonging and magnifying a natural and unavoidable infantile existence anxiety into an unnatural, culturally conditioned, essentially neurotic, personal-status anxiety. Some of the ways in which the middle-class products of this background have reacted to their status anxieties have been characterized as socially adaptive: our tremendous need for personal status keeps us striving over long periods of time for the distant and difficult goals which the middle class sets for its children (15). It also helps to make and to keep us sustainedly and "adaptively" competitive.

As a result of this need of ours for status, and of the circumstance that we tended to identify during childhood with our parents and to accept their values, we acquired an idealized picture of ourselves which was primarily that of a "successful person." Not only our parents' values but those of other adults we had contact with in school, church and community reinforced this association, as did what we read and what we saw in the movies. Surely, once we achieved the success, the status, which everyone we knew considered to be so important, our unremitting anxieties would be dissipated, and we would at last be tension-free and *happy!*

Usually by our mid-teens, we had become deeply vulnerable to our later "success" or "failure" and had acquired the touchstone fallacy—with any realization that this had occurred, nor how and why it had come about. So pervasive—and unconscious—is the subscription to the touchstone fallacy among the current generation of middle-class adults, even those professional groups who by training, values and perspective should be helping the rest of us gain insight into the inner-psychological havoc created by the fallacy, are instead every bit as much its victims as the rest of us are: psychiatrists and other psychological counselors are, typically, as competitive and status-driven in their goals for themselves and their children as are their clients.

The American middle class is paying a very high personal and social price for unknowingly fostering an infantile type of anxiety and converting it into the major source of motivation for our own *and* our children's achievement—educational, economic, social, as Part II of this discussion will attempt to document.

Another psychological by-product of constant parental pressure, in addition to our personal-status anxieties, has not been socially adaptive —quite the opposite. We developed strongly aggressive, hostile feelings for our parents. But since it was generally unthinkable in the middle-class-oriented sub-cultures for children to express their hostility against their parents openly, many of us became afraid of our own aggressive feelings. We were, as a result, rendered unable to recognize and to admit to ourselves the existence of these feelings. A psychologically logical next step among many of us was the externalization of our own aggressive feelings—the development of a tendency to project them on other people, groups, and nations (2). Having done so, we were able to express freely, in socially acceptable ways, our fears of what is actually *our own repressed hostility*. The psychological basis of scapegoating lies here, as well as many another of the expressions of reality-disproportionate amounts of hostility and suspicion increasingly evident in our personal, national and international life.

In a society as complex as ours, there are, of course, other available avenues to personal status in the middle class than that of materially based success. Examples are service to our fellow man, service to God, excellence in creative media. But unless these alternate avenues bring some kind of major social recognition to compensate for their lack of monetary reward, the individual is usually unable to feel he has achieved any real status.

The child-rearing approaches here described were widespread in the American middle class through at least the 1930s. A reaction against these patterns began during the 1940s: upper-middle-class parents, particularly, began to appreciate the emotional difficulties, resistances and hostilities they engendered in their children when they pushed them too hard to perform beyond their stage of development and when they ignored their natural aptitudes and temperamental tendencies.

In retrospect, it was infants and young children only who gained the benefits of this reaction. Acceptance of the philosophy of permissiveness was undiscriminating among many personally insecure young parents. Their reactions against their own childhood frustrations, combined with their uncertainty about themselves as persons and as parents, led them to continue permissiveness without qualification beyond infancy and early childhood. They did not appreciate that as their child's capacity for conscious control increased, their placing of rational and consistent limits on his behavior was essential to his gradual development of reliable emotional *self*-control, and was therefore just as important to his healthy psychological development as permitting expressions of his individuality.

The behavior of many of today's young people has been bearing out this earlier-edition prediction:

> If our other values concerning the importance of individual success do not change as well, these permissive child-rearing trends may ultimately do far more harm than good to our children. *Beyond babyhood,* in highly competitive urban and suburban settings, the constant parental pressure for achievement in parent-delineated areas of performance, the rejection for failure, the ignoring as worthy creative predilections which do not happen to fit into parental conceptions of group-conforming behavior seem, if anything, to be intensifying. When parental permissiveness during their child's infancy and early childhood collides with their later insistence that he compete successfully with other children in both academic and social achievement, the effect is the placing of an over-heavy psychological burden on their child. With the best intentions in the world, they maneuver him into the development of greater amounts of anxiety than they themselves were ever confronted with.[2] When parents set high, rigid expectations for their children, but provide neither concrete, graded and individually attuned opportunities for them to learn such behaviors, nor an easy acceptance of their mistakes and failures, the effect on most children exposed to such a regimen is predictable: they become highly conforming on the outside and passively fearful on the inside.[3]

---

[2]Bronfenbrenner has come to a substantially similar conclusion on the basis of an extensive review of the research literature pertinent to the "changing American child" up to circa 1960 (9).

[3] Slowly broadening understanding of that psychiatric mystery, the psychopathic— or sociopathic—personality, is telling us that it is just this kind of parent-child

A low frustration-threshold beyond childhood is a distinctive character-istic of this kind of personality organization. A startling rise in the incidence of drug (and other sorts of "kicks") addiction among economically privileged young people has coincided with its emergence; this convergence is not at all coincidental. The attraction of drugs appears to be their regression-promoting effects. They seem to induce—among some imbibers at least—a very basic, developmentally linked kind of experience, an experience which so many of today's young people were deprived of during their infancy and early child-hood by maternally-detached and accelerative patterns of child-rearing: a warmly relaxed, gut-level sense of inner well-being. The effect of LSD on those persons whose early, gut-level deprivations were so traumatic as to render them psychosis-prone is not as pleasant however: it apparently triggers off the incipient disorder.

This is not the only pattern of reaction with negative social impli-cations evident in the younger generation. Many particularly bright, urban young people have developed a typical method of coping with unremitting adult pressures on them. They first become aware of their parents' personal vulnerabilities during their normally highly self-centered early-childhood years and quickly learn to use this knowledge to their own immature advantage. They develop a refined ability to manipulate their parents, and later, other adults representing authority, through an almost Machiavellian exploitation of the older person's guilt feelings and insecurities. These highly elaborated manipulative techniques have "worked" often enough that they have been adopted as these young people's habitual method of dealing with authority figures and economic and social competitors. So long as such manipulation is used only as a defensive, "survival" tech-nique, it probably does not have an overly negative social effect. But what if this trend is carried one step further, and, as in the case of the sociopath, superior intellect, instead of being placed at the service of society in the form of ethical leadership, is habitually used to manipulate others for self-seeking ends?

A permissive trend was also dominant in the public schools during the 1950s; the earlier edition made this reference to it:

---

constellation in extreme form which lies behind the development of the split in inner and outer behavior so distinctive of this type of psychological defective: a surface mask of social conformity and even of intellectual brilliance concealing an inner chaos of infantile amorality and incapacity for emotional empathy with others (11).

Essentially the same criticism [as those of permissive child-rearing prac-
tices] could be made, with only minor variations, of the ultimate effect of
the trends towards permissiveness and de-emphasis on competition in
our schools—still assuming that adult middle-class values concerning
the importance of success remain unchanged. It may well be that much of
the current parental criticism of "new" educational methods stems
partially from their awareness of this discrepancy, and partially from the
feelings of threat aroused in them by the new philosophy's implied challenge to their own values.

This assessment has proven to be embarrassingly prophetic: in the
face of fierce post-Sputnik parental pressures, the public high schools
have reverted with almost indecent haste (and only token protest from
professional educators) to homogeneous ability-groupings, subject-
matter-centeredness and competitiveness to the point of savagery.

These emphases are even now sifting downward to the lower grades,
not only into the grade-schools but even into the early-childhood
years—with not merely the blessings, but the urgent assistance of our
current crop of psychological/pedagogical experts—who, it must be
remembered, are themselves products of, and unwitting subscribers
to, the middle-class "pressure-cooker"! I am not referring here to
Operation Headstart, in spite of this program's questionable motivation
and often inept execution in practice: our affluent society's explicit
assumption of responsibility for economically and otherwise disad-
vantaged children is long overdue—and still inadequate. I am referring, rather, to the current "teach your child to read at four so he'll
be ahead in the later, formal-schooling race for prestige-college admission" misapplication of research findings on the role of "experi-
ential enrichment" in human mental development. This research-
area has heretofore been over-narrowly conceived, both in the length
of developmental time taken into account and the range of behavior
observed. Until controlled investigations check on the ultimate effects
on later, over-all personality functioning of such one-sided early
developmental acceleration, *professional psychology is obligated to
warn against such premature applications.*[4] It may very well turn
out that such acceleration attempts, *when imposed on the wrong
children,* contribute to the incidence of emotional illnesses, as well
as to such character disorders as the sociopathic personality.

By way of contrast with the middle class, slum-reared children as a

---

[4] As the subjects used in psychological research shift from rats to human beings,
psychological investigators must be *at least* as scrupulous as medical researchers
have become with regard to the premature public release of research findings.

group are not as deprived of basic self-gratification experiences, although hunger and cold and lack of parental interest are familiar occurrences both during and after infancy. "Existence anxiety" is particularly high among this population-group, and continues as such, unconverted to any other form as long as the individual is faced with a struggle for the basic necessities which sustain life. Constant parental pressure for academic and social achievement is typically non-existent.[5] These practices probably account for the circumstance that these children have little or no achievement anxiety —a major source of exasperation to their middle-class teachers. While the middle-class youngster eventually becomes concerned about and motivated by his achievement and social status, first in school and later in the community, the slum-culture adolescent and adult remains far more concerned about and motivated by his immediate status among his peers; socially, he is gang-oriented, rather than achievement-oriented.

Recent events suggest that this generalization about slum youngsters may no longer be valid. Intensive out-group pressure to eliminate the fighting gangs, converging with in-group pressure for civil rights, a higher standard of living and "black power," has been rapidly converting Negro slum-residents from their traditional "ethic of reciprocity" to the "me first" ethic common until now primarily among lower-middle-class persons. Just at the point in time when many upper and upper-middle class individuals are becoming aware of and deeply concerned over the cumulative social impact of this middle-class attitude, many members of the slum lower class have adopted a "one-person gang" orientation—as a group-worker in close touch with such youngsters has expressed it.[6]

There seems to be a relationship between the extent of thwarting of parents' own success drives and the degree of importance they attach to success in their goals for their children. We seem to have forgotten (intentionally?) that *adults who are between 37 and 62 years of age today were 1 to 25 years old in 1930, the beginning of the Depression Decade.* How many of us currently of middle-class status were over-influenced in our aspirations, values, and personal development by the economic difficulties and status humiliations that our parents—or we ourselves—suffered during that decade?

---

[5] Current minority-group pressures on the schools are not coming from this population grouping but from lower-middle and "respectable working class" parents.
[6] Thank you, Joel Skurnik.

PART II

Effects of the Fallacy

Chapter Five

The New Slavery

THE CONVERGENCE of our internal vulnerability to higher economic status with our increasing difficulty in our attainment of that status has led to our ego-involvement in our occupational status and consumer power. As if the resulting psychological burden were not heavy enough, discouraging changes have occurred in the individual work situations in which we are investing so much of our egos.

One of these changes is the fragmentation and specialization of work to the point where most of us can gain little or no creative satisfaction from either its performance or its results: not only can we not see our puny role in the final results, many of us have come not to care, and seek elsewhere than our jobs, if at all, for our sources of personal satisfaction.

Another change, particularly from the viewpoint of those of us who are actively struggling for a higher level of occupational status, is the circumstance that although the higher level we are striving for is restricted to a relative few, we are but one of more than ever before who are similarly struggling. The result is that our striving, so essential to the maintenance of our self-respect, puts us into direct, frequently intense competition with our fellow job-holders or fellow professionals. This direct competition isolates us from them—all the more so because we try to conceal the true situation from them and from ourselves: we must, above all, be relaxed and *friendly* in our work relations!

Here, then, are the core conditions which have converged and are contributing to an inner psychological state widespread throughout the American middle classes:

our self-respect dependent upon goals difficult or impossible to achieve, external to ourselves, minimally under our direct control, and exercising only limited aspects of our complex being;

spending the best hours of our days on work which yields little or no inner satisfaction on its own merits;

direct competition with our fellow workers.

[47]

As yet, all three conditions are characteristic primarily of our large urban centers, as is the widespread psychological state which has been called "alienation" (46). Alienation is an apt rendering of a French term, *anomie* (17)—apt in that *anomie* or "rulelessness" is the outcome of alienation from our own creative and effectional needs and moral beliefs, as well as alienation from our fellow human beings.

The patterning and intensity of the reactions making up this psychological state, which I am calling the *"alienation constellation,"* differs from time to time in the same person and from person to person—from the occasional recurrent mood or emotional upset of the essentially healthy person, to the extreme and almost constant turmoil of the severely neurotic individual. I tend to a degree of overstatement in describing these feelings, both to make them more readily understood and as a means of projecting the disturbing quality of these reactions for the individual who is experiencing them. A newspaper item, "Congregation Polled," illustrates the pervasiveness of these feelings among us.[1]

First and foremost, tremendous amounts of *anxiety* stemming from our status struggle. (Aside: the first most requested sermon topic was "How To Keep Serene.") These tremendous amounts of anxiety are self-generating, like the projected atomic furnace: personal-status anxiety provides the basic fuel for our striving, yet one of the effects of our compulsive dedication to unsatisfying work and a competitive, demanding work situation, is the constant generation of fresh tensions. Perhaps here may be the common factor underlying the tendency to smoke heavily *and* incidence of heart disease.

Intermittent feelings not merely of *insecurity,* but of *helplessness* and *inadequacy,* reactions which reflect our underlying feeling of *infantile puniness.* A pervasive feeling of *alone-ness,* of isolation. Feelings of *guilt.* (Aside: the fourth most requested sermon was "How to

---

[1] Oak Park churchgoers would rather hear a sermon on serenity than any other subject, according to a poll taken in Euclid Av. Methodist Church, Euclid and Washington.

How to meet death, the second coming of Christ, miracles, the devil and the liquor problem were the least popular topics.

The Rev. Paul E. Turk, pastor, will preach on "How to Keep Serene" tomorrow.

Other topics favored in the poll will be used in coming weeks. These, in order of popularity, are: "What Protestants Believe," "Meeting and Mastering Defeat," "How to Be a Christian in the Business World."

Series of sermons on the Ten Commandments, Jesus' parables, and New Testament characters also were requested.

Be a Christian in the Business World.") Since our very selves are at stake, an increasing inability for self-objectivity and self-laughter, an apparently increasing *tendency to take ourselves too seriously,* which has been noticed and deplored by our more perceptive comedians. Associated with this defensiveness is *a latent fear of being "found out".* How disastrous it would be if anyone were to discover the scared, defenseless child we have so carefully imprisoned behind our thin façade of self-confidence!

A reluctance to recognize and to accept our deeper feelings—an over-all *incapacity to experience and to express our emotions directly and spontaneously* within the ample-enough limits prescribed by the social welfare. We tend instead to *express our feelings vicariously,* in particularly two ways—through identification with the anti-social emotions and actions of people who are removed from our immediate world, and through our use of fantasy as a means of living our emotional life entirely in the future. A future which we are rushing to meet, because "when I make that killing," "when I get that promotion," "when I get my degree," "when my raise comes through," "when we move to the *right* suburb," *then* we and those dependent on us will *really* start to live, become whole people, be *happy.*[2]

And greater and greater amounts of "free-floating" *hostility*—free floating because it ordinarily cannot be focused on the actual causes of our hostility, even if we were able to recognize and admit them to ourselves. "Cannot" because we dare not risk the increase in anxiety and guilt that inkling of the causes of our hostility might generate in us, nor the actual penalties we, and through us our family, might suffer if we decided to break the actual social and psychological mold in which we are encased. Some of our hostility is diverted to *self-hatred,* and to a kind of *sadistic pleasure* in the envy of present or potential competitors and in their misfortune, or both. Probably all of us *express our hostility vicariously,* as the tremendous appeal of

---

[2] Psychologically questionable as this "fantasy future" orientation in some ways is, it at least plays a cohesive role in ongoing personality functioning. Not even this thin glue is present for many in the younger generation: among those middle-class young people who find themselves failures in life at some point between 16 and 22 because they are unable to adapt to fiercely competitive academic requirements and/or to their parents' unremitting demands for academic and social achievement, a future orientation has been replaced by feelings of *powerlessness.* (Alien to traditional American optimism and confidence in one's ability to fashion one's own destiny as such feelings are, they have never been unfamiliar to a large group of Americans: the economically dependent poor who are trapped in—and by—their dependence and their poverty.)

themes of violence in our popular media attests. It is interesting that this prevalence of themes of violence, and, increasingly, of sadistic pleasure in torture, which is essentially an outcome or *symptom* of our inner feelings, is taken to be a *cause* of delinquency and psychological difficulty by our current crop of social uplifters (rather than a *reinforcer* of already present tendencies).

A man's work role tends to influence the focus of his inner feelings of hostility. The blue-collar worker who identifies with his union and sees management's interests as basically against his own has a different work target for his hostilities than the white-collar employee who tends to identify with management and to believe his best interests are closely tied in with those of management. For the skilled and semi-skilled unionized worker, the strike often reflects the deflection of hostilities arising from other sources than his work situation against his work situation and management; while particularly the little-white-collar employee often deflects hostilities arising from a frustrating work situation and for which management might validly be held responsible, against almost everybody else and everything else in his immediate and more distant environment.[3]

Further, *generation of an apparently insoluble conflict* which generates still further anxiety. To gain our self-respect, we strive and strive. But if we succeed to *any* measure, we threaten others who are similarly striving, and who, to preserve their own delicate inner balance, have to withdraw from us—so that to succeed or to give the impression of success or superiority usually means to isolate ourselves from others. Yet because of our inner feelings of alone-ness, we desperately need human warmth and contact: we cannot bear to be disliked by anyone. Here is an excellent example of two strong psychological needs in direct conflict with each other within us. Small wonder that under the weight of this conflict, many of us turn compulsively to our family and others in our after-work hours, seeking from them, too often fruitlessly, reassurance and recognition as a whole, intrinsically worthwhile being, regardless of our accomplishments and our salary bracket. Here is the basis of the kind of social interaction that Riesman has characterized as "the lonely crowd" (58). I believe this approach to the genesis of the lonely crowd is psychologically much more valid than Riesman's own diffuse population-trends "explanation."

Along with the highest physical standard of living in the world

---

[3] Edgar Friedenberg, in his disquieting analyses of American high-school students, has termed this order of expression of our hostilities "ressentiment." (23, 54).

has this psychological constellation appeared within us, like a cadaver at the feast. And this state tends to be self-perpetuating, because our inner pressures have the effect of reducing our creative resources and our sense of perspective, so that it is difficult for us to approach life and our problems flexibly and constructively: we have become rigid and stereotyped in our behavior.

A closed, self-reinforcing circle of reaction has been set up. Our inner pressures push us to cling tenaciously to our beliefs in the Fallacy and the Dream, the very axioms of middle-class life which have played the major psychological role in the genesis of this state within us. And then we use the core implication of these axioms for our economic and political conduct—that our salvation as individuals and as a society is entirely dependent upon each of us functioning as independent individuals—as our justification for maintaining the very pattern of economic and social life which is creating these inner pressures!

Here is a new kind of slavery: not the literal bondage of old, nor the later, symbolic bondage of a social order with everyone in his predestined place, but the inner psychological bondage of our time— slavery to ourselves. And psychological bonds, as any psychotherapist will tell you, can be far more effective than any external restraining force: whom have *we* to rebel against? For many of us, it is much more tolerable, psychologically, to project our negative feelings outward against "dangerous" ideas or groups or nations—a tendency referred to in the previous chapter.

I am not saying that our ego-involvement in our status-struggle is the *sole* source of our anxieties, hostilities, guilt feelings, rigidities. I am saying that here is one source for these feelings which is common to many of us. Each of us has, in addition, entirely unique sources for such feelings, sources related to other areas of our past experience as individuals, and to our particular psychological make-up.

Chapter Six

Those Who Succeed and Those Who Fail

The American doctrine that anyone can succeed if only he tries hard enough ignores the many economic and social factors which militate against the success of all but a relative few of those already in the middle-class who are striving for it. Far more such strivers are destined to fail than to succeed, in their own eyes and in the eyes of others. But whether we fail *or* succeed, our tremendous ego-involvement in our economic roles makes for us an ego crisis of either eventuality.

Just how negatively, and in just what ways our over-all psychological functioning is affected by our failure or success depends on two converging factors—the extent to which our earlier, family-centered experiences have made us psychologically vulnerable to our success or failure, *and* whether we eventually succeed or fail in our own eyes. I am postulating here that neither factor is *in itself* sufficient to account for a particular individual's reaction. Both the contributing psychological effects of his experiences from birth up to the time of crisis, *and* the occurrence in his adulthood of events which are precipitating the ego-crisis need to be taken into account.

So long as the striver is able to maintain hope that his goal is attainable, he is ordinarily able to keep his feelings of anxiety, of helplessness, of hostility within manageable bounds—whether his earlier experiences have placed him in the normal *or* the neurotic range. But what happens when, for the few, we seem to have reached our original status goals; or when, for the many, try and try as we have, we not only know we haven't reached our goal but are forced to admit to ourselves we probably never will? (Aside: the third most requested sermon was "Meeting and Mastering Defeat.") And what of the special case of those who decide either part-way "up the hill," or even after reaching "the top," that the personal price to be paid for attaining the heights or for maintaining them is too high?

There are a number of patterns of striving which exemplify more

[52]

intense than average effort. These patterns are worth itemizing because there is a tendency for potential as well as full-blown neurotics to adopt one or another of them.

For those whose parents were/are in an occupation with insufficient status in their own and others' eyes, self-respect becomes tied to making the jump, usually through education, to a higher-status occupation than the father's, and *not* backsliding. For those who have managed to achieve some occupational status and a reasonably high level of consumer capacity for themselves, the touchstone is expressing that status in "socially correct" fashion—spending their money in the "right places" on the "right things," behaving socially in such a way as to be accepted by the "right social group," bringing their children up "properly," sending them to the "right schools"—Riesman's "other-directed" group: for such first-generation members of the upper-middle class—that status grouping which comprises about ten per cent of the population, but to which about seventy per cent either fancy they belong or are persuaded they must belong by our advertisers—economic status is relatively secure, but subjective feelings of personal status insecurity are typically strong. For those whose parents already have high and secure occupational and consumer status, the touchstone has been to achieve at least as high a social and economic level as that of their parents.[1]

For these groups of intense strivers, family ties, whether with the parental family or with the marital family or both, typically play one or both of two very special functions. The family becomes an impregnable fortress of emotional defense against a hostile and demanding world, a fortress into which one retires, battered and bruised at the end of each personality-fragmenting day, to be made nearly whole again through the healing reassurance of strong and deep (and frequently smothering) emotional ties. And too, the "fortress family" affords dutiful middle-class sons, husbands, fathers the comfort of seeing themselves as socially responsible persons, even though the exercise of their economic roles may involve the rankest exploitation of human beings outside their immediate family and friendship circle: after all, these exploitative activities contribute to their being "good family men," do they not?

Because of this societal function of the "fortress family," those women who continue to play the traditional middle-class roles of house-

---

[1] Note that this generalization is not about the *current* generation of adolescents and young adults—who are reacting with a diversity which will be described in a later chapter.

wife and mother are, whether they are aware of it or not, in an anomalous position. Many, if not most, of these women are very much disturbed as individuals and even more as mothers by the visibly increasing immorality and disorganization of our times. Yet, by playing the supportive role described for their husbands and/or sons, they are helping to keep their achieving and/or exploitative menfolk going psychologically and, as a result, are making in the collective a *very substantial contribution to our present middle-class status quo!*[2]

As compared with those in the middle class who could be classified in the psychologically healthy range, the reactions of the neurotic individual to his status struggle differ chiefly in degree: he is far more likely to be deeply vulnerable psychologically to his success *or* failure. He doesn't have the inner resources to react in a balanced way to either eventuality: the sources for his feelings of self-worth are typically entirely outside himself, and he is particularly dependent upon outward symbols of status for whatever level of self-respect he can muster. As gifted interpreters like Karen Horney, Edward Strecker, David Riesman (30, 65, 58), among others, have pointed out, the middle-class neurotic typically escapes *into* his culture: he adopts in compulsive fashion a role or roles which his society especially values and awards status to. The status struggle of our society has tremendously great ego importance for such a person: he puts all his ego-eggs into one basket, so to speak. Resemblance to some of the figures on our current and near-past political scene is *not* "strictly coincidental."

As personal success as we currently define it becomes generally more and more difficult to achieve while remaining highly valued, the level of striving and intensive focusing of specialized skills required to succeed will come—has come—to be achieved not merely by the more gifted individual. Success will come to be achieved by the severely neurotic gifted person, because of his immense capacity for devoted singleness of purpose.

Those whose motivations for their success striving are essentially neurotic usually find, upon reaching their goals, that after all their effort and anticipation, success is not the magic touchstone they had believed it to be for so many years: they are still "hollow men." This realization acts as something of a drawn-out personal crisis. Some of

---

[2] The countless subtle as well as very much overt expressions of antagonism in our commercially subsidized mass media against women who do *not* play the traditional feminine roles acquire an extra dimension of meaning in this context.

these persons, for whom the striving itself has become an ingrained way of life, try to escape from this realization by setting up still more distant success goals to strive for: more possessions, greater personal power, more professional recognition—until the inevitable heart attack overtakes them. (How many sons of such men reveal, in their inability to become self- and socially responsible adults, a major consequence of their fathers' neurotic absorption!) Still others, in highly competitive fields, find they have to keep up a physically exhausting level of activity just to maintain the status they have driven themselves so hard to reach. Many of these men utilize the bolstering effect of alcohol during their tension-filled climb up the ladder. For these men, the transition from "social drinker" to confirmed alcoholic is a not unusual accompaniment of their success.

Another pattern is typical particularly of those who have deliberately shaken off their earlier social background. They adopt a new touchstone: the "right" ways to spend leisure time and the "right" people to spend it with, the "right" places to go, the "right" ways to dress, and so and so on, will, they hope, somehow change them into self-accepting, whole persons. Some men, who have either lost communication with their wives during their absorption in their striving, or who "never had time" for a close personal relationship, suddenly turn to intimate physical contact with a woman or a series of women as their new touchstone: the more attractive the lady, the more ego-reassuring the contact—at first. Whatever reaction-path the neurotic success adopts, he seems to have a particular external distinguishing characteristic—a certain arrogance of manner, particularly with those whom he sees as "unsuccessful."

How many of these representatives of the "fortunate few" are there? I don't know, but along with others of more lowly status but equal unhappiness, they have made New York City the mecca of psychiatrists and consulting psychologists, with other large cities rapidly catching up, proportionately. And particularly this group has helped put references to visits to one's psychiatrist in the "smart" entertainer's repertoire, country-wide.[3] I wonder how many of this "successful" group who turn to psychiatric help do so initially because they see the psychiatrist as essentially a super-fancy "happiness gadget," well worth trying, even if his fee is also super-fancy: after all, this gadget *might* just work, even though none of the others has! For these people, money is easier to come by than is reorienting their

---

[3] The inevitable reaction has set in since this sentence was written: ridicule of psychiatrists is now the order of some entertainers' day.

values and style of life. How many of these "gadget seekers" discontinue treatment when they discover *they* must do much hard, trying and painful work in order to hope to attain some measure of health—assuming theirs is an ethical psychotherapist?

How do those who had a fair degree of psychological health when they began their status struggle, whose original motives were essentially those of self-fulfillment, react to their success? By the time they "make it" in a highly competitive situation, the majority of the originally healthy are no longer able to live a relaxed, rounded life. They too have lost the ability to see wealth and position as one of many possible means to the end of self-fulfillment, rather than as ends in themselves.

What of the many when they finally are forced to realize that the economic and social status to which their self-respect is pegged is either unattainable or demands far more of them than they are willing or able to give? An ego crisis of varying degrees of intensity and duration stemming from this realization occurs at some point in the life career of most middle-class men, I believe—and of most "career women." Here again a variety of patterns of reaction exists.

Those who had a fair degree of psychological health to begin with have usually been living fairly rounded lives all along. They are likely to seek further positive compensations in other areas of living than their economic roles, without at the same time becoming apathetic in their work life—developing their roles as husband and father still more fully, extending their interest in local and broader community betterment, turning to religion as a positive emotional experience, continuing creative and personally satisfying avocations. They are able to maintain enough self-objectivity and self-humor to continue to function as positive social integers in their work and in their various personal and social allegiances. Such people are likely to weather their ego crisis without severe personality distortion. But some individual patterning of the basic reactions of the "alienation constellation" persists, probably in the form of recurrent feelings of personal inadequacy, attacks of severe anxiety, guilt, self-hatred— which strike at night often enough to make insomnia our most representative national malady and pill-taking our most representative national habit. Some of this group turn to, and are able to profit from, professional help at the time of crisis: successful psychotherapy allows them to see themselves, and themselves in relation to their world, in clearer perspective. I wonder what the age-statistics are of middle-class adults seeking such help for the first time in our large cities.

Most of us know but do not always understand those strivers who stop part way "up the hill," decide the intense competitive struggle is not for them, and settle into some relatively low-level groove with apparently few personal misgivings. Among this group are those persons who are too responsive to the good will of others and too easy-going by temperament to accept the psychological strains of direct personal competition. Such a person is frequently the stable backbone of his office, his family and his community, and yet he is often considered a "failure" not only by his fellow workers but by his wife also, if she has accepted the success values of her society.

Those who have already been rendered neurotic to a greater or lesser degree by their earlier experiences are particularly vulnerable to their "failure." The staved-off but inevitable realization that they have not reached their goals and are not likely to do so acts much like the precipitating factor in the onset of mental illness. What previously were neurotic trends kept within reasonably manageable bounds become intensified into personality disorders of varying depth and scope. Not only may the more obvious maladjustments of alcoholism (does the rate start to increase sharply in the mid- and late thirties among big-city white-collar workers?), heart disease, psychosomatic illness, promiscuity, suicide, and such crimes as petit and grand larceny, occur as reactions to their ego crisis among the initially neurotic.

Other, less obviously maladjusted reactions, may be expressed: psychological "absorption" of one's children; religion as resignation or withdrawal or emotional escape; frequent travel, physical mobility, tendency to drive at very high speeds; confirmed and constant feelings of worthlessness; sprees of self-indulgent buying; vicarious feelings of power through immersion in a powerful pressure-group; focusing of the now almost uncontrollable amounts of hostility on some safe "out group" as *the* source of one's own and the world's troubles; systematized defense reactions, such as the one Willy Loman, Arthur Miller's salesman, had developed to perfection: habitual self-deception.

Another pattern of reaction has major political implications, both now and in the future. It is common not only among those who have not been able to realize their status aspirations but also among those who are insecure in the consumer and social level they have managed to achieve after hard years of inner-self denial. These persons tend to perceive as a direct personal threat members of formerly non-competing groups who have begun also to strive for occupational status; the group which is the target of such feelings differs according to the status-level of the threat-prone individual, however. Persons hostile towards "pushy" and "undeserving" Afro-

Americans are most likely to be in the working and lower-middle classes. A concrete illustration of this datum was embodied in the results of two polls conducted by a Michigan congressman in his district, which "extends from the center of Detroit to the exclusive suburb of Grosse Pointe and includes the Polish-American community of Hamtramck." The polls were done in 1966 and in 1967 and included 10,000 respondents. The surveys' results indicated that the proportion who thought "racial integration was proceeding too fast" had risen from 44% to 53%—even though *little to no change in this area had occurred during the intervening year.* Representative Nedzi, a liberal Democrat, was quoted as saying in explanation of this finding (29):

> " 'How do you make an individual who is earning nine or ten thousand dollars a year, has his home-mortgage paid out, operates two cars and is adding a boat identify with the war on poverty? He sees only the failures in administration.' "

On the other hand, persons in the upper-middle class, even the insecure ones, are more likely to be politically and personally liberal about the upward-mobile aspirations of working-class and lower-middle class Negroes. Yet many members of the upper-middle class are not immune from competing-group hostility. Men born into working and/or lower-middle class families who are in current process of upward mobility into the upper-middle class *or* who have managed with much effort to achieve that status, are very often very hostile towards career-oriented women with equivalent or superior educational and occupational qualifications.

Individuals who have been subjected all their lives to a special combination of social pressures which appears in its most extreme form in New York City, typically develop a variety of thoroughly organized defense reactions as a means of protecting their highly vulnerable egos. This special combination represents the convergence on the individual of marked parental pressures for achievement and extreme over-all competitive pressures. For the sake of example, let me describe one such reaction-system, the one I call the "sour grapes" defense mechanism. It is typical particularly of persons who have not achieved success, but whose highly compressed egos make them exceptionally vulnerable to this inability of theirs to "make it." It involves a consistent tendency on such a person's part to belittle those who have "done better" than he has, in one or both of two ways: through attributing their success to fortuitous circumstances unrelated to their possibly greater level of ability and stronger drive; or through unearthing and dwelling on whatever personal and professional inadequacies may be present in the more successful person. It is a reaction with two self-protective functions. It serves, first, to protect the individual expressing it from the realization that he may not be in the highest level of ability; and serves, second, to console him in the face of the circumstances that he has not become "a success." Such an individual is often very much afraid to recognize just how compressed his ego is. In so bringing others down to his own size, he spares himself the trauma of an outright ego crisis, since he is not forced to admit his own puny stature to himself.

Perhaps the most frequent reaction of all to the perception of failure is confirmed feelings of powerlessness and consequent retreat into a state of apathy, with no further attempts made to cope positively with life, either in one's job or one's personal life. Here are the goal-less, face-less individuals associated particularly with the big city, drifting passively, and whose ranks continue to swell visibly. Whether we succeed *or* fail, life seems to become peculiarly empty and meaningless, *once we know into which category we fall.*[4]

These latter kinds of personal and social rot, for which there are no statistics, are affecting our society more slowly but perhaps more surely than the less widespread, more obviously distorted reactions. When realization of failure comes to a man in his 30s or 40s, the psychological impact is, at the least, usually severely disorganizing. But what of this not-uncommon contemporary situation among adolescent boys, *whose personalities are still in process of formation:* a middle-class 16-year-old confronted with the life-career implications of a poor high-school scholastic record?

Ruth Benedict, in the last chapter of her *Patterns of Culture,* has summed up in a classic sentence the nature of the ego struggle among middle-class persons and its already evident individual and social implications:

> "In proportion as success is obsessive and is limited to the few, a greater and greater number will be liable to the extreme penalties of maladjustment."

Again for the sake of perspective, a parallel statement which is more applicable to other than middle-class groups should be placed

---

[4] Srole's *Mental Health in the Metropolis,* affords a later, research-based documentation of this proposition (64).

alongside Professor Benedict's. This statement applies to many in the lower classes who never entered upon the ego struggle of the middle class, *and* to increasing numbers of those in the lower-middle class who have given up that struggle:

> In proportion as a society makes consumer-goods the major source of self-gratification, and the money required to obtain them is not as readily available to large segments of the population as they would like through socially approved channels, a greater and greater number in that society will be pushed into illegal methods of obtaining money— methods ranging from violent or stealthy theft to *corruption of the innocent.*

This statement, written circa 1955, has proven to be most prophetic. It is common knowledge among most urban and suburban senior— and junior!—high-school students that a drug-contact is present either among their classmates or waiting at the gates of their school. Not quite as common knowledge, but spreading fast by word of mouth, is that a "nice piece of change" is forthcoming to those who contribute the names and addresses of classmates towards the compilation of a nation-wide teen-age drug-solicitation mailing-list.

Essentially the same point has been succinctly expressed by Cohen in his classic analysis of the "culture of the gang" (12):

> "Our view holds that those values which are at the core of the American 'way of life,' which help to motivate behavior which we esteem as 'typically American,' are among the major determinants of that which we stigmatize as 'pathological.' . . The same value-system, *impinging upon children differently equipped to meet it,* is instrumental in generating both respectability *and* delinquency."   (page 137)

(May I add: not only delinquency but also personality disorder?)

I wonder if *this* approach to the increase in some phases of juvenile and adult crime has been presented to private and governmental investigative bodies, whether of juvenile delinquency or of the "urban crisis."

Chapter Seven

Our American "D.P.s"

The circumstance that high occupational status and consumer capacity have become primary sources for individual feelings of self-worth among the urban middle classes has acted much like the dropping of a pebble in a pool. The psychological effects on us have been steadily spreading. There are many groups in our population—women, children and adolescents, and the elderly—whose social roles do not usually involve active money earning nor participation in a prestige occupation. As a result, many members of these groups have suffered social and psychological displacement.

Many middle-class women today are psychological "displaced persons" because their former dependable and unique sources for their feelings of self-worth have either diminished or entirely evaporated, in their own eyes. Psychologically felt success for the middle-class young woman depends initially on her attainment of married status and her acquisition of an economically promising young man, rather than on status in an economic role, as in her brother's case. But once this anxiety-relieving accomplishment is behind her, she finds other personal-status problems facing her. The circumstance that the roles of mother and homemaker are no longer considered sufficient reasons for a woman's being, particularly in urban settings, acquires personal implications for her. She finds herself counting in our society almost entirely as a *consumer* only—as buyer for her family, first, and as a recruit for our society's, and especially our advertisers', "cult of youth and beauty," second.

As a result, women generally have come to accept the economic status values of their society as wholeheartedly as do their husbands and brothers. These new values have come not merely to supersede values which have contributed to a women's adequate exercise of particularly her maternal role. For many women, the new values are at present experienced as being in direct conflict with these socially older values. Only a very few women, generally of upper-middle

[61]

status or higher, because of special individual, marital and familial circumstances, are able to work out a harmonious outer and inner integration of the old and the new values and their related practices.

Most middle-class women are expressing their subscription to economic status values in one of two ways. Many have become dependent upon their husband's level of consumer capacity as the major sources for *their own* feelings of worth. The husbands of these women have the added psychological burden of struggling to "save" their wives' souls as well as their own. Perhaps this situation is one of the factors contributing to so much of the hostility between many husbands and wives today. This pattern among women seems to be so general as to cut across social-status lines. Many of these women are returning to work full-time while their children are still very young primarily to supplement their husbands' incomes.

Desire for greater family consumer capacity is not the major factor in the reaction of another group of women: many middle-class wives and mothers have fully accepted economic status values *as applying directly to themselves*. Either they work outside the home in order to have some feelings of self-worth, or they feel vaguely guilty and aimless if they do not—and become ripe for a variety of personally and socially negative behaviors, among them the kind of maternal behavior Edward Strecker has epitomized with the borrowed term, "momism" (65). Those women who work in specialized business and professional fields for much the same inner reasons as men do—although self-fulfillment motives are likely to be as yet more frequent among women—are subject to the same inner pressures as are men in regard to the self-respect meaning of success. In most instances, they carry the added handicap of having to be "twice as good as a man in order to get half as far."

Frequently, the so-called "career woman" feels the alienation from her deeper needs more keenly than do her male colleagues, because her shift in role is socially still so recent she as yet has no buttressing, social- and self-justifying tradition to fall back on, as men do. She is often regarded as an interloper by her fellow competitors, both men and women, and to a real extent, by herself too. A man finds the competitiveness in his work situation hard enough to cope with psychologically at any time, but he is particularly bitter about competition from a woman: his one dependable remaining source for his feelings of masculinity are deeply threatened by her equal or superior status in his work world. Very few career women are so insensitive as not to feel this male reaction; and each reacts to it in accordance with her over-all personality functioning—by seductive or manipulative techniques, by aggression, by withdrawal, by unflappable good humor.

Some urban middle-class wives, and mothers with school-age children, return to work part- or full-time primarily for reasons of sociability. Under the impact of the feelings of boredom and isolation fostered by their self-contained, modern-miracle "machines for living," and lacking an adequate self-satisfying and self-creative avocation, their pre-marriage rejection of their cog-in-the-wheel clerical jobs shifts to nostalgic recollection of the easy group camaraderie typical of subordinate-in-status large-office positions. This practice should be viewed alongside the statistic that the highest rate of alcoholism appears among urban housewives.

Particularly three neurotic behavior-patterns are widespread among those middle-class women who have not been able to come to terms with their social displacement. Although these patterns are here presented as separate behavior constellations, some combination of them is frequently present in the same woman, especially patterns 1 and 3, and patterns 2 and 3.

1. The "traditionalist," who continues to adhere exclusively to the traditional middle-class role of wife and mother, even though this role has insufficient personal and social meaning beyond her children's early childhood years. In doing so, she unknowingly inflicts upon herself a pervasive sense of uselessness and inadequacy, and the necessity to cope with frequent attacks of overwhelming anxiety.

2. The "competitor," who unselectively rejects all aspects of women's traditional roles and equally unselectively accepts the traditional male economic-status role primarily because of its higher societal prestige.[1] Some of the "competitor's" personality difficulties have already been mentioned.

3. The "manipulator," who has adopted what used to be the trademark of the professional prostitute—the calculated, essentially hostile use of physical feminity as a means of exploiting, controlling, manipulating men, and for similar reasons: she resents her subordination to men (itself an institutionalized expression of male insecurity/hostility), but has neither the inner resources nor sufficient occupational competence to be independent of the mink-earning male.

The hostile use of sex represented by the "manipulator" pattern

---

[1] This subscription to the "masculine mystique" quite unconsciously permeates Betty Friedan's *The Feminine Mystique* (22).

has added materially to the psychological hazards of urban male existence: urban congestion and a general lack of active physical outlets have increased men's proneness to sexual tension, at the same time that the ego-attacking social and economic pressures on them have heightened their dependency needs. As a consequence, this reactively hostile feminine pattern has aroused a great deal of un-conscious male counter-hostility—closing a vicious circle! For many in the younger male generation, rejection of the American middle-class way of life is combined with hostility towards women. This association may not be merely coincidental, for these reasons:

1. Women as sexual beings are particularly threatening to these young men's fragile masculinity, yet woman as sexual temptress is used as a selling technique so unceasingly by our advertisers, this narrow aspect of womanhood has come to symbolize our consuming-dominated way of life.

2. The "manipulator" pattern—i.e., women who push their husbands to succeed economically at whatever personal cost so *they* can enjoy a high physical standard of living—is a common feminine type: common enough to have been their mother.

The ego problem of American women today—its sources, symptoms, and personal and social effects—is too complex and too important a subject in itself for me to undertake to go into it here with any degree of thoroughness. It will have to suffice to say, for the purpose of this discussion, that many women today *are* "psychological d.p.'s" during this period of cultural transition, and that *their* personality difficulties have even more serious social implications than those of men because of the singular importance for the new generation of the maternal role in our complex society, which places so many demands on the individual.

Our urban family, as opposed to the extended-kinship family organization of our grandparents and of some other current societies, makes most children psychologically dependent on only two adults during their early, most significant in personality-formation years—their mother and their father. Because of the wide separation between the father's place of work and his home in most urban areas, as well as the other claims on the time of many a young father anxious to "get ahead," the majority of urban children are psycho-logically dependent upon only one parent and one sex, the female, during these crucial early years (nursery and grade-school teachers are invariably women too!). And if the mother also works full-time, or rejects her maternal role. . . ! (A qualification should be inserted here: as our society ages, the presence of a middle-class grandparent generation in urban settings is gradually re-creating an extended-family system; the nature and effects of this development are well worth investigating.)

Here is the most socially significant by-product of the status struggle of our day. As individually and socially debilitating as the *individual* psychological by-products of this struggle are, their influence on *parental behavior* has still greater social effects because its results, through our children, are both cumulative and expanding. Their effects on the parental behavior of many in the middle class is the topic of the next chapter.

Many children, adolescents, and old people in our economic-status-driven society have become psychological d.p.s also, for reasons similar to those causing the psychological displacement of women.

Aside from the personal value placed on them by their parents, children and adolescents in the urban American environment are accorded low social value, on two counts. First, they are economically dependent, in a culture which stresses economic independence and high consumership as the ultimate virtues. And second, they are assigned no unique, socially indispensable function, no special or valued "place" in the broader society—except, of course, as consumers. Middle-class children are learning extra-family, broader societal values at a much younger age than in that long-ago era "before T.V." For children, the distinction between "commercial" or "entertainment" T.V. and "educational" T.V. is meaningless: *all* T.V. plays a highly educative role in their lives. This mass-communication medium, to which our children are so attentive, almost uniformly portrays only one aspect of adulthood — the *consumer* adult, male and female versions.

Within this narrow enough representation, a still narrower emphasis, already referred to, is common—the characterization of the female version of the consumer adult as an overadorned, shapely body, period, who gets what she wants from others by using their weaknesses as her lever for manipulating them. As children grow older, the movies reinforce this hostile, at base homosexually inspired, representation of women. Such repeated recognition of so narrow and so negative an aspect of womanhood is not calculated to help a little girl develop understanding and acceptance of the mature woman's complex wifely, maternal and social responsibilities—particularly if her own mother does not herself accept her maternal role and is overinfluenced by the glamorous images on the screens of never-never land. Nor is such a picture of femininity likely to assist the adolescent boy in his already difficult enough task of establishing healthy relationships with the opposite sex. Similar charges of narrowness and social unadaptiveness could be made against the mass media characterization of the male version of the consumer adult role.

Small wonder that so insistent a presentation of a distorted picture of the adult world, superimposed on their parents' tendency constantly to push them beyond their level of maturity, stimulates many children with few balancing experiences in their immediate environment to become psychologically displaced: they want to be grown up in appearance and prerogatives before they have had a chance to be children! For urban little girls, the age at which lipstick must be worn and boy friends kept on a leash has been steadily shrinking. For little boys, the age at which adult privileges must be granted without commensurate responsibilities has been shrinking.

Add to these influences the insistence of middle-class parents on high scholastic achievement for their sons and on popularity for their daughters, together with teachers' pressures for conformity and high marks, and the result is children living so much in the immediate, overstimulated present that they have little or no opportunity for the inner development that a leisurely, not too closely supervised period reserved for childhood provided for—a slow, inside-out intellectual-emotional ripening, and cultivation of the habit of self-attuned self-discovery. Frequently, development of the essentially self-protective practice of thoughtful evaluation of one's experience is too long delayed among our urban youngsters who are overstimulated from external sources. They experience some deeply traumatic incident which is directly due to their surface sophistication and maturity tripping over their actual immaturity.

I must interject here that the shallowness, sensationalism, violence and just plain stupidity of so much of our "entertainment" media cannot be considered to *cause* emotional disturbances or delinquency in children in and by themselves. These media affect some children strongly because their family-centered experiences have already made them psychologically vulnerable to such distorted portrayals. Again, there is a *convergence* of influences. But such a qualification of the psychological role of the mass media does not by any means exonerate them. It is no brief in their defense to say that they have adopted policies which have the effect merely of *contributing to* the psychological and legal delinquency of some minors. Their position is even less defensible when it is realized that it is in their power instead to use their great resources and educative influence not only to assist in such "crippled" children's rehabilitation, but also to play a positive role in all children's social and intellectual growth.

Adolescents are particularly sensitive to their lack of recognition as a socially worthwhile group in our society. Their tendency to make others their own age or slightly older their supreme point of reference in their own lives is one consequence of their social displacement. An adolescent whose earlier family experiences have not given him primary feelings of worth, becomes at best over-dependent on his group's opinion of him and develops a slavish conformity to peer-group values, which is frequently carried over into adult life. At worst, such an adolescent, if his group recognizes no outside authority, becomes one of our society's increasing army of adolescent displaced persons whom we term juvenile delinquents.

Nor can we reasonably expect two particular groups of affection-deprived adolescents to conduct themselves in an individually or socially responsible manner in the face of our consumer-wooing media—those who either have no money at all to spend, and those, at almost the other extreme of the social scale, who have been over-indulged with material possessions all their lives by their always too-busy-for-them parents and have learned the compensatory, purchasable means of self-indulgence only too well. A still further factor in adolescent psychological displacement is their difficulty in finding adequate models in their immediate environment to pattern themselves after. As part of the normal process which is involved in an adolescent's emerging maturity, he seeks for such adult models. He is, as a consequence, particularly sensitive to, and affected by, the evident and increasing immorality and opportunism everywhere around him.

The more idealistic of these youngsters have as young adults been going well beyond their earlier mere "sensitivity." During the past several years, they have become civil-rights supporters and workers, Peace Corps and VISTA volunteers, recruits to the rapidly growing Roman Catholic liberal-wing, political activists and "new politics" proponents.

For most older men in large urban settings, retirement takes from them their primary, in many instances their sole, source for their feelings of self-worth. The result for many is swift psychological and physical deterioration, even though financial need may not exist. And for many women, the aging process itself destroys sources for self-regard overemphasized in their lives—overvalued partly because of their vulnerability to the ceaseless and almost exclusive glorification of youth and beauty as feminine indispensables by our consuming-absorbed mass media. The psychological meaning of retirement and the bias against employing older workers are serving to make men vulnerable as well to increasing age.

A current, thoroughly American tragedy is the behavior a great many men and women begin to express at some point during their forties. At a time of life when accumulated experience and understanding should bring some measure of insight into and acceptance of themselves and their world, and the ability to fashion a serene, gracious, and inwardly attuned pattern of living, many chronologically mature Americans are instead clinging desperately in appearance and behavior to their unsure, tension-filled youth.

The social displacement of these middle-class sub-groups acquires an added dimension when placed in a broader societal context. A large, non-middle-class group of persons in our society has also been displaced of recent years for not entirely dissimilar reasons: unskilled workers, both white and Negro. That this order of displacement has implications for the future that extend well beyond poor family-heads is a point effectively made in these excerpts from a paper titled "Who Needs the Negro?" (76):

> "The tendency to look upon the racial crisis as a struggle for equality between Negro and white is too narrow in scope . . . With the onset of automation the Negro is moving out of his historical state of oppression into uselessness. Increasingly, he is not so much exploited as he is irrelevant. And the Negro's economic anxiety is an anxiety that will spread to others in our society as automation proceeds. . ."
>
> "In short and in summary, the historical transition for the Negro is *not* occurring in a civil rights context; it is instead a movement out of the Southern cotton-fields into the Northern factories and then to the automated urbanity of 'nobodiness.' The issue becomes a question of human— not only civil—rights, and involves white and Negro alike. *For the Negro is merely a weathervane for the future. His* experience will be a common one for many whites now deprived of some sort of usefulness; *his* frustrations will become those for many others, the longer we hesitate to confront the meaning of human dignity in an automated society. As more of us become unnecessary—as human energy and thought themselves become increasingly unnecessary—the greater will be our social anxiety. Then perhaps we will become aware that racial strife today is not between black and white, but is instead a search for human rights in a world of machines that makes so many human beings utterly dispensable."

Chapter Eight

Parents as American "D.P.s"

W<small>E PAY MUCH LIP-SERVICE</small> to the sanctity of the family and to its indispensable social and psychological roles. Indeed, it would seem that no politician could hope to be elected without frequent reference to the social importance of the family. Yet two factors particularly are leading to the displacement of the maternal and paternal roles among many in our urban society—parents' own values concerning the primary importance in their lives of high consumer and personal status, and the lack of general social recognition of, and accommodation to, what is involved in the adequate exercise of the respective parental roles. Here is another major contradiction of our time.

There is a belief far too widespread in our middle-class world, a belief which is partially a reflection of the over-all material values of our culture, and partially a result, perhaps, of parents' own depression-haunted childhoods: the good parent is *primarily* one who gives his or her children material, including educational, advantages. Parents' subscription to this belief has made them particularly vulnerable to two sets of consumer pressures—those coming directly from our advertisers, who do not hesitate to exploit this parental vulnerability to the hilt; and those coming indirectly, through their children, whose immaturity is so calculatedly taken advantage of by our commercially sponsored mass media. These two sets of external pressures, combining with parents' inner vulnerability to them, have placed most parents in literal consumer bondage: there is no end to the things their children *must* have in the typically competitive urban social setting.

A new, tacit, public norm concerning what is involved in being a "good parent," as opposed to a "bad parent," has emerged in large sections of the middle class: the good parent places his children's material and physical comfort first and his own second; the not-so-good parent places his own material and physical comfort first and that of his children second. This consumer bondage, converging with parents' ego-involvement as individuals in their respective status struggles, has meant that *giving of oneself* to one's children during their earlier years, which necessarily involves the expenditure of time and interest *as needed by them,* has become an actual luxury that many young urban fathers, particularly, feel they cannot afford. Yet such child-attuned giving of self is indispensable for children's healthy psychological development in our type of family system and our type of society.

The lack of accommodation to the special problems of parents of young children in our urban economic and social practices and physical environment has also contributed to the displacement of the parental role. Our self-contained biological family unit, the transfer to the operation of the home of the industrial concept that production efficiency is prior to human social needs, the young father's absorption in his struggle for consumer and occupational status, all combine to deny the psychological needs of the mother of young children: she is physically and psychologically isolated at the very time when her children's never ending physical and psychological demands and her own inexperience lead her to need social and emotional support the most. A young family-man's struggle for an economic foothold is typically most demanding of him psychologically, physically, and in sheer time while his children are young. This culturally imposed circumstance ignores the crucial importance of the father's role in a child's personality development and character formation: by the time his strenuous efforts have made the family more secure economically, the never-to-be-made-up-for early years of his children are past.

I have so far spoken in generalized terms. Let me present, for illustrative purposes, four patterns of parental behavior which are not at all uncommon in current American life, particularly in large urban settings. Purely individual factors enter into the particular patterns of parental behavior which each father and mother expresses. But, here again, enough parents behave sufficiently similarly for a number of patterns, both wholesome and "delinquent" in effect on their children, to become evident on a group basis. I am not going to discuss those parents whose self-accepting and self- and socially responsible children offer testimony that they are doing an adequate and more than adequate job of being parents, in spite of the inner and outer pressures on them. I believe that there are still many such parents in the middle class. Probably the most frequently expressed wish of these parents is that their society were a help, rather than in so many ways a hindrance, to them in the performance of their responsibility.

Rather, I am selecting for attention patterns of parental behavior which can be considered examples of "parental delinquency" and which have their roots primarily in the parents' response as individuals to their status struggles. These are persons who, as reacting individuals, tend to fit into one or another of the neurotic patterns previously described. Two of these patterns are more typical of the middle classes, and two appear more frequently among working-class groups, the source for new members of the middle class.

Although the patterns of parental delinquency to be described are most typical of large-urban areas, I doubt that they are confined to our large cities. I am presenting each of the patterns in the form of a summary chart, under three headings:

A brief description of those characteristics of the parents as individuals which are of key importance in their parental behavior; the relationship of these characteristics to the status struggle of our time has been previously discussed.

The key characteristics of these parents' behavior with their children.

The effects on their children of the parental behavior described.

The *first* delinquent-parent pattern has been most frequent among upper-middle families, and some lower-middle, where father, and sometimes mother, is in a relatively high-status professional or business occupation:

Parents as Individuals	Parental Behavior With Their Children	CAN LEAD TO:	Psychological Effects on Their Childrenn	WHICH TENDS TO PROMOTE..
Psychologically displaced mother *or* working full-time professional level mother with young child (ren) and strong guilt feelings. *plus* Psychologically "alone" and / or job - frustrated father . . .	Their psychological absorption or overprotection of their one or two children. They react to them as extensions of their own highly vulnerable egos (27).		Their children are rendered overanxious to the point of neuroticism; frequently they become the strongly other-directed character type described by Riesman.	

It is because such a father is "torn apart" psychologically in his daily work role that he needs to make of his family life an impregnable psychological fortress and to project to and into his children his picture of his *ideal* self.

The *second* delinquent-parent pattern is most frequent among lower-middle parents who are trying to become upper-middle, or among those very recently "arrived" in the upper-middle grouping.

Parents as Individuals		Parental Behavior With Their Children		Psychological Effects on Their Children
Desperately upward-mobile parents absorbed in their respective struggles for upward status, father in his work and mother socially. Alienation from their deeper needs and emotions characteristic . . .	CAN LEAD TO:	Are either unable to react spontaneously and warmly to their children, or spend little or no time actually interacting with them, or both. Both patterns are interpreted by their children as rejection. *Along with* Assuaging their spasmodic guilt feelings over their neglect of their children with a constant stream of expensive gifts . . .	WHICH TENDS TO PROMOTE:	Emotionally-disturbed children, some of whom become socially irresponsible adolescents and adults. For many of these children, possessions come to be overvalued because of their substitute nature (for parental attention and affection) : these children tend to demand more and more, and more expensive, clothes, toys, gadgets— the producers' and advertisers' delight!

Such parents frequently harbor deep insecurities, left over from their adolescence, about their identity as a man or a woman and express these anxieties by imposing on their children premature and excessive demands for conformity to stereotypically masculine or feminine behavior. The father may insist that his adolescent son be the aggressive and dominant predator with the opposite sex that he had once dreamt of being. The mother may put both overt and subtle pressure on her daughter to be the popular and attractive "sexpot" she so much wanted to be during *her* adolescence. The not-surprising result in many instances is an almost compulsive acting-out by the children of their parents' repressed desires. Or just the opposite may occur: a slow-maturing, psychologically vulnerable boy may be panicked into homosexuality by such premature pressure.

Pattern 2 is particularly familiar to the personnel of some of our highest fee, most "exclusive" private summer camps and schools. The overanxious, overprotected child associated with Pattern 1, and the rejected, mixed-up child associated with Pattern 2 are maintaining the private practices of many a big-city child psychiatrist and child psychologist. Some of the economically privileged but socially irresponsible youngsters associated with Pattern 2 are frequently not only more than their thoroughly bewildered parents can cope with, but also thorns in the side of their teachers and community. Only their social and economic status keeps some of them from acquiring the legal label of "delinquent"—delaying the day of reckoning in some cases until they reach titular-adult status. It sometimes seems that our newspapers could not hope to keep up their circulation figures without such newsworthy "days of reckoning." [1]

The *third* delinquent-parent pattern is most frequent among young couples of minority group, upper-lower class background, struggling for upward personal and family mobility—and with apparently the best parental motivations in the world:

---

[1] Another pattern, widespread among the middle class's "best families," illustrates how difficult it can be to decide where to draw the line between parental delinquency and respectability:

Parents as Individuals	Parental Behavior with Their Children		Psychological Effects on Their Children
A mother who undertook the traditional middle-class wife-and-mother role primarily because of strong external (parental-family and general-cultural) pressures; tends to project her own strong but frustrated achievement needs onto her children. *plus* A father whose success in a highly competitive occupation has vindicated his commitment (frequently in reaction to an unsuccessful father) to unremittingly intense striving . . .	Constant pressure on their children to compete and to succeed both academically and socially. Parental approval of their child is conditional —i.e., given only upon achievement.	CAN LEAD TO: WHICH TENDS TO PROMOTE:	Two types of reactions typical: 1. Overt compliance with parental pressures and values, combined with covert and/or repressed rebellion against their parents—which is indirectly expressed in a manipulative, "operator" approach with parents and other adults. 2. Overt rebellion against their parents and even, for some, against the current American way of life.

In my eyes, this pattern is, in its essence, a variation of Pattern 2.

Parents as Individuals	Parental Behavior With Their Children	Psychological Effects on Their Children
Both parents working full-time and also, usually, father going to night school or having a second job . . .	Their spending practically no non-fatigued, non-irritable time with their children. *Along with* A tendency to be overstrict with their children when they *are* with them in order to "make up for" their lack of guidance and control while away from them . . .	The semi-orphaned, affection-starved "latch-key" child of the big city (to the uninitiated: these are the nursery and school-age children who come home to a parentless, locked apartment and have the key to the apartment on a string around their necks) who live overmuch in a fantasy world of comics and T.V. (and because vulnerable, are overinfluenced by them). Boys particularly have a difficult personality development problem, relating to their sex-role: they don't see enough of their fathers or of men generally to develop an adequate masculine image to pattern after.

(CAN LEAD TO: ... WHICH TENDS TO PROMOTE:)

Delinquent-parent patterns 2 and 3 illustrate particularly well the effects of parental acceptance of the belief that the good parent is primarily one who gives his and her children material advantages.

Pattern 3 is becoming more and more frequent as the increasing number of working-class mothers with young and very young children going outside the home to work has assumed the proportions of a social trend. This development is an excellent example of the serious social effects that an unregulated economic trend can have. This trend began when industry's newly developed machines made it necessary for the family head to go outside the home to make a living: up to then, the family had been a self-contained unit both socially and economically. In the urban working-class family, typically containing only two adults, the absence of the father from the home removed an indispensable source of experience from his growing children. But the mother, at least, remained directly accessible to them.

As food-processing and clothes-making machines outside the home have replaced woman's traditional labors inside the home, the cost of the basic necessities of living in terms of actual cash outlay has steadily risen. At the same time, producer pressures on consumers have convinced families with even the most tenuous economic base that an expanding number of home appliances comes under the category of "basic necessities." The result has been that these working-class mothers, who were originally influenced by wartime production needs to work outside the home, are continuing to do so, for the same reason the father originally did—to help meet their family's daily living expenses (67). *But these women cannot keep their children near them at the factory, as they were able to do when they worked in the home.* Who is left to perform those child-rearing functions which are indispensable to the undistorted development of members of the slow-maturing human species?

This is only the first of a series of questions that we should be asking about this social trend. Is this development strictly an individual family matter, as we are currently treating it, or do we have a stake in it as a society? Is the circumstance that juvenile delinquency rates have been rising almost directly parallel with this trend entirely a matter of coincidence? Have "socially justifiable" advertising pressures played a role in sustaining and furthering this development?

The *fourth* delinquent-parent pattern is most frequent among economically marginal and personally inadequate lower class parents who are over-stimulated by the high-pressure consumer appeals of our culture:

Parents as Individuals		Parental Behavior With Their Children		Psychological Effects on Their Children
Mother with young children working full-time and/or rejecting of her maternal role. *Along with* Psyhologically "alone" father and/or rejecting of paternal role and/or alcoholic father . . .	CAN LEAD TO:	Their inadequate exercise of their basic socializing-of-child role. *Along with* A tendency to overexercise the punishing and controlling aspects of parenthood and under-exercise the affectional and guidance aspects. Erratic, excessively brutal beatings not uncommon . . .	WHICH TENDS TO PROMOTE:	Children who feel rejected, and reject their parents as a result. Such children typically harbor a very high level of hostility. Are unable to identify with their parents, the most effective motivation for becoming socialized or "human," and *self*-disciplined. The frequent result is children unresponsive to *any* adult-dominated situation, such as school, and eventual delinquency. At the least, too many become the same kind of parents their parents were.

The children associated with Pattern 4, who have inadequate self controls and unrealistic or socially irresponsible "idealized images" (T.V. and the movies again), usually have none but their own equally rejected and socially irresponsible peers to identify with. The next step, all too often, is actual delinquent behavior, later confirmed rejection of the broader society which so clearly rejects them, and criminality. Such children, because of their psychologically inadequate family settings and because of no or inadequate provision for their special needs in our society, are usually irretrievably "lost" to that society even before they leave grade school. Their experiences in our middle-class-geared schools typically contribute to their personality difficulties. On the other hand, their presence in a public schoolroom as adolescents makes it impossible for the harassed teacher to do the job with her remaining students that society expects her to do: her total function becomes that of disciplinarian.

These are the children for whom public whippings are frequently recommended as the best and most effective deterrent to repeated delinquency! The records of our criminal and mental institutions testify to their subsequent high cost to themselves and to our short-sighted, rejecting society.

Patterns 2 and 4, although representative of families far apart on the economic scale, have not only a crucial parental personality characteristic in common—that of immaturity, but also an outcome of that characteristic of major social import. Some, if not all, of these parents' children were *not wanted, especially by the mother:* they were conceived and born either because of vulnerability to social pressure (including religious belief) or because of ignorance of or unwillingness to utilize anti-conception measures—and they continued to be unwanted after birth.[2]

When medical and psychiatric researchers and criminologists broaden their research-designs to take into controlled account such complex developmental influences, we shall have documented what many students of human development now strongly suspect: that a substantial proportion of a wide variety of social incompetents—alcoholics, the chronically ill, criminal psychopaths/sociopaths, prostitutes, so-called "sex criminals" and attackers of women—all have a crucial characteristic in common: they were unwanted by one or both of their parents, *after birth as well as before.*

---

[2] The implication of this commonality for conservative moralists both within and without the church would seem to be clear: women have truly formidable, *albeit quite-unconscious,* ways of striking back at a social order which denies them the right of control over their own bodies and individual destinies.

Chapter Nine

Creative Individualists as American "D.P.s"

Our DEDICATION to high occupational and consumer status as our personal touchstone for happiness has also come to have disastrous effects on the individualist and on creative individualism in our society. Here I am defining individualism not in the negative sense of runaway egocentrism; but rather, as true-to-oneself individuality, in which striving to become oneself in the fullest yet most unique sense is the key characteristic. Among creative people, the major means for their self-development and self-fulfillment is the practice of their creative tendencies, whatever avenues these may take, primarily because of the satisfaction and inner growth such practice brings them.

One of the most intellectually creative persons of our time, while giving advice to a young visitor, summed up the rationale of his creativity in these few words:

> The important thing is not to stop questioning. Curiosity has its own reasons for existence. One cannot help but be in awe when he contemplates the mysteries of eternity, of life, of the marvelous structure of reality. It is enough if one tries merely to comprehend a little of this mystery each day. Never lose a holy curiosity (45).

Not only intellectually and artistically creative persons function on the basis of such intrinsic motivations: the key contributions of such American industrial and business giants as Henry Ford, Conrad Hilton, David Sarnoff—much as some of us would question the influence of some aspects of their contributions to American life—are further examples of the fruits of creative individualism. It is generally conceded that acts of creation-discovery which have esthetically, intellectually, emotionally and materially enriched the world in general and our country in particular have typically resulted from the efforts of creative people so to fulfill themselves.

But this desire to fulfill oneself through creative expression is by no means confined only to such gifted persons as Albert Einstein, the person just quoted. All of us have some degree of need to express ourselves as whole and unique individuals. And all of us possess some characteristic self-expressive bent, even though constant suppression of it may have driven it from our awareness. It is my belief that this need of man to express his own individuality is uniquely human, and every bit as compelling a force in his life as his more basic physiological needs—whether the individual concerned is conscious of the existence of this need or not. I am also convinced that chronic denial of this need can and does result either in emotional problems or in pervasive hostility which may express itself in covert and overt anti-social behaviors, or both.

Yet the creative individualist, and the tendency to cultivate creative individuality, have, with one major exception, been seriously displaced in recent years. This displacement is partially due to our individual dedications to the touchstone fallacy, and partially due to today's economic facts of life in our "other-employed" society.

In our highly specialized urban world, money is absolutely necessary to obtain the basic essentials of life, let alone the status-important luxuries. There are rather short limits in this kind of economic situation to how far a man with—or even without—a family can go in pursuing creative activities which are congenial to him and which may ultimately enrich his society, but which have negligible *immediate* commercial value. "What good is happiness—can it get you money?" has long been a popular aphorism going the rounds of the less-affluent market-places of New York City. The limits are similarly short on how deviate his behavior on the job can be from the accepted and paid-for norm: most positions exist within a highly organized and complex hierarchy of human interaction. These circumstances force most of us to channel both our abilities and our behavior into those avenues of earning a living which are available to us—and these avenues are frequently not congenial either to our creative streak nor to our personalities.

There is one major group of happy and fortunate self-expressive workers in the American middle class who constitute the major exception to this situation—those whose natural creative and personality bents happen to coincide, or can be readily deflected to coincide, with the opportunities, competitive demands, and complex human maze which are involved in most of the commercially rewarded activities available to them. Whether such people are engineers or entertainers, disc jockeys or designers, office-machine operators or authors, salesmen or statisticians, test pilots or consulting psychologists, to name only a few middle class occupations, they feel rewarded inwardly as well as monetarily for doing what they can best do and like best to do.

But with all the wise vocational counseling in the world, and as amazingly adaptable as we humans are, there are far fewer people who are able readily and satisfyingly so to channel their natural self-expressive and personality inclinations than our widespread belief in the touchstone of high economic status seems to assume: available types of remunerative jobs and job settings in our highly organized and mechanized economic life cannot, I believe, provide adequately for the range and frequency in the population of individual aptitudes, preferences, potentialities, personality needs.

The continuing, almost desperate search for "sound" employee incentive plans is but one evidence of this circumstance. Further, psychology has not discovered a predictable relationship between individual creative potential in a given field and the ability to get along smoothly with other people, the personality characteristic so essential for continuing employment in the majority of available white-collar jobs. If high creativity is predictably related to any other personal characteristic, it is probably to that of independence of mind—a truly disastrous tendency in highly structured office and institutional work-settings. It appears that at least one large corporation has become concerned over the dearth of creative thinking among its employees and has applied a variation of the usual employee incentive plan to stimulate such activity (13). I seriously doubt whether its problem can be solved within the framework of current organizational thinking, which is so strongly committed to the pre-eminent dominance of economic incentives.

Large corporations—and small businesses—also overlook a major result of direct competitive pressures on their administrative personnel. A man who has run the competitive gauntlet and has managed to obtain a senior position, with all the emotional imprint this experience has left on his "insides," is not likely to "slit his own throat" by hiring or promoting a creatively promising younger man, if such hiring or promoting is within his jurisdiction. The manuals on "how to get that job or promotion" overlook that an increasingly frequent reason many a promising, well-prepared young person in creative-skills fields, particularly, does not get "that job" is not because of any deficiency in skill or personal qualifications, but quite the reverse: he is so well equipped and creative, he constitutes a direct competitive threat to his already hard-enough-pressed potential superiors.[1]

The primary and immediate purpose of our intricate modern organization of production, distribution, consumption, is, after all, to yield the owners and stockholders a profit; secondarily, to satisfy men's real and artificially stimulated material needs; incidentally, to provide a means of livelihood for the general population—but not at all to help individual workers grow as human beings nor to cater to the unregulatable unpredictability of individual creative expression and natural cycles of physical functioning. There is a basic incompatibility here which is not acknowledged by most industrial psychologists and human relations consultants.

When we adopt, without qualification, consumer and occupational status as the major means for individual status and self-respect, we are forced to accept not only the consumer-goods abundance of our economic organization. *We are also forced to accept its self-denying characteristics.* The humanity and individuality of *both* employer and employee become subservient to its profit-motive (or, in socialist countries, its production-quota) dictates. Probably the majority in the American middle class are inattentive to their own creative needs whenever these are considered to be not readily and adequately "commercial"—currently the most judgmental adjective in the language!—or otherwise prestige-giving. We are not likely even to try to work out some reasonable compromise between the demands of our status struggles and our inner needs: the gentlemen we're competing with don't take any time out, so how can we?

Many members of the younger generation who have grown up in economically secure homes are showing a different, reactive, pattern. A Spring '66 survey of 800 college seniors by *Newsweek* found that only 12 per cent planned a business career as their first choice; a business analyst commented on this survey as follows:

> "Today, it is research, the professions, academic life, and careers allow-
> ing them to help others that attract able students. . . . But the response

---

[1] Top-level management in such intensely competitive fields as advertising and the mass communications media, air and otherwise, has recently begun to recognize this middle-management "shortcoming" and to handle it in typical "economic facts of life" style: they are dismissing, regardless of their age (some are in their 30s!) middle-management persons who have become overly self-protective or "set in their ways" or so individualistic as to evince ethical objections to some more than ordinarily manipulative or bizarre offering, and to replace them with high-powered young people who are much more "manageable" because of their eagerness to get ahead at any cost.

of top business to their difficulty in hiring top students is disappointing so far. Almost without exception, the reaction seems to be: 'We must tell the story of business more effectively.' Rarely does one hear: 'What can we do to change the ways of business to make it more attractive for bright students?' The business response, in other words, leans toward doing a public-relations job instead of improving the product" (68).

(But one finds oneself wondering how the bright and idealistic young people referred to are going to react when they discover that most professions *and* the academic world have been regressing to the business mean in *their* ethics and/or layers of bureaucracy—with results described in the two subsequent chapters.)

Our own values also push us to be highly conforming in all areas of our living, regardless of what we might actually prefer to do. For most of us in the middle class, the status of our job and the size of our paycheck are our major, if not only, sources of satisfaction in life. Social respectability and acceptance at all costs are the dominant themes of our lives: how can we risk stepping out of line on anything, from the way we dress, furnish our home, have fun, and bring up our children, to the tone of voice to be used in discussing political events— if it is "permissable" to discuss them at all?

As for creative hobbies, always a respectable outlet, there is a strong tendency to have the creative element gadgeteered or pre-planned right out of them. The do-it-yourself trend is a possible exception.

But some creative people are fortunate enough to achieve commercial recognition—in fact, more and more seem to be gaining such recognition, to the extent that there is a perceptible occupational shift to careers in arts and letters and research (21). But the creative person and society are still the losers in too many cases of artistic success today. Consider the sequence of events which frequently follows in the case of the creative person in the arts whose efforts overnight acquire major commercial value.

With this practical recognition, such an individual's personal prestige rises from zero, or less, to astronomical heights. Too often a process of seduction begins, for which a sometimes unpredictable consumer public is not primarily to blame. Our fortunate little man's long-shoved-aside dream of happiness, in which comfort and personal prestige figured largely, has been given a new lease on life. Small wonder that many of our initially most promisingly creative artists, novelists, musicians, playwrights, upon practical public recognition soon abandon the serious cultivation of their muse in whatever direction she may lead them. She may, heaven forbid, lead them into channels of expression that are not immediately lucrative! They have been seduced by their own values into subserving their self-developing and self-enriching creativity to consumer power and immediate personal status —and a static, even retrogressive, personality mold.

Am I implying here that creative people should accept the curse of poverty all their lives? Not at all. I am trying to say that in a society with values and practices more attentive to the needs of human beings, such people would neither so misrepresent the personal meanings of social respectability and personal comfort, nor be poor and prestigeless in the first place.

Some people who acquire positions of high public regard in our broadcasting entertainment media become the victims of the consumer-dominated philosophy of their direct or indirect employers, the advertising industry. A spectacular if short-lived income, rather than a modest but probably much longer lasting salary is the occupational pattern typical of these media, for particularly two reasons, the second an outgrowth of the first. Such a person's value to his sponsors is measured by the cost of the program divided by the number of persons viewing it. He is accordingly forced, in our high production-cost visual media, to make one undiscriminating "pitch" to the largest possible consumer public. When it is realized that about fifty per cent of the consumer public are in Warner's two lower classes, and nearly ninety per cent in his lower-middle and lower classes combined, and since the present not the potential level of consumer taste and receptivity is the dominating criterion, the result is both predictable and understandable: the much-deplored tendency on the part of our commercially sponsored mass media to cater to the lowest common consumer denominator. Our "creative success" quickly finds himself (a) with a muse which is a bastardized caricature of her former promise, and (b) already on the "treadmill to oblivion" (3).

A further result of current programming and advertising practices on our broadcasting media has been an unexpected and disconcerting one for T.V. and radio sponsors, I am sure: it is the trend on the part of a number of publics towards resisting stock entertainment formulas and advertising messages. For these publics, the saturation point has been reached—and passed: a phenomenon which has so worried the advertising industry, our newest high-prestige professional group, that they have turned to the extensive use of another group of professionals eager for similar prestige, applied behavioral scientists. Neither of these professional groups appears to realize that in so uniting exploitative motives with manipulative skills, they are themselves setting the stage for their social repudiation.

Our commercial communicators and other entertainment entrepeneurs have yet to discover and to act on a truth that may not be quite as old as the manipulation of other human beings for personal gain, but that is nevertheless well time-tested: entertainment as a vehicle for escape from self is sterile and quickly tired of; but entertainment as a vehicle for re-creation, self-objectivity and self-emergence is, like the essentially educative philosophy it expresses, as stable and persisting as human growth and change itself.

It is not fair, nor is it intended, to leave an impression that all the creative persons employed in or supported by our various mass media are socially irresponsible—quite the contrary. The group in our country who are probably more concerned than any of us about the abysmal state of affairs in these media today are the very people who are earning their livings therefrom.

Creative individualism in the arts and letters is not the only kind of individualism which is affected by current social values and economic practices. Persons in the scholarly and pure science professions whose creative predilections run to research or to speculative thought are keenly aware of the difficulties involved in their trying to pursue a hunch which doesn't happen to coincide with the areas for which research subsidies and institutional time-allowances are available (35). Yet we are dependent as a society on this order of creativity for another Einstein and another Schweitzer!

The problem of the creative individualist in fields of endeavor not in immediate commercial and social demand is not a new one: it appears to have been in existence as long as has organized society itself. But whether or not such persons should be given broad opportunity to develop their creativity in whatever direction it may lead them, regardless of current social, governmental or commercial acceptability, can no longer be considered a problem only for the individuals concerned. The way we and other highly specialized technological societies answer this question may well play a determining role in the very survival of human society.

Whether the first motive of the creative person is to satisfy his own emerging individuality or to seek to subserve it to immediate commercial or status rewards has other less global, but nevertheless vitally important social implications. The quality and direction of our cultural and intellectual life as a nation will be—is being—directly affected by the answer which emerges to this question. The circumstance that our commercially sponsored mass-media entertainers have already become our country's major culture-carriers and -interpreters, both at home and abroad, is a testament to the quality of that culture. Also, since an increasing proportion of our population is earning its living in artistic and research occupations, more and more of us are coming to be directly affected as *reacting individuals* by the answer.

One of Ted Key's cartoons serves as an eloquent footnote here. In a six-episode sequence, we see the "progression" of a talented young American concert singer's career, from his first singing lessons as a tot, to his work with a more illustrious teacher as an adolescent, to his diligent cultivation of his talent in world-famous European conservatories as a young man, to his return to his native land of "free opportunity" and a job as a singer (whether on radio or T.V. is not clear) of the commercial, "Munchies are so good for you, so good, so good, so goodie good good . . ." in his artistic maturity.[2]

We have already become so uncreative in the arts and in ideas, one special aspect of our mediocrity will serve a compensatory function: the paper on which the various facets of current American intellectual and artistic life is printed is of such inferior quality it will have crumbled to dust within 500 years!

To those people who dismiss this problem by saying that giving people ready opportunity to do what they like best to do will breed irresponsibility, my comment is: I doubt that it will breed a fraction of the irresponsibility we have today, so much of which stems, I believe, from so many people having to do what they *don't* want to do. The *raison d'être* for our so-called "beat generation" lies here. I have already stated my belief that the creative, self-expressive needs of man, whether the individual is aware of their existence or not, are every bit as compelling in his life as are his more basic biological needs. It follows that when a society does not provide, teach, and *recognize as worthy,* channels of expression diverse enough to allow for the wide range of positive human creative behavior (in which I include creativity in human relations), *a tendency is fostered for man's creative needs to be displaced to bizarre, compulsive and anti-social avenues of expression*—as has become amply evident in the last few years. So our society loses in yet another way when it does not take man's

---

[2] In *Never on Sunday,* Jules Dassin took such exploitation of the arts a step further in a significant sub-plot, the one involving the vice-king's financial sponsorship of Illya's "reform": in a society that has gone off the rails morally, *even learning and the arts become means to further anti-social ends.*

more complex human needs more adequately and explicitly into account.

This general problem area gains even greater urgency if the predicted "second industrial revolution" of almost complete automation is as close as many informed people believe it to be. When the work the great majority of us do for our livelihood takes so little of our time and inner resources that we can no longer ascribe *any* personal importance to it, what will be our humanly meaningful alternatives? More and more commercial recreation and conspicuous consumption of leisure and LSD trips? Here is why I find it difficult to understand that the only apparent concern of our labor leaders in the face of the spread of automation is the ensuring of workers' economic security.

The questions on human creativity and individualism which have been raised in this chapter are, I believe, of such importance to our, and all human, society, we should be discussing them in every type of setting—from national conferences of our best minds in government, education, business, unions, and the behavioral sciences, to local citizens' forums, classrooms, neighborhood meetings.

Because the behavior of many middle-class young people during the past decade represents attempts, both consciously deliberate and unconsciously compulsive, to deal as affected individuals with these very questions, an examination of the younger generation's reaction to the rapidly ongoing, undeliberated and unilaterally imposed technological revolution of our time is being added as an epilogue to this chapter.

Adolescence is the life-period which is most immediately affected by the discontinuities which rapid social change builds into the individual life-career, primarily because it is the period of transition from childhood status and roles to adult status and roles: the growing young person, heretofore cushioned from the direct impact of the broader society by his family, comes smack up against the actual, not the idealized or fantasized or no longer existent world of non-related persons, situations and events. The perceived gaps occasioned by this confrontation are very frequently internalized by the young person; as such, they are accurately termed "culturally derived" conflicts.

Probably every generation of adolescents in every complex society has had to face—and to come to terms with—many such conflicts in their attempts to achieve maturity, and most have managed to do so without being destroyed psychologically. But—contrary to some platitudinous analysts—the dilemma facing the current (1960-1970) generation of American adolescents is so massive and so pervasive as to be of a qualitatively different order from those faced by adolescents of other times and other places. Especially discontinuities related to the adult male's roles, status, responsibilities, are currently on the decided increase, because unilaterally imposed and socially unexamined changes in technology *and* the size and functioning of American secondary institutions have been effecting major and widespread changes in occupations, occupational settings, and employment patterns.

The very nature of the "second industrial revolution," the narrowly self-interested manner in which it is being instituted—*and* its convergence with a period of rapidly increasing population in the United States—are combining to create so marked a conflict for the adolescent male, especially for middle-class young men, that a mass "individual confrontation" situation has emerged. The direct personal implications of the very large, bureaucratic administrative units imposed by the convergence of increasing population, uni-directional hierarchical organization, *and* massive technology, is hitting them first in our over-crowded educational institutions and second, in their work-life. This increasingly pervasive pattern is forcing two incompatible versions of the adult male role—and related personality characteristics—on them: the old, still much-preached ideal of individuality, self-direction, personal integrity, inner maturity, *and* the new necessity to accommodate to very large, hierarchically organized worksettings, which at lower levels reward the traditionally feminine and childish traits of passivity and dependency, and at higher, managerial and technical levels, necessitate the willingness to be manipulated on the one hand, and the ability to manipulate those below—and above—them in the hierarchy on the other hand.

This new definition of adulthood eliminates the necessity for a period in the individual life-career of inner transition from an immature, childish self to a mature, self-directing self, as Friedenberg has pointed out (24). And this immature version of adulthood is not merely being economically rewarded but *socially imposed,* since the young man, especially, must succeed occupationally in order to become economically self-sufficient and so be considered (and consider himself) "grown up"!

College-educated young women are also involved in this development, but in a somewhat different way. Because of the displacement of their former sources of feelings of self-worth, the traditional feminine roles, they are either turning outright to the traditionally masculine source of occupational achievement, or they are trying to combine their traditional and their newer sources. But they are in either case turning in increasingly greater numbers to the traditionally masculine source at the very time when this source is undergoing the major, technologically influenced attack just described!

In the face of this confrontation, middle-class young people have been responding in a variety of ways which may be classified first into the broad categories of "conformist" and "non-conformist," with each of these categories secondarily sub-divisible into "activists" and "passivists."

The *conformists* are adapting to the new educational and occupational situation/requirements in substantially the same ways as did the previous generation, earlier described: either as passive "fitters-in," or as active, adaptive strivers for the higher income and status occupations. The term "adaptive" is intended to signify their calculated assumption of whatever roles and behaviors are required to get ahead in a multi-layered bureaucratic hierarchy. But the overall living-pattern of both groupings of conformists is often as schizoid as was that of the older generation of conformers: their occupational compliance is in many instances balanced by a marked non-conformity in the conduct of their private lives—that is, by far more hedonistic and otherwise-infantile behavior than the previous generation dared (or perhaps needed) to express. The current big-city recreational "scene," exhibitionistic and compulsive consumerism, and the obsessively obscene character of much present art and literature are the more publicly visible aspects of these expressions; mechanically repetitious hetero- or homo- sexuality, although not as common, probably, as view-with-alarm discussions suggest, is a somewhat-less visible aspect. A quite-different group of after-work non-conformists are those who do volunteer work in anti-poverty programs and/or support civil-rights and peace -promoting organizations.

The *non-conformists* include both those who rebel actively against the society which is forcing so difficult a conflict on them, and those who passively retreat, at first from the conflict, but eventually, often, from life itself—as expressed in one of the most popular songs of 1966 (28): "I wish you'd go away and let me spend my life in Su-Su-Su-, Su-Su-Su-, Su-Su-Su-Su-Su-Su-Sugartown." [4] Initially, at least, both non-conforming sub-groupings share in common a strong

---

[4] Only those over 30 remain unaware that "sugar" is hip slang for heroin.

compensatory drive to be distinct and distinctive individuals rather than a mass-society statistic. The non-conformists also have much in common with the young ghetto-rioters, ostensibly disparate as the sources of the two groups' discontent appears to be: together they represent an entire generation's protest against the powerlessness and the "nobodiness" of urban-technological society, avant-garde, American, version.

The "passivists" comprise those who withdraw, temporarily or permanently, into alcohol- or drug-addition or some other pattern indicative of arrest at, or regression to, pre-adolescent levels of development. The "activists" include both those whose rebellion is impulsively hostile and self- and socially- defeating *and* those whose rebellion is idealistically motivated and expressed not so much against society in the abstract but against some specific aspect(s) of the present United States "establishment" or way of life: the peace-protest organizers and marchers, civil-rights workers, Peace Corps and VISTA volunteers, "new politics" activists.

Both passivists and activists are represented among the "hippies," the newest and still-widening wave of youthful adolescent revolt. Despite the romantic illusions of some of its envious-oldster observers, this peace- and love- loving sub-culture as it is being currently expressed is as passing a social phenomenon as were the beatniks—and for an inescapably blunt-fact-of-current-American-life reason. As soon as any form of dissent colorful or bizarre enough to attract popular interest emerges, it is annexed towards huckstering ends by the very status quo against which it is being expressed—and the dissent is thereby rendered meaningless, reduced to the level of yet another product- and book- selling fad.[2] (Our conservative politicians and local and federal law-enforcing apparati are obviously unaware that such containment of the milder forms of social protest forces the adoption of more and more extreme forms of expression. Might it be that Mr. Nielsen and the Mad. Ave. copywriters are the true inciters-to-violent-revolution of our times?)

---

[2] Our current Administration has proved to be equally adept at "defusing" the dissent of such politically and/or socially influential groups as the academic community and liberal Jewish-Americans. Many members of Academe who voiced criticism of one or another aspect of American life or of administration policy almost overnight found themselves either in the employ of the Executive Branch or the recipient of a large governmental research-grant—and were not heard from again. And Jews have been appointed to some of the most prestigious offices within the President's appointive powers.

Not flower-power, but something much more concrete, self-disciplined, sustained *and cerebral* is and will be required of our creative young people if they hope to have a constructive impact on how the alternatives and predictions included in Chapter 13 turn out.

Chapter Ten

Unenlightened Self-interest

Like a number of our other social responsibilities, our assumption of moral responsibility for our economic actions has become largely a casualty of our dedication to our respective struggles for social and consumer status. This abandonment of concern for the social consequences of our work roles and our economic behavior has made a major contribution to the disruption of mutual obligations among the various specialized parts of urban society, and therefore to the individual and social disorganization of our times. There are many familiar examples both of this lack of concern and of the direct social effects of it.

Where so much is at stake for the individual, socially and psychologically, it is not difficult to understand the apparently increasing number of "respectable" persons who candidly exploit not only the weaknesses of adults—a type of exploitation we tend to wink at because, after all, an adult "knows what he's doing"—but who create new and expanding markets by knowingly corrupting children and adolescents: people such as the dope peddlers' "big boss," publishers of the so-called "horror comics," and— — — (fill in your own examples here). These gentlemen also have children to be put through college!

Perhaps it is unkind to mention the increasing amount of actual if not "legal" dishonesty in today's business world, along with an increasing number of outright opportunists in almost every aspect of American life—unkind, because so many are *such* respectable people. To adjust with ease, particularly at the policy level in the highly competitive business world, has come to mean for many the ability readily to divorce's one's work self from one's moral and subtle-personal-needs self.

Our development of a native Communist movement has been attributed to the influence of depression-induced experiences on some young people. The ready opportunism, moral irresponsibility and conformity of our times strike me as being even more surely a legacy of the depression than our relative handful of native Communists. These behaviors are so widespread, so entrenched among the most respected segments of our society, *and* so carefully ignored, they raise this question: is this overlooked second legacy of the Great Depression currently and potentially far more subversive of the American tradition than a movement to whose danger we have been so thoroughly alerted?

Nor are all the respectable people with facility in splitting their work selves from their moral selves engaged in politics and government and union administration—the impression usually given by our newspapers. *Professional status and lack of social responsibility have also begun to be linked, with a good deal of justification, in the public mind.* So far, members of the medical profession have been the chief targets of open criticism by journalists and by writers of a regular sprinkling of "letters to the editor" in newspapers of every political stripe. That such criticism has entered the public domain is particularly significant: most complaining about doctors was previously done in one's personal friendship circle. I believe popular criticism of other applied science and technical professions is in the offing as well: ambivalent attitudes towards "science" and "scientists" are already apparent.

Individual lawyers, journalists, authors are showing readiness, even eagerness, to forsake the most minimal level of personal and professional integrity for any measure of status and consumer capacity. But it is the trend to social irresponsibility among those in the technical, applied science, managerial and communications professions which is particular cause of general social concern. Developments in our society have given these people a disproportionate amount of power, more than they themselves are aware they have, or even want. Our country's tendency towards increasingly large, socially uncontrolled units of economic organization and the increasing interdependence of every aspect of our economy have given the manager power over great numbers of people. Our own tendency to default on our political responsibilities has given members of the applied science and technical professions tremendous power over not only our general level of physical health and our pattern of daily living, but even over the chances for survival of the entire human species. The subservience of all our mass communications media—TV, radio, newspapers, magazines—to commercial interests is so pervasive yet so unrecognized, the term "brainwashing" is inadequate to describe its effects on us.

Many little people have come to react to the role of the technician in our society with a diffuse, low-level resentment which has remained generally unfocused until relatively recently. The fears aroused in many Americans by our development and testing of the atomic and hydrogen bombs has served to precipitate this resentment. It seems to be intensifying; and it is becoming organized into an as yet vague feeling that " 'science' has gone too far" and should be clamped down on in some way. The general public is not clearly aware of the distinction between pure and applied science, nor of the greater tendency towards a personally disinterested value system among pure scientists. It is an undiscriminating, globally irrational reaction which is involved. Many of the scholars and scholar-scientists in academic settings who during the so-called "McCarthy era" resisted formal and informal curbs on their freedom of thought and research were puzzled and disturbed by the nature of the reaction of some segments of the public to their resistance: there was not only a general lack of public support for it, but some public concurrence in the curbs themselves!

If the foregoing analysis has any validity, this scholarly group may well become the unintentional victims of their own and their antecedents' pure science value system: their devotion to their work as an end in itself and their traditional lack of concern for the social end-uses of their deliberations has created a social vacuum into which others with *far less disinterested motives* have stepped. It will be a tragic irony of our times if this sheltered, traditionally socially diffident group finds itself in the front line of those who reap the whirlwind of irrational public reaction. The Mausners' significant study on public reaction to fluoridation tends to confirm this point of view (41).

Nor will the social and personal problems raised by a trend to social irresponsibility among our professional and executive groups end with the spread of automation to the point where the average white- and blue-collar work week will be about twenty hours at the most. On the contrary, this apparently unprepared-for change will accentuate such problems: the work load and social responsibility of those in the highly trained, human-manipulation occupations will almost surely be increased by it. The current response of some of our applied behavioral scientists to the practical, profit needs of business holds out anything but encouragement in this connection for the future: they do not seem to be aware that profound moral issues are involved in their readiness to put their potentially powerful manipulative skills at the service of private-interest needs—as will be further developed in the last chapter.

We are already uncomfortably like Soviet Russia in our tendency to overemphasize and overvalue in practice the material aspects of living. If any of our behavioral, social, and biological scientists, particularly, are required to, and find it possible to, split *their* work selves from their moral selves, we shall have a very hard job to continue to justify our moral superiority over the Communists. Worse, we might find ourselves living in a society that the most sadistic of the horror "comics" is incapable of depicting. Authors Pohl and Kornbluth have grasped this latter point well in their remarkable pocket-size book, *The Space Merchants,* ostensibly a science-fiction fantasy (56). There may or may not be some significance in the circumstance that the motion picture *Metropolis,* produced by the German experimental school a decade or so before the rise of Hitler, has a remarkably similar theme.

It is not reassuring in this regard that our government raced with that of Soviet Russia to obtain the services of German guided-missile experts, at the time of the allied occupation of Germany. We seem as a nation to have had no more moral difficulty than did Russia in sponsoring the research of men who had no inner qualms about pursuing their investigations under Nazi auspices. More recently, our warfare policy in VietNam and the nature of senatorial hawks' rebuttal of criticism of our use of "anti-personnel" destructive techniques there alike show(ed) that the Pentagon *and* substantial sectors of the American public have been having/had little difficulty taking over the Germanic "might is right" style of reasoning as well.

Profound moral and social issues are involved in the case of technologists and scientists who find there is a split between their moral selves and the ends to which their skills are being put. Organized society has made a formal ruling that when socially immoral acts are committed by an individual at the behest of his employer, the individual so doing can and must be held personally responsible for his act. This ruling applies even when his employer is the state. I am speaking of the basic ruling of the Nuremberg Trials.

One of the implications of this ruling is that the individual scientist and technician can no longer take refuge behind a value system developed during a more naïve period of human history: the ends to which science's findings are enlisted is an irrelevancy to the scientist dedicated to the "search for truth." Unless the judgments of the Nuremberg Trials are to be considered historically and morally meaningless, he must make a number of decisions at the time he is asked to perform certain operations or deliberations. He must take the personal responsibility of deciding whether a socially immoral act is involved, and whether or not he can as a moral individual contribute to it. The issue is not changed by the disquieting circumstance that the individual scientist does not always know the nature of the end-product to which he is contributing his skill, nor the end use of that product. In such cases, his decision must center on whether or not he will engage in "blind work" to begin with.

Whenever pure and applied scientists and technicians are required by their employers to split the application of their specialized skills from their moral beings, and they find it possible to do so, they are following a dangerous precedent. This precedent applies whether they go along with the request as a result of conscious concurrence or *through lack of concern over the issue.* They are following the precedent initiated by the Nazi physical and biological scientists under the aegis of the not-to-be-questioned ends of the Nationalist Socialist state, a precedent continued by Communist scientists under the aegis of the equally unquestionable ends of the Soviet state.

The circumstance that some of our biological and behavioral scientists *have* done so in connection with our involvement in VietNam is what has been the most distressing aspect of that involvement to many of their colleagues.[1] This same issue, of the demands of the state versus the demands of the individual conscience, was, as I understand it, the core factor behind our most reputable and socially sensitive physical scientists' disturbed reactions to the Oppenheimer case.

Many of us are by now aware of the venality of the air mass-media and are very much concerned about its impact on American life. But few of us are as yet privy to a similar development among a

---

[1] For those optimistic people who have harbored a belief in the gradual improvement of man and of the human condition, the broken-record sound of the arguments which have been put forth by the "hawks" of both the nationalistic and the religious sub-species to justify our armed forces' use of such ultimate, "anti-personnel" destructive techniques as napalm and wholesale devastation of the VietNam countryside, has been even more distressing. These justifications are, in essence: (1) the goodness of our side's ends lends sanctity to *whatever* means we use to accomplish these ends; (2) the enemy deserves everything we are giving them and much, much more: first, because they were so unenlightened and wicked as initially to resist us "defenders of the free world," and second and still worse, because they have had the utter gall to mount counter-aggressive measures against us, and (3) (a variation of 1) the enemy is also doing terrible things, and if we have to do even worse things in order to win, so what—war is war, and isn't victory all that really matters?

growing number of reputable book-publishers (college-graduates, all!): they are quite calculatedly soliciting and publishing pornographic and/or sadistically violent, written-for-mass-sale "put-ons"— and citing as their justification for doing so, such books' subsidization of their other, "really worthwhile" books. One wonders whether it is merely a coincidence that both this publishing practice *and* its rationalization were not-at-all uncommon in pre-World War II Germany and France. The comment of a knowledgeable young European, librarian on a trans-Atlantic passenger-ship of west-European registry, comes vividly to mind in this connection. A book in his very much "au courant" collection, one of the first of the obscene cum homosexual cum sadistically violent American-new-wave big moneymakers, prompted him to quote older-generation friends to the effect that the current trend in the United States towards discarding all standards of taste and morality reminded them very much of the atmosphere in Germany during the period of the Weimar Republic.

Another example of creeping venality among the communications professions is the eagerness on the part of large-circulation magazines, TV and radio to cater to the American public's desire for oversimplified, personally uninvolved answers to the complex problems and issues of our times. Mass-media commentators, interviewers, book-reviewers, feature-article writers have the power to "make" a book of ideas by bringing it to the attention of their mass audience— or to let it expire at the journal-of-opinion level merely by ignoring it. An example of a book they chose to make was one which implied that nationalism is a fundamental human drive stemming directly from the mammalian instinct of territoriality—a simplistic order of reasoning that the anthropological and sociological disciplines discarded nearly half-a-century ago. Marshall McLuhan's contribution is another example: he was/is thoroughly within his literary/artistic rights to present his sociologically and historically unsophisticated— yet original and useful—thesis in as reductionistic and over-stated form as he wished; but its adoption and mass propagation in uncritical, unqualified toto by our Madison Avenue "intellectuals" is quite-another matter.

Nor does the chain reaction of social irresponsibility as it applies to the highly trained end here. Higher education has become almost the sole predictable avenue of entry into higher-status professions, with all the psychological "loadings" such entry represents to the individual. Also, another instance of that inverse snobbery which permeates the middle classes of the greatest democracy in the world is gaining ground—the philosophy that everyone who *wants* a college degree is, in a democracy, entitled to have it; level of intellectual ability is an irrelevant consideration. When the majority of our college population are enrolled primarily for the purpose of ego-enhancement, and secondarily, if at all, for reasons of intellectual curiosity and inner development, bastardization of college and university programs and standards and loss of professorial integrity are inevitable. What has already occurred along these lines "ain't nothin'" compared with what is yet to be.

The end results of these developments may well be the actual antithesis of the original purpose of higher education in a democracy. Only graduates of certain institutions will come to be regarded as adequately qualified for our top-level policy-making jobs in business, education and government: those very few, prestige-full, highly selective and high-fee colleges, universities and professional schools which continue to maintain high scholastic standards. Shall we not then again have the old "élite class" who achieve their status not primarily through individual worth, but through wealth and family connection?

Those who are less economically privileged typically gain entry into such status-giving institutions through a few competitively awarded scholarships. The amounts of anxiety and hostility which competition for the few scholarships available already engender among the many who try for them are appalling to contemplate. The level of mental health among our college population is currently a source of concern to many responsible educators. The state of affairs visualized is not calculated to promote the mental equilibrium of the most capable of our college students.

This intense competitiveness is only one of the byproducts of the "vocationalization" which, together with compartmentalization, has always been a major theme in higher education in these United States. But what was formerly no more than a theme has assumed the proportions of a dominating trend right along with the rapid expansion of big technology—to the point that our colleges and universities have become primarily avenues of entry into the higher-income and higher-prestige positions, while their former, higher *education* purpose has become secondary, even vestigial. More specifically, their major function now is to serve as training facilities for big-business, big-industry, big-government (hereafter big B-I-G) along these three lines:

1) to serve the personnel-needs of big B-I-G by training technical and managerial and professional workers;

2) to make major contributions to the exponentially increasing volume of technical and scientific knowledge, especially in those areas of science/technology in which the three "bigs" are particularly—and very practically—interested;

3) to train the research-workers who will "deliver," in both academic and industrial/governmental settings, the knowledge referred to in 2.

This accelerating advanced-education trend to compartmentaliza-tion-cum-vocationalization has affected the lower schools: at the insistence of ego-involved middle-class parents and with the enthusi-astic cooperation of the great majority of (also middle-class) high-school teachers, this trend—and its accompanying intense competitive-ness—has been extended downward into the secondary schools. It is beginning to influence grade-school—and even pre-school!—cur-ricula as well (but with somewhat less enthusiastic teacher coopera-tion). This shift in the dominant function of our college-university establishment is particularly evident in the proliferation of liberally funded research institutes on university campuses (one of these, at the University of Pennsylvania, was devoted to the continuing secret development of biochemical warfare techniques); in emphasis upon, and generous funding of, careers chiefly in applied science but also in those areas of pure science the eventual applications of which may be to the "national interest;" in accelerated-degree programs in those technological and applied science specialities most needed by and/or profitable to big B-I-G. It would seem to be necessary to update former President Eisenhower's outgoing warning against the military-industrial complex by warning against the military-industrial-*universi-ties* complex![2]

There is an ironical aspect to this compartmentalization cum vocationalization of American higher education. It has occurred at just the time when we are coming to realize that most big-technology jobs are highly specialized, routinized, and afford little personal satis-faction aside from the consumer-power provided by one's pay-check. It is, rather, one's after-work, leisure, hours which are potentially of real personal meaning. Yet most of us do not know how to use our

---

[2] Another statement to this same effect, recommended to the reader, came to my attention after the foregoing was written (31). I subscribe to Doctor Hutchins' "diagnosis" but am not sure I can go along with his "cure."

outside-of-work time in ways which are either or both self-fulfilling and socially contributive: knowledge which represents the *traditional* teachings of higher education! What should be complementary themes in American higher education have become competitive ones, with the societally and individually more important theme currently losing out.

The intimate tie between higher-technical, managerial and lesser-professional occupational eligibility *and* enrollment in our higher-education establishment, a kind of explicit link formerly characteristic only of the trades and the specialized professions, is having a predictable effect on student attitudes towards college attendance, on professor-student relationships, and on the learning process itself. A model of the on-rushing future in these areas is already present in the shape of current programs of teacher-education offered both within and without the liberal arts and sciences framework. The curriculum of these programs, both undergraduate and post-graduate, are dictated directly and explicitly by state and/or municipal requirements governing not only the appointment but also the *retention* and the *promotion* of teachers. Students' reactions to this direct tie-up are thoroughly adaptive. On the one hand, the aim of the great majority is to obtain the highest possible grade in each of the prescribed courses commensurate with the lowest possible expenditure of time, effort *and thought*. On the other hand, since "education-course" instructors are perceived as little more than deputies of the job (or promotion) -dispensing establishment, and are evaluated primarily if not entirely in terms of their role as grades-assigner, students put tremendous overt and subtle pressures on their teachers to minimize the effort and thought required in course assignments.

This conception of higher education—as primarily a barrier between the higher-paying-job aspirant and the job—is a direct outcome of the academic trend towards vocationalization. It is also one of two concurrent developments that are having a negative impact on the status of the college/university professor. The other is an outcome of academic compartmentalization: college-teaching is increasingly being done by "ignorant Ph.D.s" with minimal orientation to the art of teaching and to areas of knowledge outside of their field of specialized competence. To the extent that these two developments obtain and converge, to that extent the college professor:

> has lost whatever independent, socially mediative function and moral authority he once had;
>
> is replaceable by technological substitutes, such as a centrally located

TV lecturer or an instructional program, which are more efficient conduits of factual knowledge than he can possibly be;

is becoming an obedient civil servant, which is already the status of his lower-school counterparts.

Certainly college professors have been reacting like civil servants in the face of these academic developments. They have organized as a professional group, yes, but for higher salaries and pensions and occasionally for better working conditions—not to overcome their powerlessness as a profession. Some are beginning to deplore the erosion of their role as educators in the old sense, yes, but the institutional-level solutions they envision (4) fail to recognize that the sources of the problem lie in social and economic trends well beyond the college-gates. Some younger faculty-members have helped to develop and many have attended one of the most effective new public-education techniques in a generation, the "teach-in," yes, but have not used this technique to inform the middle-class about the social and political implications of what is happening to higher education in the United States. Many instructors are very active at the departmental and institutional and professional-organization levels, yes, but at building their own private little empires, using colleagues and students as means to their narrowly personal ends, not at developing a genuine academic community in cooperation with colleagues and students—a community which would strive to act as a societal counter-force against the spreading whirlpool of centralized power into which the higher education establishment is being—has already been! —engulfed.

There are of course heartening exceptions to this generally depressing picture, but the over-all situation may be summarized as: the great majority of the highly educated elite of our society are as busily tending to their own individual status struggles as any middle-executive in General Motors or a Madison Avenue advertising agency.

It would be misleading to leave the impression that compartmentalization/specialization and its negative social impact is a very novel, very American development, however. Consider these passages, translated from their original Spanish:

"When by 1890 a third generation assumes intellectual command in Europe, we meet with a type of scientist unparalleled in history. He is one who, out of all that has to be known in order to be a man of judgment, is only acquainted with one science, and even of that one only knows the small corner in which he is an active investigator. He even proclaims it a virtue that he takes no cognizance of what lies outside the narrow territory specially cultivated by himself, and gives the name of 'dilettantism' to any curiosity for the general scheme of things. . .

"Experimental science has progressed thanks in great part to the work of men astoundingly mediocre, and even less than mediocre. That is to say, modern science, the root and symbol of our actual civilisation, finds a place for the intellectually commonplace man and allows him to work therein with success. The reason of this lies in what is at the same time the great advantage and the greatest peril of the new science, and of the civilisation directed and represented by it, namely, mechanisation . . .

"Previously, men could be divided simply into the learned and the ignorant, those more or less the one, and those more or less the other. But your specialist cannot be brought in under either of these two categories. He is not learned, for he is formally ignorant of all that does not enter into his specialty; but neither is he ignorant, because he is a 'scientist', and 'knows' very well his own tiny portion of the universe. We shall have to say that he is a learned ignoramus, which is a very serious matter, as it implies that he is a person who is ignorant, not in the fashion of the ignorant man, but with all the petulance of one who is learned in his own special line. . . The result is that even in this case, representing an apparent maximum of qualification in many—specialisation—and therefore the thing most opposed to the mass-man, the result is that he will behave in almost all spheres of life as does the unqualified, the mass-man. . .

"[Such men of science] symbolise, and to a great extent constitute, the actual domination of the masses, and their barbarism is the most immediate cause of European demoralisation. Furthermore, they afford the clearest, most striking example of how the civilisation of the last century, *abandoned to its own devices,* has brought about this rebirth of primitivism and barbarism" (55).

The "rebirth of primitivism and barbarism" Professor Ortega spoke of in 1930 referred to aspects of the history of Europe between 1910 and 1935 (and later!) familiar to all of us. Are we Americans as exempt from the historical process as we seem to believe we are?

That the higher-education developments discussed in this chapter raise serious questions about the proper function of advanced education in a complex, avowedly democratic country is obvious. Just what these questions are—and their answers—is not as obvious. Here are only four such questions—and no answers:

1. Granted that education and vocationally oriented training are *both*

needed and valid functions of higher education, how can both themes be served more satisfactorily than at present?

2. Should some other academic organizational principle than compartmentalization/departmentalization be adopted instead of, or in addition to, it?

3. The imposition of standards of performance can be argued as necessary for courses which are vocationally oriented. Should compulsory attendance and *any* kind of grading system be maintained for "molding of human beings" learnings?

4. Should non-church-affiliated schools and colleges explicitly undertake to teach values as well as facts and skills? If yes, which values, and how?

Chapter Eleven

"That Which We Call Freedom"[1]

THE TREND TOWARD personal opportunism among individuals in the highly trained and highly placed occupations deserves special attention because this upper-middle-class group holds a leadership role well out of proportion to their number in the population (about ten per cent.). Disinterested social leadership has traditionally been an important concomitant of professional status. Indeed, the exercise of such leadership in the past is a major reason for the high social status enjoyed by the professional occupations in the present.

But professionalism can, under certain social conditions, lose its socially responsible roots and, as a direct result, become a symptom of pathology, rather than a positive social force. For some of the applied-science and technical professions, three such conditions have been in joint operation for some time now.

The first condition is the general public's dedication to the proposition that the fruits of applied science and technology are in themselves synonymous with social progress in the highest sense. The second condition is that these professions have acquired, because of our own values and practices, a disproportionate amount of power over other people in our society. The third condition is the individual professional's dedication to his striving for personal status and material success at any cost. "At any cost" typically means his tacit willingness to exploit fully, or assist his employer in exploiting fully, the public's commitment to its "dream of comfort," physical and emotional.

A number of special factors seem to me to be operating in this

---

[1] This title is taken from the following passage in Kahlil Gibran's *The Prophet:* "And how shall you rise beyond your days and nights unless you break the chains which you at the dawn of your understanding have fastened around your noon-hour?

"In truth, that which you call freedom is the strongest of these chains, though its links glitter in the sun and dazzle your eyes" (26).

increase in personal opportunism and social irresponsibility among those in the higher-status occupations.

One such factor is that such occupations have come to exert a strong attraction for a certain kind of neurotic personality. In a society where entry into high-status occupations has become one of the few avenues to higher social status remaining to the individual, and where higher status has great personal meaning, such occupations are particularly appealing to persons with strong feelings of personal inadequacy: too often, a young man's motive for choosing to enter a professional occupation is this desire to acquire some basis for a feeling of self-worth. Such a person is more likely to be willing to discard at least minor moral scruples, if such discard is necessary to maintain this status, than is the person who has more dependable bases for his feelings of self-respect.

In previous years, those with primarily self-seeking motives seem to have been in the minority in the higher-status professions, while those with substantial amounts of social idealism and a desire for self-fulfillment were in the majority. It would seem that in highly competitive urban settings in particular, this former balance has been reversed.

A second factor is the long and increasingly difficult and demanding courses of training required particularly for the applied science professions—a circumstance with ramifications which most laymen cannot fully visualize. By the time the individual professional graduates, he has had a great deal of practice in self-alienation: he has had to endure many very trying and personally meaningless experiences for the sake of reaching a long-delayed goal. As scientific and technical knowledge has increased and will continue to increase, the sheer amount of information and techniques to be continually assimilated by one individual is of staggering proportions. Here is the major reason for the tendency towards the often-criticized trend to specialization in the pure as well as the applied sciences—a trend that at least pure scientists are themselves concerned over. Nor are universities showing a strong enough tendency to improve this situation by instituting much-needed changes in their curricular and administrative organization.

The carry-over for the individual professional of such demanding training within the context of our self-interest-first value system is frequently a certain selfishness, well justified in the professional person's eyes: many feel society owes them something for this long, trying and expensive period. And particularly for the professional who has chosen a prestige occupation primarily for personal-status reasons, the habit of separating his work self from other aspects of his personality, well practiced during the arduous training period, is readily carried over to job or professional practice. I feel the criticism of medicine for the trend to specialization of practice is misplaced: increased knowledge and skill in diagnosing and treating illness can under proper conditions be of almost uniformly greater advantage to the public. Rather, it is the competitive, high-fee, uncoordinated, public-be-damned aspect of a good deal of individual specialist practice that is chiefly responsible for the criticized abuses.

The intense competitiveness of every aspect of American life, converging with the trend towards specialization earlier referred to, has yielded yet another development with particularly unfortunate societal effects: the intra-science "pecking-order," in which the oldest and methodologically most exact, natural and biological, sciences are considered to have the highest prestige, and the youngest and methodologically suspect behavioral and social sciences have the least prestige. These attitudes are endemic not only within Academia but also among persons in the professional and research occupations who are the products of Academia. Because the applications of the older sciences have paid off handsomely *and* tangibly in creature-comforts, in control of disease and of the physical environment, *and* in corporation profits, this prestige-order is also subscribed to, if not by the general public, certainly by our political representatives.

This inner-circle value-system has contributed to these expressions of professional ineptitude:

1. Individual investigators, practitioners, and administrators in the natural and biological sciences have the tendency to assume that merely because they are individual human beings who live in a society, they are fully qualified to make judgments and recommendations concerning the impact on society and on the individual not only of developments in their specialized field but of any new scientific knowledge; they react, that is, as if the extensive bodies of knowledge bearing on man-in-society were non-existent.

2. Those sciences whose province is, theoretically, the exploration of the human condition, have for so long followed the analytic and reductionist approaches of the older, prestigious sciences, they are able to tell us a great deal about various "bits" of animal and human behavior and of the human organism per se mechanism, but very little about man as a unique form of life.

3. There is virtually no recognition of the urgent need for dialogue across discipline-boundaries concerning such scientifically and socially

vital problems as: the actual *vs.* the desirable social role(s) of scientists and technicians; the impact, *in a competitive economic system,* of applied science and technology on society and on the individual; the social responsibility(ies) of the scientist and technician; the problems now being and most likely to be worked on in the next 5, 10, 20 years *vs.* the problems of greatest relevance to and within each discipline *vs.* the most socially vital problems requiring attention within the next 5, 10, 20 years; the priority-order of research-areas on the basis of *both* disciplinary and societal considerations.

There is another reason for a lack of social responsibility among many in high-status occupations, one which applies particularly to those who have just completed successfully the difficult climb from lower-middle "old American" or from upper-lower "recent-ethnic" status. These are usually especially capable, active individuals who have deliberately used their education and occupation as an avenue of escape from the cramped "little man's world" into which they were born and which was so confining to them physically and psychologically. Such a person is not likely to identify with those who continue to live in a world he has put behind him. On the contrary, a person with this background who has climbed to the higher executive echelons of business, particularly, frequently has no difficulty in adopting the values and world picture of those who have a candidly exploitative and manipulative attitude towards the very human mass from which he has extricated himself.

Whenever this situation occurs in the fields of advertising and communications, a peculiar social tragedy has been enacted: the middle classes' own values have led to their loss of those individuals who are best equipped through intelligence and direct experience to interpret to them what is happening to them and why. Still worse, we have lost these people's superior energies and intellect to those very groups who have an active interest in maintaining and intensifying the middle classes' psychological status quo.

All of these "special instances" form a sub-group within a much larger group, a group to which nearly all of us in the highly trained and highly placed occupations belong. For reasons already discussed, most of us in this larger group have channelled our drives for achievement, for self-expression, for self-fulfillment into the very avenue which is most closely associated with the rewards of our society: our occupation. "Doing a good job, the best job I know how" has become the ultimate personal ideal of our most dedicated, responsible, and respected persons in the professions and business.

Like Captain Nicholson in *The Bridge on the River Kwai,* who had the same absolute value-ethic, it has not occurred to us of this group to ask ourselves *what social ends our excellent job performance is furthering.* Shall some of our most gifted and dedicated technicians and scientists one day "come to" and cry out, as did the captain, "My God, what have I done?", too late for their society and themselves?

These various inner psychological factors mean that many highly placed individuals bring to their jobs a latent—or even manifest!—willingness to accommodate to whatever is demanded of them by their work role. Unfortunately, changes in their work situations have added up to the circumstance that what *is* demanded frequently requires of them socially irresponsible activities and decisions.

The aspect of slavery that led civilized man eventually to consider it socially immoral was not the nature of the work done by the slave, but its forcing of the slave to submit to a will other than his own. When a man has to do for a living what he does not want to do, when he is required to go against his basic moral beliefs in order to make that living, when he is required to contribute to the de-humanizing of his fellow human beings in order to make that living, there obtains in each instance a kind of immorality. *It is immoral even though such situations have come about without anyone's deliberate intent.*

But *we* live in a free society: if anyone finds himself in such a work situation in our land, he has the choice, if he wishes to do so, of changing to another employer or type of work!

Unfortunately, this free choice is more fictional than actual in our highly organized industrial society where only one-fifth of those who work were self-employed as of 1940; the last thirty years have seen an accentuation of this trend to employment by another. It is no longer only the little- blue- and white-collar workers who are affected by these limitations. The old small-town small businessman had some control over the day-to-day decisions he made in carrying out his economic function; the individual corporation executive or small-business sub-contractor has no real control over company policy. The university-employed chemistry professor and researcher had sole responsibility for his extra-curricular research activities; the corporation- and government-employed research chemist works at problems not of his own choosing and cannot suppress or falsify any of his findings in the interests of the broader social welfare—at least not for long, as Dr. Oppenheimer discovered.

Take for example an executive who finds himself with a moral objection to some aspect of his company's policy affecting the con-sumer public. Theoretically, he has the free choice of changing to an employer whose level of social responsibility is more to his liking. In actual practice, however, such a choice is virtually non-existent because he usually cannot locate another employer whose policy is at all different, and/or he has become so specialized in his work that practically no other job for which he might be suitable is available to him. And starting another business in competition is in most instances either foolhardy or impossible, and would in any case require his eventual practice of those very abuses which he could not tolerate originally.

And so, such a person spends part or all of his work life on a job to which he inwardly objects. In so doing, he is literally an economic prostitute—and is usually only too well aware of it. Is this circumstance one of the reasons for the striking preponderance of packaged liquor stores in the succession of "highly exclusive" suburban "villages" of southern Connecticut?

As a related example, I recall the problem of a young lady in a very different position on the economic and social scale. On the verge of abandoning her education as a teacher after an occasional modeling stint had expanded into steady work, she said:

> I think teaching is a far more important, worthwhile occupation. I'm not particularly impressed with the glamor of being a model as some of the other girls are. My own values tell me I am doing the wrong thing from a social point of view. But what can I do? I'm helping my husband through law school and I get $45.00 an hour—*$45.00 for one hour of posing!* Compare that with what I'd get as a teacher—and even that I wouldn't earn for years yet. I don't think I have any real choice.

This young lady's situation illustrates not only a personal dilemma, but also expresses the extent of disorganization in our society: we currently accord a sheer luxury occupation far more status and income than a function which is socially indispensable.

A comparison of the amount of time, money and brains currently spent in designing, consumer-testing and merchandising new commercial packaging, with the amount of time, money and brains now devoted to research into the causes of war (but one of many possible examples), yields a directly analogous instance of the deterioration in social perspective in our society.

The problem of lack of choice also encompasses those highly trained professionals who find they are overprepared for the jobs they eventually settle into: a far greater proportion of their work proves to be routine and far less of it creative than either their training or their own preferences and expectations prepared them for. If attempts to reverse this balance fail and family pressures or lack of availability of a more satisfying job at a "decent" salary (or any salary at all) make a job change unfeasible, only two relatively dependable sources of job satisfaction are left—the status of the position, both in the immediate job setting and in the general community, and the size and dependability of consumer capacity provided by the pay-check. Both of these sources of job satisfaction tend to maintain and to enhance an inner state of alienation and an over-all tendency towards social irresponsibility.

R. H. Tawney made the recommendation in 1919 to "professionalize" industry and the new technical occupations as the key means of rescuing English industry from the self-interested, socially irresponsible pit into which it had fallen (66). He was not able to foresee that the pendulum would instead swing the other way, in the United States at least—that the professions and unions would regress to the industrial norm. He was not able to foresee these trends of our time and place:

1. Professional ethics have tended to regress toward industrial ethics— from pride in profession, dedication to the social welfare, maintenance of high professional standards and the exercise of internal discipline towards that end, more and more members of more and more professions have adopted the frankly exploitative attitudes of private industry, along with its penchant for internal suppression of "mavericks."

2. Union leaders have contributed directly to the solidification of the economic status quo by working within it and not challenging it; by, instead, adapting the exploitative, self-interested attitudes and techniques of management to the end of worker self-interest—although in the present situation of unequal power and "interest," one's sympathies tend still to be with "David" rather than with "Goliath."

3. The "brain-worker" group in industry has vastly increased in number. But these people, instead of directing their professional values towards general social-good goals, as Tawney recommended, have identified with the parochial self-interest goals of management. Where such a man is a "true professional," he has tended to make the advancement of the company's welfare his "higher good." Where he is not, he has adopted the frankly exploitative, irresponsible attitudes of the rank and file worker. When a manager or a co-owner is also a technician— a spreading development in industry—there has been little evidence of even a minor struggle between professional and business values.

4. Self-interested management's answer to increasing competition and its continuing difficulties with self-interested labor, inevitable under the present power-bloc system, has been elegantly simple and direct. It has created a new category of small business by turning to a highly specialized group of brain workers with the urgent request that they invent a new kind of machine—machines which replace troublesome and expensive unionized workers with a smaller number of brain-work "professionals." This latter category has up to now shown far greater willingness to identify with, rather than organize against, management.

An American reporter just returned from a trip to the U.S.S.R. commented during a radio interview (78) on the high degree of irresponsibility at the lower echelons of Soviet officialdom. He compared the situation to that of a military organization, a situation thoroughly familiar to "anyone who has been in the Army." Inefficiency, buck-passing and influence-peddling were the rule in the conduct of affairs in Russia, he said, with one major exception— the handling of those few top-priority matters of vital concern to the nation.[2]

It is not only military experience which makes this description hauntingly familiar to us, nor even currently reviving polemics against spreading American governmental bureaucracy. The reaction of the individual employee and minor administrator to a big, hierarchically organized work situation is here described, and large business units cannot be omitted from the list. As more and more of Soviet urban society is revealed to us, we seem more and more to be seeing a mirror-image of ourselves.

What is perhaps another condition contributing to the growing pathology of professionalism and our social and economic life generally, has stemmed, with exceptions to be referred to presently, from omission where commission is badly needed. The sacredness and inviolability of the human personality, and related problems of ethics and morality, have traditionally been matters of primary concern to the various organized religions. Yet the larger American denominations have tended to show little if any inclination to lead in attempts to analyze and to recognize the nature and the sources of the social and economic irresponsibility widespread in our society. There has been no "second look" at the American churches' long-propounded

---

[2] *We* are no longer able to boast of even this one exception: viz. the National Aero Space Administration's suppression of reports of serious defects in the North American Aviation-constructed Apollo space-capsule.

thesis that our nation and the economic philosophy which made it great have alike been singled out for God's especial favor. Nor has there been a willingness to consider the possibility that the recent "return to religion" may be at least partially occasioned by our inner reaction of guilt to our failure to reach the success goals we had set for ourselves as individuals and to the bad things we must keep doing to each other in our highly competitive society. This load of guilt-feeling has become unbearable for more and more of us, and the only institutionalized, respectable avenue for lightening it which is readily available to us is organized religion.

Quite the contrary: instead of challenging us, their present and potential middle-class parishioners, to become adult enough to face squarely up to our anxieties and to examine our assumptions, our values, our way of life objectively and constructively, most of our organized religions were until recently urging without qualification our unquestioning, childlike return to the tradition and authority of each particular religious faith. Our misery among plenty was taken full advantage of—it was cited as proof that secularism, rationalism and "science" have failed. Only through our acceptance of the irremediable weakness of man and the essential futility of all his works could we hope to find that boon beyond price, "peace of mind."

In so preaching, these religious faiths are compounding our personal and social problems by providing us with yet another readily accessible avenue of escape from ourselves and our situation. In so preaching, they are themselves placing church attendance on the same psychological plane as the viewing of whodunits on TV, going to a night club, driving at ninety miles an hour, or attending a boxing match. Further, the "curative powers" of church attendance are being sold us by hired hucksters in much the same way that these same hucksters promote various patent nostrums.

But, fairly enough, this latter partnership is not one-sided. Our advertising agencies and business community have been quick to recognize in the current "religious kick" an effective emotional handle for consumer and social manipulation. On the one hand, religious themes and symbols have been put to good use selling cigarettes and socks and soap. On the other hand, much of the institutional advertising and public service announcements sponsored by some of our biggest corporations have taken on a pronounced "return to religion" flavor.

Both these developments showed conspicuous convergence in a now-vintage, but too prototypical an example to discard: *Life's* 1955

Christmas-timed issue on Christianity (38). This issue, aptly enough, was fronted by a sensitively executed Christ suspended in agonized resignation on the Cross, and backed by a Coca-Cola ad depicting two carefree, attractive young Americans taking "time out for a coke" from our currently most popular conspicuous-consumption winter sport. What more unconsciously appropriate portrayal could there be of the deep split between our inner and outer selves? The latter, "official" American version of our outer selves, incessantly and undeviatingly projected by our advertisers, has contributed to our self-alienation in two ways: it has set up a uniform, one-dimensional standard which, in a period of other-directedness, particularly our young people feel obliged to emulate, no matter what their inner inclinations may be; and, by studiously ignoring the existence of our tortured inner being, it has influenced us to do the same.

Finally, let me quote the full text of each of the three full-page (in one case, double-page) ads of the institutional-message type which appeared in this same issue:

1. Peace of Mind (spread over two pages) . . . may you have it abundantly in 1956. (*State Farm Mutual Automobile Insurance Co.*: More car owners insure with State Farm Mutual than with any other company in the world.)

2. Wise Men Still Seek Him: Moses sought Him on a mountain; St. Augustine in his books; Washington at Valley Forge; Albert Schweitzer in the heart of the African jungle; President Eisenhower in his own heart and the hearts of his people; Konrad Adenauer in the Cathedral of Cologne. And one cold night long ago the Wise men found Him—and Angels singing, Glory to God in the highest, and on earth peace to men of good will. (*Hilton Hotels, Conrad H. Hilton, President.*)

3. We forget these things too soon . . .
   That other men died to keep us free
   That Christian ideals created freedom
   That our children cannot live by bread alone
   That a nation can be no stronger than its faith
   That our future can be no greater than our vision
   That the quality of our daily work is a measure of our character
       [sic!]
   We forget these things too soon, yet—
       who will remember if we forget?"
   (*Olin Mathieson Chemical Corporation*)

This issue's promisingly titled editorial, "The American Moral

Consensus," proved to be a discussion of the essentially unreal question of the wisdom of our Constitution's provision for the separation of Church and State, rather than of the very real problem in morality posed by the annexation of religious themes by big-business-getting-bigger.

A more contemporary *Life* editorial might well take as its subject the moral issue posed by the conduct of important sectors of two of our major faiths with respect to the continually increasing number of parochial schools. These faiths have chosen to accept at face-value, and to turn to their own sectarian advantage, urban middle-class parents' stated rationale for enrolling their children in increasingly greater numbers in parochial, rather than in public, schools: that they want their children to receive sectarian religious and moral training. Both religious representatives and parents are well aware of the real reason behind the parochial-school boom—at least for the great majority of such parents: they do not want their children to be exposed to the increase in what is carefully termed the "undesirable element" in the public schools, nor to the lowering of academic standards frequently associated with this increase under current conditions of public-school staffing and financing. That is, more and more middle-class parents are using parochial schools for the same reasons that affluent Americans have always used private schools: to interject social distance between themselves and those below them in the socio-economic scale.

Instead of inveighing against the fundamentally immoral—not to speak of hypocritical!—character of this social development, the faiths involved are turning it to their own indoctrination and fund-raising advantage and are becoming increasingly militant politically over the issue of the allocation of public tax-monies to parochial schools. Knowingly or unknowingly, this church-parent coalition is serving to create the same sort of dual school-system that the Supreme Court acted to abolish in the southern states in 1954—but in this instance, the segregation is along primarily socioeconomic rather than color lines. It may be that they are pushing to go even further back—to 1850, when:

> "the poor of New York did not have . . a public-school system to which to send their children. New York had private and charity schools only. To send their children to charity schools, parents had to sign a pauper's oath. Parents too proud to be thus humiliated kept their children at home" (7).

There are important individual and denominational exceptions to these generalizations concerning the social role of our organized religions, fortunately, and they have grown during the last decade to include more than a few individuals connected with university faculties and liberal denominations small in membership. The breeze still blowing from the window opened by Pope John, the clerical leadership of and involvement in the Civil Rights movements, the "heresies" of James Pike, the revolt of the nuns and of the younger clergy of most denominations—all have transpired since all but the last two paragraphs of the foregoing polemic was written.

But the evidence is plentiful that this clerical awakening has come too late to influence a substantial portion of the present adult generation of church-attenders and supporters—who constitute the very backbone of the American middle-class. These persons' need for "that old-time religion" is fundamental: it permits them to maintain their schizoid way of life and therefore their emotional equilibrium. This need is so great, many have been turning against the moral authority and leadership of their own, in their eyes overly liberal, clergy. A December '66 advertisement in the *New York Times* sponsored by the Presbyterian Lay Committee (the membership of which includes some of the United States' most substantial businessmen) concerning the "Confession of 1967" (57) provides an articulately apt example of this sort of situation. It is a "call to every United Presbyterian" *not* to ratify the new Confession, which is intended to supersede the Church's 300-year-old "Westminster Confession." [3] The sentiments expressed in this "call" are by no means characteristic only of conservative Presbyterians; here are three excerpts from it:

"Are you willing to give up your belief in the Bible as the true and infallible Word of God? Are the Scriptures a divine guide or is the Bible a human and, therefore, unreliable document? The new Confession now attempts to answer these questions in a way that weakens the concept of the Bible as we have always accepted it. It claims to be a modern document necessary to challenge the modern age. But careful study reveals a close parallel between the criticism of the Scriptures as stated in this new Confession and the criticism of atheists and extreme liberals down through history."

"Do you accept the belief that your church should take whatever posi-

---

[3] The Confession of 1967 was ratified three months after the publication of this advertisement by two-thirds of the voting presbyteries: obviously, its sponsors were outnumbered—*but they abide!*

tion on any political, social or economic issue the governing body of the church decides is the proper one? Who decides what issues are to be opposed and what are to be supported? On what basis are church leaders qualified to make a judgment on such secular problems of the day? 'Render therefore unto Caesar the things that are Caesar's; and unto God, the things that are God's' is the way Christ answered this whole question (Matthew 22:21). The Westminster Confession states it clearly: "Synods and councils are to handle or conclude nothing but which is ecclesiastical, and are not to inter-meddle with civil affairs which concern the commonwealth. Protestant denominations generally have limited themselves in their jurisdiction to ecclesiastical and spiritual subjects."

"The 1967 Confession does not ring true. It is so filled with ambiguities, undefined statements, involved meanings, and obscure language that it becomes possible to rationalize almost any point of view the reader seeks to establish. The Westminster Confession of Faith, on the other hand, is so clearly and succinctly stated that anyone who can read can understand its meaning. It does not require a group of intellectuals to explain it."

At the point when the leaders of the various organized Christian faiths have belatedly begun formally to recognize each other's existence and to discover how artificial most of the old religious dichotomies are, a new, much more basic religious distinction is coming to the fore. Unless our churches, lay-members and clergy alike, face up very soon to a reality imposed by today's shrinking world, the major religious division in these United States may shortly be that between the few participants of *every* denomination—and the much greater number of non-communicants.

Just as churches of an earlier day in many countries re-won people's good will and validity as a social institution as an almost direct outcome of their separation from the state, so today's organized faiths must for the same reasons sever their identifications with any one nation or any particular economic philosophy. If they do not, they will be contributing to the emergence of a new feudalism, just as they did to the old. When the continuance and expansion of man's humanity (that is, his divinity) comes into conflict with any particular status quo, organized religions above all must place human needs first.

But the defection in their social responsibility of many of our churches and professional persons cannot in fairness be viewed apart from the defection of nearly all of us.

Most of us, whether or not we are parents trying to give our children some semblance of moral training, have at one time or another deplored certain practices which represent various gradations of the social immorality of our times. Whether or not we prefer it to be so, our visual "entertainment" media play a most important educative function in the lives particularly of urban children. These visual media have an even greater educative function than printed media, chiefly because children are not usually able to read until middle childhood. Many of us feel very strongly about the low level, moral and intellectual, of too much of the fare presented to us and to our children. A number of us criticize the stress on the sadistic, the violent, the sensational—and the just plain stupid—in so-called comic books and in other mass media, including our daily newspapers, readily available to children.

Some of us deplore our advertisers' calculated exploitation of the most intimate and tender of human experiences and sentiments—or of the more brassily sexy—for the commercial ends of their business clientele. Still others of us are disturbed about the glad—and well publicized—hand of the insurance salesman or banker or lawyer in community affairs. A few of us, because the funds are derived from the patronage of the general public, criticize the large amounts of money some business interests give to sponsor pressure for special privilege.

We deplore these lapses in social morality not only on their own merits but because we recognize their negative influence on the character development of the next generation. But not many of us would, I believe, consciously criticize these unformalized but pervasive American beliefs which constitute the credo for our own individual status struggles:

> The progress we have made as a nation and will make is primarily due to the operation of unhampered competition between individuals and between business concerns.

> Every individual has an inalienable right to "make a buck" any way he can, so long as he isn't actually breaking a major law (better, if he isn't *caught* breaking it).

> The privacy of private enterprise, even in those areas of its functioning which directly affect the public welfare, is a sacred and inviolable principle.

> It is better to go without a service needed by a large proportion of the population, or to put up with the irresponsible exploitation of an impor-

tant public medium or resource, than have the service supplied or closely
supervised by an agency supported by public funds. [4]

On the contrary, a great many of us would consider criticism of these
beliefs to be un-American.

*Yet it is the application of these beliefs, singly or in concert, by
individuals like ourselves, which must be held accountable for one or
the other of every lapse in social morality which we deplore.* We of
the American middle classes must learn to ask, and try to work
through the implications of our answers to, such questions as these:

> Do we logically have the right to criticize individuals and corporations
> when they behave in consonance with beliefs which are not only theirs
> but *our own?*

> How many of us in the lower-middle class would do almost anything to
> be in the expensive-leather shoes and the Florida-in-season hotel suite [5]
> of the man who has "succeeded," *regardless of the basis of his success?*

> Can we legitimately expect to have *both* untrammeled practice of the
> belief that it is right to produce and sell *anything* people will buy or can
> be induced to buy, *and* a high level, or even a low level, of social co-
> hesion and morality?

Our clinging to the beliefs enumerated has been a major factor in
our failure to assume the "universal parent" responsibility: *there
is a mutual incompatibility between the social effects of these beliefs
and the possibility that the next generation will grow up psychologically
whole.*

As here predicted, it is evident a decade later that a great many of
the next generation have *not* been growing up "psychologically whole."
But so strong a hold do these beliefs have on the "established middle-
class," they have even led to a double standard of reaction to young
people's varying ways of responding to their problems. Extreme
conspicuous consumption fads, such as his and hers bathtubs with
gold-plated fixtures and $15,000 custom sports-car convertibles (52)

---

[4] Exposure of CIA foundation-funneled subsidies to the international programs
of various opinion-molding groups such as the National Student Association and
the American Newspaper Guild, which occurred as this chapter was under re-
vision-review has prompted an addition to this list:

> Even when an activity can be demonstrated as being manifestly in the national
> interest, it is better to finance it secretly than to work towards an open-subsidy
> arrangement: such a program-request would undoubtedly raise the political
> kiss-of-death cry of "socialism"!

[5] The updated version appears to be Acapulco-in-season cabana—at least momen-
tarily.

prompt, at the most, amused exasperation; and the use of LSD, which was reported in Feb. '67 as spreading among west-coast college students at a rate "alarming to doctors and police" (53) arouses feelings of mild discomfort. But ah the cries of outrage and alarm over the young political activists on college campuses and the rioters in the Negro ghettos! (Yet the former youthful behaviors are usually indicative of far more serious individual-psychological difficulties than are the latter ones.)

We have also mishandled the "teacher" aspect of our parental role. We have delegated this function to other agencies of our society, but we have not assumed informed responsibility for maintaining the social and the economic conditions which would enable these agencies to perform these functions effectively.

Nor can we fairly expect our schools, community centers and youth organizations to nullify the consequences of our own failure to appreciate that the use-tested knowledge of and about mankind is *only one aspect* of the accumulated cultural heritage of man which must be passed on to each new generation. The ethical and moral checks on social relationships which the "highest form of life" has built into his group life so slowly and with so much pain over the millenia are also part of that heritage. The teaching of *this* aspect of man's dual cultural heritage *cannot be delegated to anyone else*: our children first learn it through observing our own active practice of it. Our generation seems to have overlooked that it is *both* aspects of man's heritage which make it possible for the potentially human infant to become the actually human adult.

The degree to which we in the middle classes have defaulted in recent years in our exercise of that active political responsibility which makes self-government more than a lip-service concept is the subject of many analyses. Our dedication to our struggle for personal status and "security" is keeping most of us too busy or too fearful to do more than cast a secret ballot—and for a great many of us, not even that restricted aspect of our citizenship responsibility.

We are not only denying ourselves personally enriching experiences when our eternal busy-ness, self-absorption, self-escape prevent our active practice of those responsibilities which center around our implicit obligations as human beings to our fellow humans beings, be they members of our family *or not*. When it becomes customary for each of us to overlook or deliberately ignore taking moral responsibility for our own actions, from the work we do to our most casual relations with other persons; when it does not occur to us that the social consequences of our own beliefs and activities may be making it difficult for the next generation to grow up to become psychologically as well as physically healthy; and when we do not in large numbers involve ourselves in focused, mentally open attempts to formulate, examine and try to solve current and urgent social problems, we are illustrating the degree to which the "American way of life" has already become a myth rather than a practiced reality. We are demonstrating that we are rapidly losing, if we have not already lost, all sense of "community."

Chapter Twelve

Comic Books or the Tattered Web?

Whether or not the individual feels he has obligations towards his society is related to his conception of the role that the broader society plays in his life. When an individual has a fairly definite idea of his society as a "positive something" beyond and above his immediate daily concerns and private interest, when he feels supported by his society and is able to have a kind of inner allegiance to it, his social acts are affected by this allegiance. He tends to keep in mind what this "higher something" would think of his actions, and as a result, he voluntarily makes them moral in the social sense.

But when the individual feels no support from his society, when his picture of it is so vague or so negative that beyond his immediate associations he feels "nobody gives a damn" about him, his social acts tend to be governed by a different set of considerations. When he feels alone and pitted against a hostile world, his credo is frequently like that of the fabled gunmen of the lawless West: "The best thing is to draw first, before the other fellow gets you." His economic and social behavior, under such circumstances, tends to be governed by his immediate self-interest in what he sees as a dog-eat-dog world.

As a result, his social and economic relations, beyond family and friends, are more often than not of an immoral character in the social sense. His exercise of his citizenship and other broader social responsibilities tends to be characterized either by apathy or irresponsibility. If he feels unqualified identification with the firm which employs him, or the union or professional group to which he belongs, or with his church or a special-interest organization, he is at least governed to some degree by the self-interest of firm, union, profession, church or organization. But if he is ambivalent about his job and does not identify with any organized group, he does not have even this narrow allegiance as an intermediate tie to his society. And it is questionable whether an executive whose ultimate personal allegiance

[119]

is to his employer is any more socially responsible than the man who has no such identification. Such fragmented relationships between the individual and his society seem to be more the rule than the exception in our very large cities.

Here is an example of circular social reaction: the trend to social disorganization reinforces and perpetuates the trend to social immorality on the part of the individual, while our individual lack of concern for the social effects of our actions contributes to the tattering of the web of mutual obligations. The disruption of relationships between the individual and his society and between the various specialized parts of our society has in turn resulted in a number of major contradictions in the life career of middle-class adults.

Adulthood in any society brings with it a kind of anxiety which is as indigenous to the late adolescent and adult stages of human development as "existence anxiety" is to infancy—a "cosmic" kind of anxiety (47). It stems from the adult's perception of his minuteness in physical, social and cultural space and time, and it has been increasing in direct proportion to the increase in the complexity of society and in man's knowledge of the universe and of himself. Since it is reality-centered, cosmic anxiety cannot be considered as neurotic in and of itself. Cosmic anxiety has grown markedly in the last few decades due to increasingly widespread literacy, and to technical advances in communication and transportation. As a direct result, it must be an explicit responsibility of the educational, religious, and mass-communication media of the respective modern societies to assist the individual to understand, tolerate, channel and control his share of cosmic anxiety as he becomes old enough to acquire it.

But our society does not merely *not* provide the growing individual with such focused assistance; it is instead contributing directly to an increase in the individual's load of cosmic anxiety, in particularly two ways:

> The personal-status anxiety induced in us by our early family-centered and later childhood and adolescent experiences is already present before our cosmic anxieties become intense. The result is that this unavoidable, adult type of anxiety must be superimposed on an already high level of culturally conditioned anxiety which stems from infantile sources.

> And the life-career contradictions brought about by the tattered social web of our time, in combination with the markedly stepped-up rate of

societal feedback [1] brought about by advancing communications technology, serve to reinforce our personal-status anxieties and increase our level of cosmic anxiety.

The life experiences of the middle-class adult continue to be as much at variance with experiences which are believed to promote inner integration and continuing emotional, social, intellectual growth, as were many of his childhood experiences. Ideally, there should be some degree of consistency between the various social roles the individual must perform at each stage of his development, in order that he may learn each role and integrate it into his personality functioning with no, or a minimum amount of, inner conflict. And there should be enough consistency between what is expected of him at each successive stage of development, so that he can progress from one stage to the next with no, or a minimum of, sharp breaks in the continuity of his experience. But for the middle-class adult, neither of these social conditions obtains.

In our complex society, the adult middle-class individual functions within several social contexts at the same time—the family in which he is a parent, his work setting, his friendship group, his consumer group, his lodge group, his church group, his political group, his professional group or union, the family in which he was a child, and so on. He has a different social role in each group, partly because he has a different function in each group and partly because the different personnel of each group contribute to different psychological relationships.

In our disorganized society, the various functionally-specialized parts are frequently at cross purposes with one another. What is the result of this circumstance for the adult who participates in a number of such functional groups? He finds that his various social roles and the values connected with them are more often than not in conflict with one another, some of them in marked conflict. For example, many a middle-class woman finds the "good mother" role conflicts with both a high-level consumer role and her role as a rounded, self-respecting individual. To be a "good provider" for most middle-class men is frequently at odds with being a "good father" and a "good citizen." Our various economic roles and interests

---

[1] *This* is the sociological (and the moral and the political!) significance of the new electric media—contrary to McLuhan's naive thesis that these media's content is irrelevant.

are also at cross-purposes. Many a middle-class adult is simultaneously a low-cost-seeking consumer, a high-wage-seeking worker, and a profit-valuing small shareholder!

The 1967 annual RCA share-holders' meeting prompted this additional illustrative contradiction. Many, probably most, middle-class men and women adhere to a double standard in their economic vs. their political judgments: as corporation stock-holders, they vote unhesitatingly for any merger with another company which will result in immediately or eventually increased dividends—so contributing directly to the concentration of power in fewer and fewer, larger and larger companies; yet in their role as citizens, many investers complain bitterly about the trend towards increasing centralization of power in the federal government!

Conflict between simultaneous social roles is not the only set of contradictions our fragmented society forces upon the individual. There are also life-career incompatibilities which stem from inconsistency between means and ends as we grow up. Overrapid and unguided technological, economic and social change has led to the increasingly frequent circumstance that a person's experiences and training while growing up bear little relationship to the type of life he is expected to lead as an adult. Many of us were, for example, raised to believe that initiative, originality, "openness," and hard work made up a sure-fire formula for economic success and for "getting along in the world" generally. In actual practice, we are in many cases finding such characteristics to be a handicap to us in our adulthood. We have had to develop the ability to follow directions accurately and cheerfully, to be a "good fellow" in every situation, no matter what our actual feelings are, and to say "yes" at the right times to the right people.

The marked break between our childhood experiences and moral training and what we must do in order to hope to gain and to maintain status as an adult is one of the major sources of confusion and difficulty for our teen-agers and young adults. The break is so marked for some that if their earlier experiences have already made them insecure and overvulnerable to failure, they cannot hazard taking the giant steps into adulthood our society expects them to take during adolescence and early adulthood. Many retreat entirely into their own private world: the rate of commitment for schizophrenia makes a sharp upward spurt during these life periods in our society. The number of teen-agers in our urban society who have to pick their bewildered way from childhood to adulthood through a process of almost sheer trial and error—lacking even one socially mature and responsible adult in their immediate environment who is interested in them and whom they can identify with and are willing to be guided by—makes me wonder why teen-age crime and behavior difficulties are not even more widespread than they currently are.

As has already been mentioned in Chapter 8, family functioning has also been affected by the disorganization of our times: there are many discrepancies between what the family is expected to do and what our actual social practice permits it to do. An additional discrepancy involves the child's development of moral concepts and of self-discipline, characteristics which are particularly essential to the maintenance of a self-governing political system. Our development of these characteristics is pretty closely tied in with the father's role in our kind of family system. Yet, for the majority of families in our urban population, the father is almost an absentee figure, or is himself confused on moral issues—or both—during his children's most character-formative years. Is this contradiction related to the widespread popular desire for a father figure, which is both a symptom of our times, and a warning?

The consumer pressures of our time also add to the emotional hazards of adult middle-class living—in two ways, both related to the commercial annexation of our various mass media. In an earlier time, when people were not as status driven, resided in smaller communities, and lived a less fragmented, more inwardly satisfying life than most of us do today, advertising pressures played little or no role in the emotional life of most middle-class individuals because they were not psychologically vulnerable to them. But at the same time that our values, inner tensions and unsatisfying daily round of life have combined to make us vulnerable to the consumer pressures of our advertisers, the mass media have markedly broadened their role in our lives. Commercial subsidization of these media has led to our being constantly bombarded, by eye and by ear, with the deliberately high pressure, manipulative messages of our production-dominated society. Those of us who are alarmed or simply bored to tears with these media's recent shift to catering not just to youth but to the most heedless and hedonistic and self-centered aspects of the current "youth culture" are wasting our emotional energies; this youth "kick" is due to this simple fact-of-program-sponsorship statistic: nearly half of United States consumers are under 25 years of age and are considered to be more "brain-washable" than their elders.

Our broadcasting media have added to the hazards not only of middle-class living in yet another way. When our personal life space was pretty much bounded by our immediate physical and social environment, the people we associated with were, when we compared them with us, just as likely to be equally or less capable, talented, good-looking, as they were to be more so. The generally competitive values of our culture have combined with intentional commercial stimulation of our material desires to place constantly before us the "best" of everything—the most successful, the most talented, the best looking, the apparently totally immune from errors, failure, pettiness, tension. We are led to compare ourselves with only the most superior in skill, appearance, possessions, ability, charm, and knowledge.

Since our other life experiences have already made us dependent upon just such chiefly external symbols of status for our inner feelings of self-worth, the psychological effect on us of this situation is well-nigh disastrous. Among other reactions, we typically develop a tremendous inner block against doing anything at which we might fail: we cannot chance the increase in fear, self-hatred, self-rejection such failure would induce in us. The social evidences of this blocking are legion. The growing disinterest of the majority of our young people in participation in sports is only one such evidence; this lack of interest is due, I believe, to the convergence of the individual psychological situation just described with the exclusively competitive emphasis we have traditionally placed on athletic participation.

The current role of the mass media in our lives illustrates yet another social contradiction of our day. Instead of using their remarkable coverage and influence to help us adults understand, contain, control, and channel our anxieties, which are unavoidably high in a complex, expanding world, they are playing a major role in compounding them.[2]

Further instances of the contradictions which stem from the social fragmentation of our times are so numerous, only a few additional ones are listed below:

> Ortega's "ignorant mass-man" (55) has emerged in our country at a time when the mass media have become world-wide in scope and instantaneous reach and when books and advanced education are more widely available than ever before.

> As the population expands and people are getting closer and closer physically, they are going further and further apart psychologically.

---

[2] Indeed, it is the tremendous power these media have put in the hands of those who control them which is forcing us to make deliberated choices concerning the future direction of our society much sooner than anyone had anticipated.

Public interest in the arts and in drama is increasing, at a time when all but a few artists and actors are unable to earn an independently creative living.

While Americans' feelings about John F. Kennedy's assassination continue to be intense enough to make any and all discussion of it and of his widow and children front-page news everywhere in the United States three years after his death, legal curbs on the sale of firearms remain more lax than in any other democratic country.

Concern about the technological pollution of our physical environment has increased to the point of instituting programs to combat it, at the same time that we are accelerating governmental and private financial support of applied-science research and decelerating/omitting research and social programs bearing on the individual human being who is supposed to be the beneficiary of all these technological advances.

As the "middle-class crisis" deepens, many middle-class persons, rather than facing up to it, are using the plight of our rediscovered poor as an avenue of escape from their own multi-faceted dilemma: while some are using the poor and the weak and the unadapting as their psychological scapegoats (après Ayn Rand), others are choosing the diametrically opposite course of actively participating in "anti-poverty" programs.

Most civil-rights leaders are pushing for full economic opportunity for Afro-Americans and for their unqualified acceptance into the white middle-class social establishment, at the very time when that establishment cannot afford to be generous either economically or psychologically because it is experiencing the severe strains that are the subject of this book.

Slum youngsters as of Summers '66 and '67 were rioting supposedly because they do not enjoy the advantages of the middle class, at the same time that more and more privileged young people were opting out of their middle-class paradise into hippy-land.

Complaints about the low amounts of social leadership, personal courage, creativity and independence of mind on the part of our school-system's teachers and administators are being increasingly expressed, at the same time that a particular community's and/or institution's core criterion for retention of educational personnel at every academic level continues to be their capacity to be good civil-servants—i.e., their willingness to carry out the dictates of local school-boards and/or to fit 'smoothly' into a mammoth bureaucracy.

So abundant in contradictions are the interrelated areas of changing sex-roles and attitudes towards women, a whole sub-series is necessary:

More and more women are calling for full competitive/occupational equality with men at a time when the male-dominated occupational world is not only becoming increasingly immoral but is on the verge of collapse in the face of automation/cybernation; and when men and women should alike be turning toward the cultivation of unpaid roles and activities centered in home and family and community and creative and self-fulfillment—traditionally the cultivated-feminine domain!

Decisions concerning matters which fundamentally affect women's life and being—e.g., curbing the population explosion, liberalizing abortion laws—are continuing to be made at male-dominated highest-policy-making levels.

Expressions of hunger for the warmth, affection, nurturance, traditionally associated with women's traditional roles, are on the increase, at the same time that expressions of hostility towards, and denigration of, women are endemic in our mass media—to the point of affecting negatively women's capacity and willingness to continue to accept and to practice these functions.

We continue to give lip-service to "individualism" even as feelings of powerlessness are spreading to persons in positions of supposed power and as we make little to no effort to develop and to institute supplementary democratic forms and processes which would permit *some* degree of individual citizen influence and responsibility.

These multiple contradictions and inconsistencies permeate the the growing-up experiences of nearly everyone in our society. Each of us is faced with the staggering psychological burden of integrating social demands which are frequently in both simultaneous and serial conflict. Nearly all of us in the middle class are finding this load a heavy one. At the least, it predisposes us towards developing the "alienation constellation" of Chapter 5. It promotes what is probably the most ultimately negative manifestation of our times, a manifestation seldom noticed by us because of its quiet, undramatic pervasiveness. Our inner conflicts force a great many of us to expend all or nearly all of our psychic energies in just keeping ourselves going from day to day. Many of us have little or no energy or motivation left over for our own positive inner development, as a result.

When a great many of us are denying ourselves by not cultivating in a calm, reflective, deeply experienced way the many-faceted aspects of our being, we are not harming ourselves only as individuals. Our society suffers as well: when each of us is not what we can be, everyone is the loser.

If the jokes we tell one another constitute evidence, at least some of us are becoming consciously aware of the impossibly contradictory life we are expected—and expect ourselves—to lead. One such joke has as its central character the prototypical doting grandmother out shopping for a toy for her three-year-old grandson. The saleslady, after showing her several fascinatingly complex toys, finally demonstrates one that is *so* complicated, it cannot, by design, be put together to form any sort of coherent entity:

> *Saleslady:* You see—no matter how hard your grandson may try to put it together, he can't.
>
> *Customer:* Oh good, I'll take it. That's just the sort of toy that will fit him for today's world.

Those of us who are interested in the promotion of human welfare have generally accepted the principle that physical conditions of living which allow deprivation of the basic physical needs of man must be eliminated, if the human expression potential of human beings is to be raised, if immature levels of adjustment are to be discarded, and if war is to be eliminated. For myself, I have become convinced that human welfare efforts must for the same reasons seek to minimize as well distorting blocks on individual psychological development which have their sources in the very make-up of one's society.

On the basis of socially based supportive emotional experiences, American middle-class children, adolescents, adults, old people, are among the most seriously underprivileged in the world. Coincident with our acquisition of an ever greater number of gadgets and the steady increase in our physical-comfort standards, the new urban middle class, *when compared with the old American middle class*, has in psychological and general environmental standards been regressing steadily towards these characteristics of *life in the slums:*

> progressively less space and privacy per family and per person;
>
> fewer and fewer socially unharmful opportunities for psychologically-expansive experiences, including those which stem from contact with the open countryside and the world of nature;
>
> progressively less time and inclination for the inner cultivation of self as a unique and sensitive human being;
>
> progressively fewer opportunities for supportive and mutually rewarding human relationships, coincident with
>
> progressively more personality-attacking and -fragmenting experiences— to the extent that the general latent level of fear and of vulnerability

towards external "stress events" is steadily rising, while our threshold of resistance to frustrations and ego-threats is steadily dropping;

an increasing tendency for the father to abdicate from nearly all aspects of the paternal role—with the single exception of that of economic provider;

emergence of tendencies towards overt, directly destructive violence and/ or withdrawal into drugs on the part of young people, as the conditions formerly associated with slum living spread to the suburbs: manipulations by forces beyond one's control and consequent feelings of helplessness.

We Americans may have achieved the highest physical standard of living in the world, but we have achieved it at the price of creating for a great many of us what is in many respects a psychological slum. We should hesitate a long time before we export *this* facet of the American way of life to any industrially backward but often more psychologically privileged nation. And these nations should, in turn, hesitate a long time before they inflict on themselves the social and individual effects of the wholesale adoption of economic materialism and technological advancement *as ends in themselves*—whether they choose the communistic *or* the capitalistic blueprint.

It is the complex interdependence of social trends and individual functioning which leads me to question the effectiveness of our current Administration's "band-aid" approach to such problems as the "crisis of our cities." Our political representatives, highest planning levels in our federal and state governments, private/voluntary programs are all persisting in an almost compulsive adherence to more and more of the same remedial approaches that have failed in the past.

This interdependence also leads me to question the constructiveness of a number of popular middle-class cause-groups which represent well-intentioned and often well-informed people who are justifiably concerned about one or another aspect of the sickness of our times. But their concern has led them to an overhasty diagnosis of that illness: what they have selected as *the* important problem has relevance, but this selection is either one-sided in approach or constitutes what is in actuality a symptom of the illness rather than a contributing cause of it. Their recommended "cures" reveal the same tendency towards oversimplification. In so espousing an oversimplified solution, they are diverting themselves and their society from undertaking more thorough and comprehensive—and undoubtedly more personally and socially painful—analyses. Two examples of such "causes," both wisely supported by middle-class persons, are:

the various censorship groups, who urge elimination of genuinely objectionable themes from comic books and widely distributed pocket-size books, radio and TV programming;

the various mental-health groups, who urge major expansion of psychiatric, psychological and social work personnel to serve the real and increasing needs of individual sufferers.

The censorship groups owe their appeal to their legitimate belief that the violent, salacious and sadistic materials which our adult hostilities make popular are not particularly wholesome fare for our children, whether or not they happen to be psychologically vulnerable to such materials. The weakest link in their argument seems to me to be the circumstance that most of our newspapers, under the opportunity for license granted by our belief in the freedom of the press, print on their front pages far more salacious, violent and perverted accounts than any comic-book writer could hope to get by with: after all, that sort of "lead story" sells more papers, doesn't it?

I agree with the civil-liberties groups that "voluntary" *or* legal censorship of books and motion pictures may lead to potentially more negative social results than overstimulated children. But many parents will continue to consider the civil-liberties argument an essentially negative one, so long as they (*and* the civil-liberties organizations!) are not helped to see that censorship cannot solve a problem which stems from an immorality which has come to lie at the very core of our society—an immorality to which they themselves are contributing through their own values and practices.

These cause groups would make a far greater social contribution if they sponsored studies by qualified personnel to discover *who* habitually reads those materials which are most objectionable from the middle-class moral and psychiatric points of view, and *why* these people do so, in psychological terms. Such studies just might make the disconcerting discovery that horror comics and perverted "thrillers" are actually contributing to the maintenance of our society "as is." Surely inner distortions which are partially an offshoot of the operation of social factors in these people's lives are more "safely" siphoned off in the reading of horror comics than in more violent and socially rejected behaviors, such as theft and the destruction of private property! (Or are they?)

The "solution" recommended by mental health groups invites comparison with the medical profession's approach to a patient suffering from an infectious disease in its pre-Pasteur days. These groups' emphasis on the necessity for expanded therapeutic means and services without *at the same time* acknowledging and trying to discover the role of social factors in the spread of psychological difficulties in our society, compares with the pre-Pasteur practitioner's belief that his professional responsibility did not extend beyond efforts to treat the infected individual. It also emphasizes the conceptual and research handicaps imposed by professional specialization and lack of communication among those disciplines which deal with one or another aspect of the living person: our scientific approaches to the individual have, until very recently, been so fragmented or so slavishly imitative of the physical sciences, we have difficulty in formulating meaningful problems about his functioning as a purposeful human being.

I readily admit, in spite of my apparent certainty on this point, that we do not as yet have anywhere near as exact knowledge of the relationship between general social trends and individual psychological difficulty as today's epidemiologist has of the relationship between physical-environmental factors, individual susceptibility, and the spread of infectious disease. I acknowledge, further, that social factors seem to play a secondary role in the incidence of the psychoses, which are believed to have an important organic-susceptibility component.

But when qualified psychotherapists and cooperating research personnel are not willing to go beyond their responsibility to and concern for the individual sufferer, nor beyond the search for medical palliatives "after the fact," their reluctance is postponing that day when the complexities of the relationship between social factors and individual psychological difficulties are discovered and made available to us. Certainly this area is much too complex to give our population the impression that pill-cures for "mental illness" (the current catch-all of catch-alls) can be found which will operate as quickly and painlessly as the (for example) preventive vaccine for polio. To add insult to injury, we have been "sold" this idea by the very industry which has contributed more than any other single source to the high level of tension of American life: executive officers of big-city mental-health societies typically include top-level advertising personages in hot pursuit of a "socially responsible" image.

When professional researchers take so simplistic and manipulative an approach to human behavior, we should be neither surprised nor punitive when some of our unhappy *and* quick-learning young attempt to attain instant nirvana and/or wisdom through the use of LSD or other "mind-expanding" drugs. And haven't our advertisers been reiterating to them all their waking hours all their growing-up years that any problem, even the most difficult of one's inner "hang-ups," can be solved merely by the buying and using of some product or other?

Some of the most socially responsible and concerned people in our society are members of mental health groups. If we, the better informed of our society, are not able to focus our eyes beyond the immediate, urgent needs of individual sufferers and delinquents— to see this step as but one of many essential parallel steps—we shall shortly be living, as someone has perceptively remarked (Agnes Meyer, I think), in a society where one-half of us will be either looking after *or* protecting the other half of us. New York Police Commissioner Stephen Kennedy's Valentine's Day 1956 request for 9,000, and Commissioner Leary's Christmas 1966 request for 1000, more foot-patrolmen for New York City provide but one of many possible foot-notes for this comment.

Chapter Thirteen

Imminent: A Time of Testing?

As YET, THE more extreme economic and social pressures and the more extreme individual reactions to them tend to be concentrated in our very large cities. Assuming that our values and practices continue to be at odds with the actual economic and social facts of life, and that our daily round of living becomes more and more "prepackaged," it seems valid to predict that the various described patterns of individual reaction and of social immorality will spread to smaller centers of population as well.

It is further warrantable to predict that the level of anxiety required for most middle-class individuals to remain socially adaptive—that is, to reach their goals of high consumer and occupational status—will steadily rise, so that:

The successfully adapting middle-class person will have to cope with greater and greater amounts of anxiety and hostility within himself.

A greater proportion of us will not be able to tolerate psychologically either the high level of compulsiveness and anxiety necessary for success, nor the psychological backwash resulting from our perception of failure, so that more and more of us, proportionately, will either develop psychological and psychosomatic distortions of varying degrees of severity, or escape into social irresponsibility and apathy, or both. The always-present tendency to blame others who are even more vulnerable than we are for our troubles will intensify into a socially divisive search for victims—i.e., into scapegoating. Our cities' "skid row" populations will not only increase markedly, *they will include a much higher proportion of young ex-middle-class men.*

The more extreme types of individual reaction will increase in rate for all levels of the population—juvenile delinquency; crimes of violence; crimes of violence of a bizarre and perverted nature; the psychotherapeutic case-loads of private practitioners and public agencies; increasingly unstable marital relationships; homosexuality; cases of child neglect and child assault; drug addiction; alcoholism; severe emotional disturbances among children; heart disease and other ailments which stem primarily from hypertension; suicide; psychopathic and sociopathic personality.

The various expressions of social immorality described earlier will spread and become more acute.

Unfortunately, the over-all situation will first have to get worse in order for it to get any better. A broader base of the middle-class population all across the United States will have to experience directly the more extreme psychological and social residues of the status struggle of our times before sufficient grass-roots impetus for change is built up.[1] The great risk in this connection is that the increasing anxiety, frustration, hostility, apathy, occasioned by current trends actually militate against our capacity for, and likelihood of, changing our beliefs and our practices in a rational and responsible manner: these psychological pressures force the individual to become increasingly rigid and stereotyped in his inner reactions and in his tendencies to escape from, rather than face up to, his life problems. Also, the advertising and publishing industries' annexation towards commercial ends of milder forms of youthful non-conformity and dissent is serving to remove an important social safety-valve—and so is contributing to the emergence of the kinds of increasingly violent forms of dissent that induce panic among the solid citizenry.

If we are unable to re-accept for and within ourselves this nation's more than adequate social ideals, and *if* we are unable creatively and rationally to develop personal values and implementing practices which are far more consistent with these ideals than those we have today, then we may well experience as a nation one or both of two types of seriously traumatic social happenings.

First, we may have a political escape from freedom so well described and analyzed by Erich Fromm (25). I have an impression that is not at all reassuring in this regard. The great majority of the middle and working class population are so absorbed in the urgent, demanding, immediate present, they are quite unconcerned about what system of government they live under so long as it functions in such a way as to permit an apparently stable or increasing consumer capacity. A sharp, obvious change to an autocracy of the right or of the left would probably cause a counter-reaction prompted primarily by fear

---

[1] The rate of cultural feedback has increased so rapidly, the continuing use of the future tense may well be already inappropriate: viz the circumstance that this book is being re-published—with great enthusiasm—by a house located in *St. Louis.*

of the unfamiliar. But so long as their relative prosperity holds and the change is gradual, and accomplished and maintained behind the screen of familiar political forms, I do not believe there will be—is!— any protest worth speaking of from the great majority of urbanites and suburbanites, in spite of their traditional role as a politically sophisticated and liberal sector of the voting population.[2]

The measures taken to prevent the possible emergence of an autocracy of the left have been so effective, it is not realistic to anticipate such a political change of direction in the United States. But the very measures so taken may at the same time have diverted public attention from a development which is far more likely during this period of unregulated bigness: initiation of steps toward an autocracy of the right.

There are a number of evidences that quietly powerful groups and individuals, acting on the conviction that "we know better than they do what is best for them," have begun to take full advantage of the lack of interest of the bulk of our citizenry in their own and their neighbors' political and civil obligations and rights. Four such evidences are:

1. American very-big business' unabating penchant for placing its parochial aims—continuing expansion and refusal to countenance over-all economic or social planning—above any and every other societal and national consideration, and its possession of sufficient influence to be able to implement both these goals. It is doing so first, by encouraging, through its subsidization of our printed and air mass media, more and more luxury/conspicuous consumption and irresponsible escapism at home; and second, by influencing our government to assume western Europe's old role of economic imperialism in underdeveloped cum politically unstable areas of the world.

2. The emergence of a new feudalism, of which the foregoing represents

---

[2] The circumstance that the first unmistakable expressions of social protest have begun to come not from members of the middle or working classes but from our slum dwellers—who happen at this period of American history to be chiefly people of color—may prove to be disastrous for the United States. Popular prejudices may obscure this important fact of latter-twentieth-century life: that the desperate youngsters of the central-city constitute merely the *first portion* of that eventual human mass which is being rendered occupationally and psychologically displaced by the *second,* equally unplanned, industrial revolution. If at least the liberal members of the politically dominant middle-class are not able to perceive the rioters in this broader context, this avant-garde group may instead provide a fortuitous excuse for a nation-wide wave of political reaction we may not be given the opportunity to rebound from—and the coming decade of political crisis discussed later in this chapter may begin as much as seven years earlier than predicted.

only one evidence. Contemporary, mass-society-style feudalism is headed not by an absolute, hereditary monarch but by big-business-getting-bigger, and is maintained first through big-B's coalition with big-government and higher education earlier referred to, and second by big-B's massive control over the mass communications *and entertainment* media. So far as the air mass-media are concerned, the line between performer and huckster has been so thoroughly breached, even the most established TV actors and singers and "personalities" introduce and/or deliver their show's "commercials," and highly respected news analysts and commentators are required to deliver a chaste statement identifying their radio-program sponsors. Further, two types of business subsidies to the higher status entertainment media are the latest good-public-relations ploy. One type involves large, direct—and well-publicized—grants for opera, theater and ballet performances; the other is the provision of exceptionally high remuneration for individual artists who are willing to participate in spot commercials: viz. Robert Merrill's beer "spots." (So pervasive is this total-environment brainwashing process, not even our nation's teachers—and those preparing to be teachers—are aware that it is occurring nor that it has significant political implications.)

3. The current Administration's official manner of describing Americans who oppose our country's VietNam "action" as a " 'small' minority" without further qualification—when that substantial minority's majority is drawn from the best educated and informed groups in our society.

4. The lack of real political choices in the last two national elections and probably in the next two. The expansive post-war temper of the American people, in combination with Communism as a fortuitous target for internally generated hostilities, has contributed to the development of so strong a middle-of-the-road political trend, both parties have been jostling one another for the coveted center position for over a decade. The marked changes both at home and abroad which have been occurring during the past several years have not been adequately reported to the American public nor have they evoked a corresponding responsible-political mirroring of the intra- and inter-national meanings of these changes. So, very much like the situation in authoritarian countries that we habitually deplore, practically no real political choices are available to the thoughtful but non-doctrinaire voter. This lack of realistic and responsible political choice has made a major contribution to the current tendencies in the United States towards polarization at the political extremes, intensified inter-group hostilities, and social fragmentation. [3]

---

[3] Had our VietNam intervention caught emotional fire with Americans, it might have served the customary "external aggressor" unifying function: indeed, this

Further, we are currently nurturing a whole generation of urban youngsters the majority of whom probably accept what the "ads" and the mass entertainment media tell them, and what most of their parents believe: that self-worth is measurable by one's material possessions and the glamor or the institutional status of one's occupation. If enlightened social and political leadership does not emerge as a counter-force to these pervasive mass-media influences, what degree of social responsibility can we expect these children and teenagers to display during both the competitive-race phase of their early adulthood and the later, post -success or -failure phase? How many of the next generation of American middle-class citizenry will fall into two rather clear-cut *and highly manipulable* categories of "arrogant irresponsible" and "defeated irresponsible"?

Although only the passage of time can yield the full answers to these questions, I think the summer and fall of 1966 can be pinpointed as having initiated a period of steadily increasing political crisis in these United States, a period which will reach its climax during the decade 1975-85. Provided that the middle class continues as a group to cling to its reality-dissociated value-system, this decade appears to be a climatic time, for these interlocking reasons (36)[4]:

1. The generation born between 1935 and 1945 will be 30-50 between 1975 and 1985. Large numbers of this particular generation spent their early, most formative years under wartime conditions of family instability—a circumstance already showing up in the weak ego-structure and inner controls of many of our young people. It is conservative to say that many, probably most, of this generation is characterized by a high degree of psychological vulnerability to external social pressures.

2. It is between the ages of 30 and 40 that the middle-class individual usually knows "for sure" whether he is, or is going to be, a "success" or a "failure." Assuming that a far greater proportion of those to whom success has major ego meanings fail than succeed, most of the 1935-45 generation will be subjected to an extreme inner stress experience beginning about 1975.

3. If this generation crumbles psychologically under this combination of inner and outer pressures, our democratic practices may well crumble

---

hoped-for eventuality was one of the reasons it was embarked upon, I believe. But this gamble was lost: VietNam has instead played/been playing an intensely and increasingly divisive role in American life.

[4] I am indebted to this reference for the basic conception behind this analysis.

with them, because 30 to 50 is, in a democracy, the life period when the burden of responsibility for decision-making in every public sphere of life—social, political, economic—must be seriously assumed by the individual.

Second, we may experience as a nation one or more of a number of fanatic or hysterical manifestations such as: the psychosomatic hysterias which occurred during the Middle Ages; a wave of religious fanaticism (some of our most respected churchmen have already expressed fears that this may be occurring); rejection and active suppression of a minority (that is, scapegoating)—which, in our minorities-composed society, is more likely to be differentiated on the basis of values and social role than of religion or ethnic origins and tends to represent a projection of the suppressing majority's feared or rejected inner reactions.[5] I do not believe that extension of our current anti-Communism quite fills this last bill, although exploitation of irrational fears of Communism as an aggressive threat against the status quo may be contributing to a social reaction of major proportions.

Manifestations of scapegoating, although relatively minor as yet, are visibly becoming more common; here is a survey of the most socially divisive of such manifestations:

The tendency to turn our backs on those who are unable to adapt to the intensely competitive middle-class way of life—the poor, the weak, the old, the imprisoned, the mentally ill, the non-conforming young—has always been endemic in these United States. But such ignoring/rejection has begun not only to change to outright hostility among substantial sectors of the middle class; it has been raised to

---

[5] My heretofore nebulously developing hunch that *the poor, and especially the colored poor,* fill this bill's specifications remarkably well, was sharpened just as this edition went to press by this finding of a four-year study of the elementary school children, parents and teachers of the phototypical suburb of "New Village" (80); directly pertinent passages have been italicized:

"Finally it appears that one area of human difference is almost completely ignored in the American suburb. Many parents and teachers were found eager to bridge religious differences; many recognized, however uneasily, the need for discussion of racial differences. But with a few notable exceptions, *neither parents nor schools were facing up to economic inequality.* Occasionally, a social-studies class would take up the poor of other nations, or a fund-drive would focus attention on the less fortunate in the United States, but *the fact that there were impoverished families within a stone's throw of New Village was seldom noted,* and how they got there or what kept them impoverished was seldom investigated." (page 14)

the level of a philosophical position by that guru of the "far right," Ayn Rand.

A further, similar-order danger-signal is the spreading tendency of social groups who are themselves socially vulnerable to direct their aggressions at other groups who are even more vulnerable than they are. Thus, women are at least as much victims of the dislocations of our times as are men, yet much denigration/hostility is being directed against them by those whose fragile masculine-self-hood is most threatened by the ego-destroying pressures of our time. This "underground campaign" could be dismissed as only a limited and a passing aberration were it not for the circumstance that many of these confused persons have acquired influential roles not only in literature and in the arts, but also in the mass media. Hostility towards the civil-rights movement on the part of persons of working- and lower-middle class background—who make up the bulk of the "white backlash"—is another example of a vulnerable social group reacting against a still-more-vulnerable group. Probably the most pathetic example of vulnerable social targetry is our public-school teachers, who are currently caught in a withering societal cross-fire. From one direction, teachers have become the scapegoats of minority groups who are not being permitted to join the (to them) "charmed circle" as rapidly as the TV commercials stimulate them to demand as their inalienable right. From the opposite direction, the same upper-middle-class charmed circle—with whom teachers identify with a loyalty so unswerving as to merit the attention of a first-rate satirist—has placed them on the expendable front-line of social tension without adequate professional or institutional "ammunition," nor back-up social support.

Another order of intergroup hostility was experienced during Spring '67 by high school students in an affluent suburb of New York City. As part of a professional exchange-program between their school and a Harlem school, a group of "inner-city" teachers presented the protest play "In White America" to these suburban students. The performance was followed by a discussion between the "actors" and their student audience. The visitors' hostility towards these privileged young people was very evident during the discussion; one young (white!) teacher expressed feelings of outright hostility so openly and directly, the students were both startled and puzzled. Perhaps a better example, because well-publicized (during August '67), was Chet Huntley's charge that major, repeated acts of vandalism had forced him to sell his 300-acre New Jersey cattle-fattening ranch.

Further examples of expressions of intra-societal hostility are now legion in these United States. Shirley Jackson's *The Lottery* may turn out to be a more acutely prescient anticipation of our society circa 1974 than even she herself realized (32).

The most ominous indicator of all for the future is the variety and the pervasiveness of evidences of a *reaction against rationality* at every level in American society, even among the highly educated—a trend which I am dubbing the "severed-head syndrome" after Iris Murdoch's perspicacious book-title.

One of the ways this reaction is showing up was partially predicted in this passage from the earlier version of this book:

> The real contribution to current anti-intellectual reactions of those persons of superior ability who misuse that ability has already been referred to in Chapters 10 and 11: to manipulate and to exploit others for our own shortsightedly selfish ends in the present is to incur these same people's hostility in the not-long-after-future.

Rational, "depersonalized" thinking is itself—not just as utilized by scientists—coming to be seen as most to blame for the elimination of the older, simpler, psychologically encompassable way of life. The more meaninglessly complex and anxiety-filled daily living becomes, the stronger the feelings against the factors considered to be responsible for removal from an earlier "Eden." Evidences of a rebellion against the authority of depersonalized intellectuality include: the feeling among many people, precipitated by our A- and H- bomb tests, that "science has gone too far" (contrast this reaction with the partially educated middle-class person's usual sanguine picture of applied science as an omniscient and omniversatile "magical fixer"); a widespread distrust of the professional and of scientifically derived evidence, shown in the Mausners' significant study referred to earlier; the lack of public support for scholarly concern over attacks on intellectual freedoms; [6] the popularity among the middle class of a book

---

[6] This public reaction during the mid-1950s provided a lesson which the executive branch of our present Administration has quickly learned—and applied. It has not only felt free to ignore the organized, continuing anti-VietNam protests of major sectors of the academic and scientific community. It has also, and perhaps more significantly as already mentioned, referred in its official pronouncements to this best informed and educated sector of the United States population as "only a small minority of the American people" without further elaboration. And it has permitted the CIA freely to use towards nationalistic political ends, student and professional organizations formed for purposes of scholarly inquiry and advancement, without the knowledge and considered consent of these organizations' respective memberships. (Just what *is* it we are supposed to be fighting *against?*)

with as Nietzschean a sub-theme as *The Caine Mutiny* (79): the motion-picture, based on the play, based on the book, which was nominated as one of the "five best films of 1954," made the dichotomy between the simply noble man of action (Van Johnson, no less!) and the deviously despicable man of intellect its major theme. Perhaps the most significant evidence of all is that which must underlie the authorship of such a book as *The Caine Mutiny*—the sickness of an intellectual who, in coming to reject the manipulative application of his own superior intellect, has rejected intellectuality altogether.

Another source of evidence, too easily overlooked, is the continuing growth in the rate of new adult memberships in churches and/or sects which stress either that "God can and will perform miracles," or that "This sinful world will soon come to an end, as prophesied." Contrary to the impression held by many, this new membership is coming primarily from respectable working-class and small-white-collar young adults with young and growing families—not primarily from the emotionally unstable and dispossessed persons usually associated with such religious groups.

Many little people are convinced, with a good deal of justification in our exploitative society, that they are being manipulated by forces beyond their control. A diffuse and ordinarily unfocused blend of fear, hostility and resentment is their typical reaction to this suspicion. Leaders of irrational movements on both the right and the left are able to focus these feelings on individuals and groups whose social function can be rationalized to epitomize the "sinister forces" which control these little people's unsatisfying lives. The day-before-yesterday it was the Wall Street bankers; yesterday and today it was/is the Communists; tomorrow it may well be dissenting scientists and intellectuals. To those who may feel I am somewhat overdrawing the picture I commend the viewing of a motion-picture of the "McCarthy period" which was excellent box-office among some groups in our population: *My Son John,* ostensibly anti-Communist, only, in theme.

Although the majority of those who distrust rationality and the intellect are ordinarily lower than middle class in social status, those who *lead* anti-liberal and anti-intellectual movements are usually middle class in background. Run-of-the-mill lower-middle-class persons are also displaying anti-intellectual leanings. What has happened to the traditional middle class respect for those of high educational attainments? This respect is of course still present, but distinctly less so than in the not-too-distant past. I believe part of the reason for this change is an overall diminution of regard among Americans for higher education: it is no longer as sure a ladder for upward social mobility as it used to be.

I also believe that a more fertile emotional soil for the growth of anti-intellectualism is present in some sections of the middle class than has been appreciated. Two sub-groups particularly are prone to such reactions—persons who have moved into "lower-middle" status from a working-class family background, more because of fortuitous circumstances external to themselves (such as the qualitative changes in the occupational pattern occasioned by urbanization and industrialization) than because of their own focused and adaptive striving for higher status, and persons trying very hard to make the jump from "lower-middle" to "upper-middle" status, but who just can't seem to do so—and to whom secure upper-middle status has tremendous emotional meanings.

The egos of such people tend to be in a constant state of threat; a typical manner of expressing these feelings of threat is their inability to accept that anyone is or can be "above" them. Their striving for greater consumer power stems not so much from a desire to surpass oneself or one's peers, but from the emotional imperative to be equal with the "top people"—"top" interpreted by them as the most obviously "successful" people. By acquiring and displaying the things the "top people" have, these persons are able to see themselves as "equal to anybody." To create and to maintain their self-made myth of equality, all they need to do is keep on making enough money to buy an increasing number and variety of "equalizing" things.

People with such a life rationale deeply resent the intellectually able—as well as, for that matter, anyone who is manifestly superior in a self-expressive medium which requires both a high level of innate capacity and long, disciplined years of education or training—because such a person's very presence gives testimony to the circumstance that there is a good deal more to being or becoming "equal" than the mere purchase of external symbols of status. The existence of such a person forces them to consider the possibility that there are inner qualities of excellence which can neither be bought nor manufactured nor counterfeited. This reminder threatens to subvert these people's entire ego rationale. Their reaction is thoroughly logical, psychologically: they reject the highly able person as the apparent source of threat.

It is not surprising, in light of this analysis, that teachers in some of the new, solidly middle-class suburban areas speak of the arrogance and patronizing attitudes towards them of many of their pupils' parents. It also should not be surprising if many middle-class persons join actively in movements which express distrust and rejection of dissenting intellectuals and scientists.

Certain American parallels with Europe have already been mentioned. If the present United States "establishment" and value systems continue in substantially unmodified form, and if competitive pressures and related "ressentiment" continue to increase, it is not inconceivable, in light of some interesting circa-1958 tabulations (8) that another aspect of European history may be repeated in these United States. Consider the pattern drawn by this religious breakdown of statistical data on occupation, amount of education and income of family-head (44):

Index	Protestant	Catholic	Jewish
Proportion of the population of the United States:	66%	26%	3%
Persons having four years or more of college education:	9	7	22
Professional, managerial, clerical, sales, occupations:	32	32	70
Crafts and semi-skilled occupations:	39	46	19
Household-heads with income of $10,000 and over:	5	5	19

Jewish-Americans would appear to have a more than routine interest in the sorts of social change that will arrest the present rapid growth of "ressentiment" in American society.

Another of the ways in which the "severed-head syndrome" has been manifesting itself is in a refusal or an actual inability on the part of some chronological-adults to assume, beyond their occupational obligations, adult roles and responsibilities and self-disciplines. Arrest at childhood levels of impulsivity and of inability to endure even minor amounts of frustration and stress have in the past been traits frequently present among slum-lower-class adults; they are now showing up among middle-class persons as well. Among such individuals, if a task or a goal turns out to entail more than minor amounts of sustained mental effort or delay of gratification, it is quickly abandoned and some other, less taxing, activity resorted to: we are now living in an era of instant knowledge, instant happiness, instant "mind-expansion"!

McLuhan to the apparent contrary, complex ideas (including McLuhan's!) require hard thought and persisting effort on the part of the learner to be grasped by him. This "instant" urge is affecting the higher learning situation: if those dominated by it are unable easily and immediately to understand an idea or to reduce it to a superficial generalization, they are driven to reject either or both their mentor or the entire learning situation.

Professor Fromm had not, perhaps, been long enough in this country at the time he wrote his book (about 1939) to recognize the beginnings of a characteristically American evidence of escape from freedom, responsibility, maturity—evidence which has become a well-defined trend during only the last two decades. From the ethically justifiable development of *labor*-saving devices, we have moved to an addiction to any and all *effort*-saving ones. We are all familiar with those glowing, consumer-aimed accounts of the latest technological "advances" for the home of the present—changing a TV channel without having to get up from one's chair, cooking a meal likewise, etc., etc. (as a Mr. Delaney of General Motors put it during a radio interview: "We are constantly trying to reduce the physical effort of operating an automobile and to increase its comfort.")—and of the entirely push-button world of the near future. No one ever seems to be curious about what more worthwhile things we are going to do with the time and energy and muscle-power so being saved!

It was one of these accounts which prompted me to put these questions to myself: What is the end-point of this trend towards our every desire being attended to without any effort on our parts? What, probably unconscious, psychological need lies behind it? The answer which I have arrived at has been more than a little shocking to myself. Far from showing signs of developing the thoroughly adult level of behavior essential to the exercise of freedom, Americans are being driven by outer pressures and inner anxieties stemming from infantile deprivations into a *compensatory mass movement back to the womb!* To date, this movement is evident in our consuming behavior, in consequent production emphases and advertising "pitches," and in some of the ways we prefer to spend our leisure time. Tomorrow . . . ?

Twelve years later, tomorrow—and with it, LSD, and Hugh Hefner and his bed-womb[7]—seems to have arrived!

Still-another way in which the "severed-head syndrome" is showing

---

[7] I am indebted to Winifred Colton for this bon-"pon".

up—actually a variation on the foregoing one—is the current trend, modeled, appropriately enough, after our country's warfare-policy in VietNam, to reject not merely formerly accepted standards of value and of conduct but to abandon *all* beyond-self reference-points: under such "convenient" circumstances, bothersome guilt-feelings are no longer aroused when one gives in to one's first, infantile, impulse, or does absolutely *anything* that will draw attention to oneself, or makes and sells *whatever* will bring in a profit, or uses other persons towards one's own self-centered ends. Convenient in the short-run, that is. It will not take long for us to discover that in a world where all abstract, beyond-self moral standards are dispensed with, and only expediency and/or power determines what is right, *all of us are victims,* sooner than later.

If a widespread and extreme reaction against rationality spreads and grows, it may well serve as a "time of testing" for our nation[8] from which we may or may not recover as an essentially self-governing social unit. *If* such a socially traumatic event occurs and we do recover from it, it may serve an ultimately constructive purpose: it may lead to our re-acceptance of, and re-dedication to, ideals of social justice and respect for the human personality perceived as of prior inner significance to any immediate individual or group self-interest. Such widespread inner commitment and dedication to a commonly compelling goal seems to be a basic requirement for the maintenance of an indispensable level of socially responsible behavior —indispensable among not only the self-seeking and the immature, but among all of us.

---

[8] Evidence is rapidly accumulating that such a time of testing will merely *begin* here and spread in intermittent waves to the rest of the planet. Our country's omnipresent military power and aggressive style of salesmanship and merchandising, in combination with the global scope of the various communications media, are imposing the second industrial revolution and its accompanying social and individual disorganization on the rest of the world much sooner and more quickly than anyone, including this writer, has foreseen. (It is this marked cultural discontinuity, converging with the obsolescence of many of the most cherished conscious and unconscious tenets of western civilization, which is sparking the forthcoming global convulsion—not a confrontation between "capitalism" and "communism": if written history continues, future generations will be as baffled over the present era's bitter hostility between two such marginally different economic and social systems as we are today over the religious wars of seventeenth century Europe!)

PART III

New Values for Old

Chapter Fourteen

We *Learn* To Be Human and Ourselves

For us of the American middle class to regain some measure of control over our own lives and of our national life will require no less than a deliberate, studied attempt on our parts to reorient our values and ways of thinking and reacting. But for us even to consider such a course will mean that marked changes in our habitual ways of thinking about ourselves have occurred. And these changes will be most difficult for us to accomplish because they require a marked shift in the point of reference for our individual and social value systems.

Instead of our current twin tendencies of

evaluating ourselves and others in accordance with how closely we and and they conform to the particular existing values and practices of the social group with which we identify, and

considering the human organism as but another gadget created primarily for economic and technological ends, and therefore as infinitely tinkerable and "improvable,"

we must learn to do just the opposite. We must make our own emerging humanity the reference point of our economic and social life: *we must learn to understand the nature and the ingredients of our own and others' humanity and individuality, and then we must use this growing understanding as the basis for evaluating—and changing—our economic, social, technological, political, legal forms and practices.*

We shall have to learn to do this kind of thinking in order for us to hope to develop a picture of a humanity-promoting society. We shall have to learn to do this kind of thinking in order for us to conceive and to apply the means for our realization of such a society. We shall have to learn to do this kind of thinking if we hope to control the development and applications of technological innovations, rather than be controlled by them. We shall have to learn to do this

[147]

kind of thinking and acting in order for us to make any real progress towards becoming integrated, "whole" individuals. We shall have to learn to do this kind of thinking in order for us to be able constantly to re-appraise the nature of our humanity as man's understanding of himself grows, to reconceive a new social ideal, to rebuild in light of this new ideal—and to keep on repeating this process indefinitely.

I believe we already know enough about the real, not the ideal, nature of human nature to start as a nation to make constructive social use of this knowledge. For illustrative, not prescriptive, purposes, I am going to describe selected areas of our knowledge of man and then I shall try to show how this knowledge can be applied to developing an idea of the ingredients of a viable society. I shall not be referring to Freud's contribution alone: some modern social philosophers give the impression that the gathering of psychological knowledge about man both began and ended with Freud—an approach that would have appalled Freud himself. The last three decades particularly have seen a tremendous spurt in our knowledge about man as a physiological and psychological entity, and Freud's contribution must be evaluated in its *historical* perspective.

Perhaps the most important knowledge we have about man for social purposes concerns the role of experience and learning in human development. As a member biologically of the human species, the nature and the quality of our humanity and our individuality are *not fixed* at birth. Contrary to most other, lower, forms of life, we do not fulfill our innate species potentials merely as a result of instinct or of maturational unfolding. We begin to learn to be human shortly after birth through our experiences with, and the conscious teachings of, older persons who have already been made human by *their* social experiences. When compared with other, lower animals, man exhibits three general classifications of behavior: unlearned behaviors we share with other mammals, learned behaviors we share with other higher mammals, and learned behaviors we share with no other form of life.

Species-determined patterns of physical growth do play a basically important psychological role during our earlier years in particularly three ways: they impose limits on *what* we can do, experience, learn *when;* they make the infant and young child totally dependent on other, more mature persons for his continuing existence; and especially during the first several months of life they impose, as a result of the mammalian principle in our species dual genetic inheritance, the necessity for certain kinds of direct, "gut-level" experiences with another responsive human being if later patterns of psychological development are to emerge and develop normally. If such "responsive relationship" experiences are provided during this early period, innate developmental forces are able to take firm hold and to provide a natural impetus for increasing maturity: psychologically healthy children require no "pushing" in order to grow up (and, certainly, for disturbed children, such pushing is a most ends-defeating incentive for growth). Genetically determined individual growth patterns also play a fundamental role: they impose limits on the nature and the quality of each person's experience and learning at every stage of his development, and as a result have much to do with his individual uniqueness.

But the consistent *direction* of individual behavioral development is from expression of behaviors which are determined by innate maturational forces relatively uninfluenced by experience, to the expression of behaviors which emerge only as a result of highly individualized experience and learning. Freud, whose therapeutic work with upper-middle-class adults led him to his almost exclusive interest in the role of early emotional frustrations in later psychological development, did not adequately appreciate the role of culturally determined learning both in these early experiences and in later development.

Underlying this developmental shift from maturation to learning as the dominating force in the development of human behavior are certain developmental changes in the human nervous system. The direction of these changes is from little or no direct involvement of the higher brain centers in the behavior of the newborn child, to these centers' participation in nearly all human functioning beyond the sheerly vegetative processes in the mature human organism. It is not a young child's "natural stubbornness" nor his possession of "original sin" which can be held accountable for his "refusal" to comprehend and to behave at the more mature level we may want him to behave. His innately determined stage of neural development and his directly related level of experience make it either difficult or impossible for him so to behave.

Paralleling this pattern of nervous-system development and of the shift in determining dominance from maturation to learning, is a trend from a very small repertoire of distinctly human and individually unique behavior-patterns in the infant, to a very large repertoire of distinctly human responses, organized in highly individual patterns, in the biologically and socially mature adult. Very early behavior, which occurs at a stage of development when the higher brain centers are barely functioning, and when the infant's learning has scarcely begun, is characterized by lack of physical and emotional coordination and control. His complete dependency upon others at this stage accounts for his development of some degree of what I have called "existence anxiety." When higher brain functioning and attendant learnings have begun but are not advanced, primacy of self-centered motives, lack of inner-directed emotional control, incapacity to delay voluntarily the satisfaction of basic bodily needs, incapacity to see oneself as one among many, are all developmentally characteristic of the older infant and young child. As such, they are thoroughly normal behaviors for this developmental period. To insist that a young child behave more maturely than his developmental status permits him to behave is to instill in him anxiety and hostility.

Such more mature and exclusively human behaviors as self-directed communication through spoken and written language, more complex abstract thinking, the more subtle emotions and appreciations, increasing self-discipline and self-direction, ability to conceive of and be controlled by goals and concepts beyond our immediate personal welfare, increasing organization and individuality in the ways we perceive, structure, and react to reality, are all mediated by neural circuits inclusive of the now-functioning "human principle" higher brain centers—*behaviors which develop as a result of our learning, chiefly of socially derived learning.* Presence in adulthood of behaviors typical of the early childhood period are, except during moments of extreme stress, not "normal" for most people because they are not imposed by developmental and intellectual limitations, as they are in the child. When they are so present, it is because the adult concerned was not allowed to behave as a child when he was a child, *or* just the opposite—because he was given no real opportunity to learn adult ways of behaving as he became developmentally able so to behave.

Because of its social and political implications, let me describe how one of the mature behaviors just mentioned develops through the individual's opportunities to have appropriate learning experiences as he grows up. The individual's ability to conceive of and be governed by social goals beyond his immediate welfare depends largely on his having developed a concept of "group" which embodies something at once personally meaningful *and* larger than self. He begins to develop such a concept as a child through his direct experiences with concrete instances—that is, through his direct participation in group life. Participation in the family group and in play and friendship groups are basic group experiences which we all ordinarily have, no matter what our social status. We acquire our primary emotional associations with group life through these childhood and adolescent experiences.

Whether or not we are able to cross over from this rudimentary and self-referent concept of group to the far broader political-social concepts of "community," "nation," "organized society," "world community," seems to depend on the presence of a bridge which is partly of our own and partly of our society's making: the nature of the experiences we have as we mature in such group-units representative of organized society as classroom and school, work group and work setting, community-centered association groups; *and* our own individual ability to project intellectually and emotionally beyond our direct experience.

The over-all developmental trend from dominance of maturational forces to dominance of learning in individual behavior has an innate basis directly related to the pattern of development and functioning of the human nervous system. As such, *this trend is biologically characteristic of the human species.*

Our humanity is a constantly emerging phenomenon, in both a social and an individual sense, in the light of this circumstance. History and anthropology document that specific societies throughout the course of their existence gather up and pass on to each succeeding generation—and to succeeding societies—the cumulative experience of that society and of the societies before it. In so doing, they increase constantly the available "cultural reservoir" of uniquely human expression and the products of that expression (50). Man, as Korzybski has put it, is the only "time-binding" form of life (34). (Question: has the reservoir of *inhuman* expression remained stationary, or is it too increasing in directly parallel manner?)[1]

Our humanity is constantly emergent in the individual in three senses. It tends to accumulate throughout our life span. We may approach, but we seem never quite to reach our individual upper limits for learning and expressing the higher human behaviors. These limits themselves seem to be receding for mankind in general as an increasing depth and range of human expression is gathered up and

---

[1] Since raising this question, I have come to believe that the range of inhuman *attitudes* has been stationary for millenia, although our *techniques* for implementing them have been getting more and more deadly.

passed on through the cultures of human societies. *Particularly creative people, who are able to make the jump from the already known
and experienced to the previously unknown and unexperienced, contribute to the enlargement of the common reservoir of human expression.*

Although some Congressional committees have ignored the existence
of this process of change and emergence in individual human beings
throughout their life span, this process has gone on and will continue
to go on in spite of the dictates of demagogues and of political expediency—and of Skinnerian learning theory. The biological and
psychological forces which underlie it are far more permanent and
powerful than any inquisitorial body—difficult to believe as this asser-
tion was during the McCarthy period and the still-extant McCarthy
era.

But a very important "but" has to be inserted here. At every stage
of individual development, the role of learning is complicated by particularly two considerations—individual differences in constitution and
environment, *and* the effects of strong and prolonged inner tension.

Wide variations in such a personality characteristic as social maturity exist at chronological maturity because there are wide individual
differences in the experiencing-learning process through which each
of us becomes at once human and unique. The interaction of individual constitutional and environmental factors contributes to individual differences in this learning process.

On the one hand, lack of opportunity to express and to practice
physical and psychological capacities as they emerge developmentally
has the effect of retarding learning and the growth to maturity process.
For example, environmental deprivation of responsive human contact during the first several months of life can, if extreme, permanently
handicap the individual's expression of his innate psychological potentialities. Such lack of opportunity is not always, however, due to
an impoverished human environment. Parental overprotection and
overindulgence can contribute to lack of appropriate stimulation and
so retard the child's expression of his naturally increasing capacities
for physical, emotional, intellectual independence, and for self-control
and self-direction. And, on the other hand, constitutional influences
can be so marked in some individuals' development that they are
unable to become mature social and psychological beings, no matter
how favorable their physical and social-emotional environments. I
am thinking here not only of instances involving mental retardation
but of those cases of childhood autism and schizophrenia which
apparently stem from organic deficiency.

It is the complexity of interaction between constitutional and environmental factors which accounts for the range and subtlety of individual differences, as well as for group similarities, in individual psychological functioning.

A physiological state of tension, whether it arises from a basic physical need such as hunger, or from an emotional reaction such as fear, causes changes in the chemical balance of the body, which in turn affects the functioning of the nervous system. If emotional stress is intense and prolonged, it tends to have a blocking or distorting effect on the individual's learning, and hence on his continuing balanced growth to intellectual and emotional maturity. (Milder, non-disorganizing tensions usually provide incentives *for* learning.) Experiences with others which induce such prolonged emotional reactions as severe frustration, conflict, anxiety, are a more typical source of tension in our middle-class society than is the long-standing deprivation of such basic physical needs as food and warmth.

Arousal of strong inner tensions typically affects the individual in one or both of two ways. Either it causes him to cling to his present level of learning and adjustment to reality, and to resist the acquisition of new learnings in the areas of behavior affected by the stress. Or it leads him to regress temporarily or permanently to less mature ways of behaving in these areas. Whether one or both of these reactions occurs, and how permanent each is, seems to be related partly to the intensity, duration and developmental timing of the arousal of stress, and partly to individual constitutional factors. For example, most children who have been consistently denied responsive attention and affection during their very early years when they naturally need them most tend to be arrested in their subsequent social development: it is difficult for them to go beyond the infantile stage of pre-occupation with and concern for themselves. Yet different children respond differently to what seem to be similar objective amounts of deprivation.

The retarding effects on individual psychological development of prolonged emotional stress also have an innate basis related to the integrated nature of the functioning of the human organism.

Still-another large body of research indicates that the nervous system requires a sensation- rich and varied external environment, not only to develop normally but to function normally at every successive stage of development. The drably monotonous urban and suburban physical environment most Americans now live in may well be a major factor in the almost-frantic hunt for sensory experience which has become one of the distinctive trade-marks of our time.

Man's growing knowledge of the development, organization and functioning of the human nervous system, particularly, has made the old philosophical dichotomy between "mental" and "physical" meaningless beyond its continued retention in either the academic or the popular self-and-world view. We now know that each of these former "incompatibles" represents the respective functional roles of the higher and the lower parts of the *same* coherent entity, the human nervous system. Reluctant medical recognition of the physiological principle of "organism" led to the coining of the term "psychosomatic"—a singularly unfortunate artificialism. This attempt to dispense with the ancient dichotomy by pasting its two aspects together has instead tended to encourage the retention of old thought-habits—rather than to promote fresh, more adequate ways of conceptualizing individual functioning, which an entirely different term, such as "organismic," might have done.

Since the major source for what we learn, including what we react to emotionally, is the human environment into which we are born, *the core responsibility for the younger generation's progress towards humanity, individuality, and inner integration rests squarely on the shoulders of the older generations,* who represent and reflect the society into which the new generation is born. Whether we are aware of it or not, we teach our version of human-ness and our social values and practices to younger persons through our relations with them, *not through lip-service, word-magic, admonitions*—whether these relations involve direct personal interaction, or are indirect, as in the case of adult-controlled mass media. At the same time we are so teaching, we are providing them with the social experiences from which their own unique personalities are derived (42).

Contrary to popular belief, the survival and the perfectability of the human species do not depend primarily on biological laws of natural selection operating on a simple individual basis. *The circumstance that the pattern of development of the human nervous system makes individual experience subsequent to birth of major importance in human development, complicates matters for the human species.*[2] This circumstance means that the advancement of the human species, including the wide possibility of inner psychological health among structurally normal human beings, has at our evolutionary level come

---

[2] Here is why that popular pastime of the semi-knowledgeable, to apply lower-mammalian data on the expression of a complex instinct such as sex or "territoriality" directly to man, must be considered just that—a pastime. Here is why, also, genetics investigators who speak of being on the verge of controlling the genetic make-up of man and thus, by implication, of man's behavior, are revealing the limitations—and grave dangers—of scientific over-specialization.

to depend upon social factors. To put it plainly, *our species' advancement depends primarily upon our capacity to develop, and constantly to redevelop as environmental changes require it, humanity-promoting forms of child-rearing and social living.*

It is regrettable that a brilliant young European of the caliber of Colin Wilson failed, as do many brilliant young American writers as well, to recognize the implications for individual development of this basic social-psychological principle (77). Individual self-hood is not merely impossible apart from society; there is an intimate relationship between the inner life of the apparently autonomous adult and the society in which he has grown up. Here, again, there is a circular relationship: *in order to improve himself, the individual must improve society; in order to improve society, the individual must improve himself.* This is not to deny the possibility that a few unusual adults are in their maturity able to achieve inner functional integrity, apparently in spite of the functioning of their society. But even the particular personal "salvation" such individuals attain bears the ineradicable marks of their background of socially derived experience.

The respective roles of learning and of emotional stress in individual development make it possible to develop a yardstick for evaluating a simple society or a sub-culture within a complex society. We can arrive at the "humanity quotient" of a particular culture or sub-culture by asking these two related questions: To what degree do the *actual* values and practices of the various aspects of this society promote the growing individual's emerging humanity and inner integration? To what degree do they help him outgrow his earlier, developmentally imposed immaturities, no matter what his level of ability and perceptiveness may be? [3]

I submit that when the dominant working values of a society are that:

it is all right to offer for sale, and keep on selling more and more of, *anything* that people of any age level can be induced *by any means* to buy:

individual and group immediate self-interest comes first;

immediate expediency and self-interest are adequate principles on which to base major economic, political and personal decisions,

then that society does not merely have a low humanity quotient—it has already traveled far along the road back to barbarism.

[3] This line of reasoning—concerning the possibility of developing a *biologically anchored* picture of an optimum social environment for human beings—has been developed further in another, more technical, publication (48).

Chapter Fifteen

Elements of a Viable Society

Basic social realities can be considered to be imposed by the nature of the process through which each individual becomes at once human and himself, and by the outcome of this learning process—the wide individual differences in actual and potential self-discipline and social maturity which inevitably exist among the citizenry of a heterogenous society. It is my belief that the degree to which these realities come to be ignored by a society's values, forms, and practices, is the degree to which that society has progressed towards its own disintegration. Conversely, in order for a society to remain viable, it must increasingly take these realities into account in its forms and practices. Let me review a number of these realities as I see them—again, not for prescriptive, but for illustrative purposes.

Because of the family's indispensable biological and psychological roles, a society must have *some* kind of stable family system. A large part of the family's social function of passing on the group culture to each new generation may be delegated to other agencies of society, as we are discovering today. But the long period of physical and emotional dependency characteristic of the human species means that the family's basic biological function of sustaining the helpless infant and child physically and psychologically can be dispensed with only at the price of destruction of the whole social group.

Second, the society's technology, and industrial and business practices must operate in such a way as to permit—better, to assist—the family to perform its indispensable functions. This supportive relationship can be taken for granted in simple societies where family life, economic practices and technology are all closely inter-connected. It is not sufficiently appreciated by us today that although the ability to beget and conceive children are primarily biological, species phenomena, *appropriate maternal and paternal behavior are, in the human being, almost entirely dependent upon socially-provided learning and support.* Complex, industry-centered societies can overlook this most basic "fact of life" only at their own great peril.

The personal development of the girls and women of any society has its greatest social relevance within this context. The key personal dilemma of emancipated womanhood today must at the same time be seen as a core problem for all humanity because of the basic psychological role of the mother for every member of the next generation. The individual woman must learn to employ her development as a growing, autonomous individual as a means of complementing and enriching her maternal role; she must also learn to employ her maternal role as a means of enriching her development as a growing autonomous individual—rather than to be forced, as she is at present, to approach these two necessary aspects of her being as incompatibles because of current social values and practices. It is not merely coincidental that as socially-provided learning of and support for the exercise of mature, warmly maternal and paternal behavior has decreased in our society, the number of psychiatrists and other welfare and guidance personnel have been steadily increasing.[1]

Although the need for self-fulfillment is a diffuse one, it seems to be characteristic of maturing human beings everywhere, and is almost surely a function of our unique higher species capacities. The receiving of some kind of social recognition seems to be as universal a way of satisfying this need as is the need itself. A society can provide means of social recognition which are good or bad in terms of their individual and social effects. The avenues for social recognition which have the best psychological and social effects are those which recognize and reward the individual either for his exemplary exercise of roles and behaviors which make a positive contribution to his society, or for his own creative products. The avenues for social recognition which sooner or later seem to have negative psychological and social effects are those which depend upon the individual's acquisition of external-to-himself status symbols, symbols which can be achieved only through the accident of birth or by direct and intense competition with other contenders.

Our society makes use of both these kinds of social recognition, but it makes far more dominant use of the second type, status symbols achieved through direct competition or through birth. The "external symbols" means to social recognition is exacting far too great a psycho-

---

[1] The influence of Freud's Victorian-era background on certain aspects of his theoretical system is a source of amusement to me in this connection. While leaving a legacy of his own unresolved oedipal anxieties and hostilities in his concept of "penis-envy" among women, he overlooked that psychotherapeutic psychiatry represents a culturally sanctioned expression of male "motherhood-envy."

logical penalty, both from those who succeed in achieving the requisite symbols and from those who are unable to achieve them. The widespread and continuing use of this means denies the possibility of feelings of self-fulfillment to great numbers in our population. Such denial ignores basic human psychological realities.

Even a cursory study of the world's cultures impresses one with the tremendous scope and flexibility of the behaviors which *homo sapiens* is capable of expressing, including the amount of psychological stress to which he can accommodate. But *history tells us time and time again that there are limits to the amount and duration of the stress which human beings can tolerate without some kind of extreme reaction on both an individual and a mass basis.* Although the amount of stress which can be borne without psychological or physical breakdown is a highly individual matter, it is also acknowledged that everyone has his particular "breaking point"—a circumstance on which those skilled in "brainwashing" have apparently skilfully capitalized.

If the majority in a society are to be able to progress toward the goal of becoming individual *human* beings with some consistency and without personally disorganizing amounts of emotional tension, the lifelong process involved would seem to have to contain in sufficient measure the positive psychological ingredients enumerated in Chapters 4 and 12. It seems possible for a society to develop a pattern of daily living and feeling so inappropriate for human beings that the emotional stress promoted by it results in breakdown among too many in that society for it to continue functioning in a self-responsible manner. Not only do I consider this possibility to be a third "basic reality," I believe our own values have already contributed to our society's currently rapid development of economic and technological and social practices which are imposing just such an inappropriate living pattern on us. Nor will this impasse be eventually resolved more or less automatically through the operation of the biological mechanism of "survival of the fittest." This order of resolution, so often propounded of late by even highly educated persons, represents a confession of individual passivity, powerlessness, irresponsibility, rather than a realistic solution: as mentioned earlier (page 154), this evolutionary mechanism does *not* apply on a simple, individual, level within the human species.

We must come as a society to emphasize means of social recognition —and consequent feelings of self-worth—which are at least *supplementary* to those we have today, and which fulfill these basic criteria:

they can be learned and expressed by the great majority of the population;

they involve functions which are biologically and socially positive and adaptive;

intrinsic satisfactions are gained from their practice.

Particularly two types of activities fulfill all three of these criteria:

the "responsible member-of-the-community" function—recognition of, and preparation and opportunities for, the lifelong exercise of this function should be available to every social level and every age period beyond infancy;

the "next-generation nurturing and rearing" function—recognition of, and preparation and opportunities for, the lifelong exercise of this responsibility should be accorded everyone beyond the preadolescent developmental period by his immediate community.

I believe we must come to consider these society-centered functions to be *inseparable from our biological status as human beings,* and therefore as prior, or at least equal, in inner importance, to our self-centered activities.

Further, if my hypothesis that cosmic anxiety is an unavoidable aspect of adult human existence is correct, the mass media of a complex society share with its educational institutions an unavoidable obligation. It becomes one of their basic social responsibilities to help adolescents and adults both understand the nature and sources of human anxiety, and channel their cosmic anxieties into personally and socially constructive avenues of expression.

Similarly, the middle class needs as a sub-culture to develop a wider variety of substitutive yet direct (rather than vicarious) outlets for expressing strong inner tensions: although we can hope to minimize the incidence of such tensions, we cannot—and should not—hope to eliminate them altogether. Anger, guilt, sexual need, fear, hostility which cannot be directly expressed at the time of arousal should not be consistently repressed because a sub-culture is lacking in socially-accepted substitute channels of expression. There is no simple answer to this problem, but I would like to suggest that we consider particularly the deliberate use of creative, self-expressive dance for such a purpose, from early childhood on throughout the life span.

Complex societies seem to me to have a far greater potential for self-regulation and survival than do simple societies. If, for any one of a number of internal or external reasons, the various component aspects of a complex society become so divergent that its basic "organic equilibrium" is badly disturbed (the present situation in our own society), it is more capable than a simple society of developing new, more viable social, political, economic, legal, educational, and techno- logical forms and practices, because of the "self-regulating" potential that it possesses. This potential is made up of the wide variety of creative persons in that society—creative in leadership and in ideas in every area of human expression: political, scholarly, humanitarian, religious, esthetic, human relations, pure scientific; as well as tech- nological, economic and applied-scientific. When a complex society gives encouragement ranging from minimal, to active discouragement, to the exercise of creativity in the former fields, while at the same time giving unrestricted opportunity and encouragement to technological, business and applied science creativity, that society is interfering with its own capacities for self-regulation. It is disturbing seriously the very "mechanism" which is capable of keeping not only itself, but nowadays all human society, functioning as a continuing entity. Here is a fourth "basic reality."

We have come to accept that such physical requirements of man as food, water, shelter, sanitation, must be available to some basic degree if a minimal level of physical health is to be achieved and maintained among a society's population. It is not yet generally recognized that both physical and psychological health require a basic living-working routine which is sufficiently under the individual's own control to allow him to adjust it to his particular cycles of physio- logical strength and weakness. I see this requirement as a fifth basic reality which many middle-class men are ignoring or are being obliged to ignore, with serious physical and psychological cost to themselves.

I prefer to put the sixth basic reality on my list in the form of a question. It has been implied in the previous chapter that physical and intellectual effort and opportunities for practice provide stimula- tion which is essential for the growing child's rounded development, as well as for the maintenance of mental alertness and physical tone throughout adulthood and old age. Can we carry the present tech- nological trend towards eliminating any and all physical and mental effort in the individual's daily round of living so far as to promote human deterioration?

I believe, as a seventh "basic reality," that there are psycho- logical limits to the degree to which the social functions and responsibilities of the human individual can be delegated to specialists or to gadgets and machines. When we surrender the active exercise of certain functions at particular stages of our development, we are giving up the very building materials from which our individual personality is structured. I have already mentioned the exercise of the "universal parent" role, the "creative citizen" role, and the "moral responsibility" role as providing, among other social functions, such psychologically indispensable experiences.

Let me use the current fragmentation and specialization of the universal parent role as an example here. We may have no question that nursery-school teachers, social workers, group workers, guidance counselors, marriage advisers, audio-visual teaching aids, educational T.V., do a much more competent job of those services which, in a less complex age, every socially mature and responsible adult performed for younger relatives and friends as these roles were required of them. Nutritionists recommend vitamin pills as a supplement to, *not as a substitute for,* a basically adequate daily diet. So I have no question as to the value of such specialized professions as I have enumerated if they are seen as having a supplementary rather than a substitutive function in our complex society.

We can no more afford to give up, personality-development-wise, our active exercise of the universal-parent responsibility than we can afford to give up the exercise of such other basic human relations as friend, husband or wife, son or daughter, father or mother, productive worker, leader, follower, and still expect to fulfill our particular potential for humanity and for individuality. And we cannot give up the exercise of our responsibility for passing on *ourselves* to those younger than us and still expect *them* to become human beings. It is through their interaction beyond the early years with (preferably) a wide variety of other human beings that children develop a rich and complex personality. So much daily human interaction centers around economic transactions and mutual services of various kinds, that the delegation of these transactions and services to machines eliminates a very important source of social learning for the child. The images on the T.V. screen, a major source of stimulation for children today, can never compensate psychologically for this loss of *responsive* social *inter*action (48).

Let me carry this general point one step further by suggesting the following interrelated social conditions as most conducive to the development of as complex *and* harmonious a personality organization as each individual member of a particular society is genetically capable (49).

| Presence in the society of a wide variety of possible experiences— of interpersonal relations, social roles, knowledges and skills— as stimulation for maximal development of the higher brain centers (which includes development of a wide range of emotional sensitivity). | ALONG WITH: | A social value system which lays stress on the fullest development of all socially positive human potentialities; *plus* institutions (including our industrial organization) and personal and social practices *which operate in accordance with these values with a high degree of consistency.* | WHICH SHOULD INCLUDE: | Family values and practices in rearing children which will promote individual psychological ability to profit from the wide range of experiences available in the society. |

Family and general social practices should result in frequent opportunities for all in the population to experience the wide range of roles, feelings, ideas, skills, values, appreciations, as they are developmentally ready for them.

It is worth evaluating our current urban trend towards segregation into one-class, age-restricted housing projects and suburbs in the light of this formulation. Such segregation is at least as contrary to democratic ideals and inimical to the provision of a broad learning environment for our children as is segregation along ethnic and "racial" lines —perhaps even more so, since we have come to recognize, at the verbal level, at least, the social dangers in the latter type of segregation. How can we expect our overprotected middle-class children to gain some idea of the complexity of values and behaviors in our society if they are not exposed to values and behaviors other than those of their own class and generation? How can we expect lower-class children to learn the more controlled and socially responsible behavior of the middle class, if they do not have opportunities for direct observation of such behavior? How can we expect the elderly to retain feelings of social and personal worth when we exclude them from the main activities of their society?

Study of the functioning of small groups is indicating that there is an optimum size range for human association groups. Face to face interaction is the key characteristic of the association group which functions optimally in terms of both the psychological effects on the participants and the quality of group outcomes. This generalization seems to hold whether a group's explicit function is production or planning or learning or psychotherapy or friendship-recreation. Further, when an association group is set up so that its members participate both in the setting (and any subsequent resetting) of group goals and in the activity directed towards realizing these common goals, personal involvement of group members in group purposes develops. Such personal involvement has been found to promote the participating individual's identification with group interests and his readiness to acquire attitudes, behaviors, knowledges which serve to further the group interest (37). I call this latter effect the "principle of participation."

These findings raise the possibility of an eighth basic reality—that such representative units of organized society as classroom and school settings, work groups and production settings, neighborhood and community, can become so large that they do not provide the individual with the bridge of direct and emotionally positive experience through which he can cross over from his limited childhood concept of group to a socially and politically mature group concept; that they contribute instead to the feelings of apathy and powerlessness which are becoming increasingly prevalent in American society. The individual is further handicapped in his transition to a more mature concept if the values and practices of each of the society-representative groups in which he participates are in mutual conflict—a typical situation in our disorganized society; or if they are widely divergent from his previous life experiences, as in the case of the lower-class child in the middle-class school. This particular area of lack of appropriate learning experiences seems to me to have important implications for especially our continuing practice of self-government.

The circumstance of wide individual differences in social maturity among our citizens imposes another basic reality which our society can no longer afford to ignore. To continue to function, totalitarian governments require basic attitudes of fear towards law and government on the part of their people. Our disapproval of this state of affairs does not mean that we can dispense with restriction and control. Rather, in a self-governing society, we must depend upon the individual citizen's *self-imposition* of control and responsibility— the ideal situation. But what about the immature, the self-seeking, the vicious, who typically interpret their inalienable right to liberty as their inalienable right to license and irresponsibility? I agree that to impose legal penalties on irresponsible behavior is to begin a chain reaction which can too easily lead to everyone's loss of civil liberties, and of self-government itself, as civil liberties groups rightly point out.

I submit that there is another way out of this dilemma, but one which requires a rather marked digression on our parts from one aspect of our national tradition. In that tradition, we are as a nation still rebelling against the rule of a tyrant-king—a rule our fore-fathers dispensed with nearly two centuries ago! It is this tradition which sems to me to have contributed to our insufficient appreciation that:

> restriction, control, order are prerequisite to the functioning of any society, simple or complex;
>
> restriction, control, order are necessary for any degree of individual freedom *and to any dependable degree of inner freedom within each individual in that society;*
>
> if we reject externally imposed means of social control such as an absolute monarchy or a dictatorship or a behavior-foreordained caste system, we must *willingly* accept self-imposed and self-directed methods of social control.

The continuing functioning of a society based on the principle of self-government requires the individual citizen to view law and government, and agents of law and government, with basic attitudes of respect, no matter what his station and level of social maturity. Conversely, agents of organized society have the obligation of carrying out their responsibilities in ways that merit respect.

It is essential for our continuing existence as a self-governing, self-controlling society that we develop a voluntary doctrine of responsible leadership and responsible followership—and that we "break through" to its active application: my ninth "basic reality." We are going to have to learn to relate to each level of government much as a responsible employer relates to a responsible employee— to set for each level (local, state, national) whatever tasks we collectively believe will contribute in some meaningful way to our realization of our basic goal of becoming increasingly more human beings, and then *allow each government body whatever scope and freedom it needs to accomplish its respective tasks.* We are going to have to recognize the necessity for a high-caliber career civil service not subject to political pressure, at every governmental level. We are going to have to become mature enough to select and vote for a far greater proportion of political representatives whose level of personal integrity, intelligence and social maturity is *higher,* rather than equal to or less, than our own. And if big government develops those bureaucratic tendencies towards insensitivity to individual rights and overbearing exercise of power that were formerly characteristic only of big business, the answer is not to resist being governed, but first, to improve archaic mechanisms of representation and of governing, and second, to develop avenues of citizen participation supplementary to those we have today.

Government must integrate and control the diversified activities of the social "organism"; profiting from its own past history and that of other governments, it plans wisely for the present and for the immediate and distant future; it carries out the plans so made efficiently and in ways that are not harmful either to its own society or to other societies; it revises its plans and procedures as changed circumstances warrant such change. The social results of our not giving the executive aspects of government freedom to act is analogous to the effects on the individual of the removal of major sections of his higher brain centers: his basic bodily functions continue, but his own experience no longer has any coherent meaning to him and his behavior beyond the physiological is lacking in even elementary levels of coordination and effectiveness.

Perhaps no other major democracy's citizens are as reluctant as are we Americans to grant a responsible social function to our government and to accept and practice voluntarily a doctrine of responsible leadership and followership. Our semianarchy has "worked" until recently primarily because the very multiplicity of our conflicting interest groups has had the effect of a mutual "canceling out." But the circumstance that this behind-the-scenes arrangement has worked fairly well up to the recent past does not guarantee that it will continue to do so: we are now living in an era of increasing concentration of "interest" into fewer and larger units; *we no longer live in a power-diversified, agrarian and small-business society.*

Chapter Sixteen

Green Shoots are Showing

IT WOULD BE neither fair to the American middle class, nor accurate, to leave an impression that the current picture is uniformly negative, that no trends of a more adaptive nature exist. I want to mention a number of currently developing trends which seem to me to hold positive promise for the future: they are going in the direction I believe we must go if we hope to continue to fulfill our emergent potentialities for human behavior and self-realization and if we hope to survive as a self-governing society. It is the existence of these trends which led me to use the suppositional "if" in my earlier prediction of possible future negative developments. My list is by no means exhaustive; many readers will be able to add to it.

There is a growing tendency in the middle class for adults with common needs, interests, problems, to meet in local, regional and national conference groups—not for purposes of chest-beating, self-congratulatory awards and political pressure, but for serious and creative face-to-face consideration of some common problem. Sponsoring organizations are typically universities, churches and other religious bodies, professional organizations, college student groups, labor unions, leadership-training institutes. A growing trend on the part of these conference groups is to make on-the-spot use, *on a consultative rather than a directive basis,* of experts with special knowledges related to the content of the problem being studied. This practice has by now become firmly established in American organizational and governmental life.

Many of these citizen groups have also begun to make use of those professionals whose special knowledges and skills are in the human relations and communication aspects of the problem under study and of the conduct of the conference itself. Particularly in this latter development, these self-motivated groups are well ahead of their own political leaders and representatives. One of the major consequences of this kind of cooperative relationship between citizens and human relations specialists has been the increasing, and increasingly effective, application in the organization and conduct of such conferences of the "principle of participation," referred to in the previous chapter. Another concrete example of this type of citizen-specialist mutual aid is the "community self-survey." It involves applied social-scientist guidance of a survey-research procedure, which is planned and carried out by interested citizens of a particular community. This special application of the principle of participation has been found to promote fundamental changes in social attitudes and practices among those who were active in it (63).

These trends are socially fruitful in my eyes not so much because the relevant and objective knowledges and know-how provided by the applied behavioral scientist are a real and immediate advantage to such problem-solving and social-application attempts. It is the social-political implications for the future of this kind of cooperative, mutual aid relationship that are more significant than are the immediate outcomes of this association. The cooperating behavioral or social scientist is frequently overly technique- or gadget-minded in his approach to human relations and behavior situations, or is committed to some *a priori* theoretical orientation. This kind of participant citizen-professional liaison provides him with invaluable opportunities for the growth of personal, conceptual, and working skills. For their part, lay citizens are able to meet the "experts" face to face and discover *through their own experience* the real advantages of a cooperative relationship of this kind.

These first hesitating and sometimes mutually traumatic citizen-scientist working-planning associations are setting what in the not too distant future may be considered a social-political precedent of major importance—a precedent of potentially much greater importance in the world of our children and our children's children than the development of a moon rocket. A few of the organized deliberative approaches of this genre that have emerged since the foregoing paragraphs were written warrant description.

The "teach-in" derives its name from the circumstance that the first one, a student-faculty organized examination of the American involvement in VietNam at the University of Michigan, was convened after regular class hours and, with qualified faculty-members speaking in relays, lasted the entire night. It has since been adapted for use on other controversial issues and has spread to university campuses across the globe. Its usual format consists of an initial formal presentation by a panel of scholars and/or practitioners who represent differing approaches to the interpretation and resolution of the problem under analysis. Thereafter, members of the audience enter into informal, spirited and, often, prolonged interchanges with panel members.

DEADLINE, my second example of recent concerned-citizen activity, departs from the premise that new initiatives and methods for keeping the peace are of top priority. Its rationale and organizational procedures are given in these excerpts from a folder titled "DEAD-LINE: A Call For Convergence on the Future of Man on the Planet," prepared by Mrs. Eleanor Garst: [1]

> "Global unrest erupts over resource-distribution, human rights and liberties. The time has never been more urgent for people of goodwill and global outlook to come together to determine what can be done to make our planet fit for human life. . .
>
> We cannot look only to governments; too often they are trapped in archaic machinery and rigid traditions. Nor can we look to experts in any one field or leaders of any single group. Rather, we must speak out as individuals whose mutual interest in human survival transcends every other consideration. Therefore, let us convene individuals of every persuasion, speaking not for governments, organizations or groups but fo themselves—and for man. . .
>
> First there will be a series of local and regional conferences on an agenda now in preparation; your suggestions are welcomed. Then there will be a national and an international conference—*not a series of talk-fests but action-planning meetings.* . ."

Robert Theobald, departing from concern over the impact of advanced technology on society and on the individual, is in active process of developing and organizing two citizen self-education-towards-informed-action techniques. The first one is a national network of "depth-education" groups—DEGs. To quote from material describing their rationale:

> "It is now generally agreed that failure to change the present socio-economic system to meet pressures arising from new technologies and attitudes will lead to profoundly anti-human developments. Many initiatives have been started which aim to invent a future in which the true humanity of man can be achieved. Those involved in these initiatives appear to agree that our present systems and styles of debate, discussion and education are not well suited to achieving fundamental rethinking of issues.
>
> Those supporting this new approach—often called dialogue—believe it has passed beyond theory and is in the process of emerging. *It is based*

---

[1] From whom further information concerning DEADLINE is obtainable; her address: c/o Aberman, 80 LaSalle St., New York City 100-27.

on a study of problems rather than disciplines, on a recognition that authoritarian relationships cannot exist in real education, and that faculty, students and citizens must cooperate in the creation of new knowledge. . .

It is proposed that all those developing dialogue across the country should join together to encourage the formation of Depth Education Groups to examine problem-areas of particular interest to those involved in each group."

The initial task of each DEG is to undertake to prepare a "dialogue-focuser," a problem-centered document which is a compilation of a wide range of materials bearing on the problem: the second of Theobald's techniques. Such a dialogue-focuser explicitly "recognizes the reality of disagreement and provides an opportunity to state this disagreement with a maximum of clarity." [2]

Another positive social development seems to me to be our constantly increasing attempts to apply, on a *preventive* basis, our growing knowledge of the nature of individual human development and behavior throughout the life-span in the home, in the school, in industry, in recreational agencies, in the church—spotty, inconsistent, and misused as many of these application attempts undoubtedly are. An outstanding example of such a preventive attempt is the Headstart program; some civic groups are urging that this program be extended to all American pre-schoolers. Another aspect of this trend is the social-work profession's development of a preventive philosophy, and its application in two relatively new social-work specialties of recreational group-work (as expressed particularly in the community-center movement), and of community organization. The current self-help approach in the slums is an offshoot of this professional development; one cannot help but wonder why this approach is being applied only in the slums: persons trained in community organization are very much needed in *all* urban and suburban neighborhoods, as well as in small cities, towns and rural areas.

Some colleges have incorporated volunteer service in a community center or settlement house as part of the requirements for graduation in such fields as sociology and education. This practice suggests a time when junior and senior high school students will routinely do some part-time community service which is genuinely needed and which is suited to their level of maturity—on no other basis than their implicit duty as residents of their community. VISTA is a major step in this direction.

Related to the group problem-solving trend is the growing num-

---

[2] Further information on DEGs and dialogue-focusers may be obtained from: Karen Jones, Room 758, 475 Riverside Drive, New York City, 100-27.

ber of member -initiated and -conducted adult study-discussion groups. These groups are arising as adults begin to appreciate that their stage of maturity and learning readiness during their earlier, formal schooling period did not allow them to formulate many questions of genuine personal meaning, particularly questions of value. Nor were their motivations and skills for seeking personally meaningful answers adequately developed at a younger age. Parent-education groups, world politics discussion groups, summer music, art and dance camps and seminars, neighborhood political study-discussion groups, older-adults forums and academic study activities, short-term special-problem institutes—all testify that some of our most important areas of personal growth, and an emerging awareness of the need for such growth, occur well beyond the period our society has arbitrarily designated as our "educative years." In too many cases, they were vocational training years, even though we may have been awarded the traditional Bachelor of Arts degree. If this adult-education trend continues, we may yet dig up and make real social use of the scholarly treasure presently submerged in many of our college faculties!

The pressures of American urban living may be losing us our childhood and adolescence, but a longer life span, medical advances, shorter work hours and earlier retirement are winning us a whole new life period in which we can continue to grow mentally, esthetically, personally—the period of later maturity. I am looking forward to the early formation of small-in-size higher education institutions in every part of our country, with curricula and teaching methods especially planned to meet the needs of an "over 40" student body—Ford Foundation, please note. I believe that the newer educational methods and emphases will prove to be far more successful with such intrinsically motivated students than with inwardly unready teen-agers.

Increasing travel abroad is a current middle-class trend in which the motives of those participating seem to me to be far more significant than is the social value of the trend in itself. If travel abroad is undertaken as yet another item of conspicuous consumption, as the "smart" or the "right" thing to do, and if the traveler returns with no greater addition to his life than: confirmation of his most cherished prejudices about the inferior sanitation and the lack of good old American go-getiveness in the foreign lands visited, or a new and chic wardrobe, or a hangover and a fresh crop of bawdy stories; or (at the opposite extreme) an unselective rejection of everything at home merely because it is American and as such prosaic and "uncultured"—then the social value of this activity is negative, in that such a traveler confirms widespread foreign prejudices about "thoughtless" and "shallow" Americans. Unfortunately, most conducted tours tend to ensure such sterile outcomes: very few such tours are organized to give Americans anything but a most superficial and biased picture of life in the countries visited.

But if the traveler is able to approach and to use the experience as an opportunity for informal self-education, for development of greater perspective on his own values and of those of his culture, then travel abroad is a definitely positive social trend.

Riesman has described some members of the American upper-middle-class as modern pioneers and as such, committed to endure the many mental and emotional hazards of the pioneer (59): among a people almost entirely lacking in a creative leisure-time tradition, they are seeking out, adopting, adapting and testing such after-work activities as community theater and ballet, music groups, art shows, new tastes in interior design, clothing, food, vacations. The decline of a strong family tradition and the prevalence of the other-directed character-type in the middle class has led to another, related development: the emergence of the new professional groups of taste setters, interpreters, and advisers.

Again, it is the motives of those who undertake such activities and such occupations which would indicate whether these trends have negative or positive social implications for the future. If activities traditionally associated with the world's leisure classes are undertaken primarily as a means of placing as much social distance as possible between oneself or one's group and other people and social groups— as yet another item of conspicuous consumption—this trend has the effect in a competitive society of promoting fad-seeking and consequent bastardization of standards in the creative arts and artist.[3] Similarly, professional taste-setters and interpreters tend to provide additional impetus towards a uniform mass culture and an undiscriminating, unattuned-to-self "herd" conformity, if they are motivated by no higher end than "plugging" a sponsor's product or service or their own exhibitionistic needs.

Fortunately, the tendency of these upper-middle-class pioneers to

---

[3] Precisely this process, predicted in 1955, has been occurring since—"in spades." For example: the first "pop" art (*and* underground film) efforts were no more than time-filling "doodling" by bored young art-students and were placed on exhibit as a prank. No one was more surprised than their creators—nor quicker to jump on the money-making bandwagon—when these "put-ons" were bought at a fine price by those members of the new smart-set whose avocation is to maintain their reputation for being avant-garde, no matter how.

contribute to the current trend to uniformity holds within its own self-corrective. These people are beginning to realize that no matter what *external* symbols of social distance and status they may seek out and adopt, mass production, the mass media, and professional taste interpreters will shortly make it available to great numbers of people. The time-lapse between the initial American taste-setter's adoption of a "casual jacket" worn by upper-class European sportsmen and its appearance on a teen-ager on a street corner in Flatbush has already narrowed to about a year. Under such circumstances, the entire psychological rationale behind acquisition of external status symbols is subverted. In spite of himself, the upper-middle-class pioneer is discovering that he has only one last frontier of individual difference and social distance left to him—not escape to outer space, but the discovery, exploration and development of his unique inner self. This frontier has the great advantage, furthermore, of being a constantly receding one.

This realization on the part of our more perceptive taste and value leaders will be assisted by a related self-corrective development among the coming generation of young adults. As the general upgrading of income and physical living standards permits more and more of the younger generation to attain while still relatively young the consumer status their parents and our advertisers taught them to want, many will discover "in time" how very limited and inwardly unsatisfying are the life goals they had set for themselves.

I have so far selected for attention primarily negative aspects of our situation as it applies to today's and tomorrow's young people. But the reaction of today's more sensitive, gifted and emotionally hardy teen-agers and young adults against the obsessive materialism and inner denial of the times in which they are growing up cannot be overlooked as a major hope for the future. I believe these young people, from whom our future leaders will be drawn, will be more able to place the material aspects of life in balanced perspective than our past and current leaders in ideas and political life have been able to do— partly because their material environment during their formative years has been a relatively secure one.[4]

But something more complex than a background of material security is influencing the thinking and actions of such young people. I shall not readily forget one twenty-one-year-old's reference in the presence

---

[4] In light of subsequent events, the reader should know that this and the following four paragraphs remain just as they were in the original edition.

of his peers to the "bitch goddess success"—not with bitterness nor with envy, but as a result of evident attempts to develop a dependable set of personal values.

I do not believe that all of the current tendency on our college campuses towards conservatism, conformity, political inertia, renewed interest in religious traditions, is negative in implication, as many analysts are taking it to be. Concealed within this generalized trend is a sub-development not easily discernible by the casual observer. I believe that the more thoughtful and sensitive of our student population are engaged in an active process of re-examination of the values their parents, their culture and they themselves have taken for granted for so long. A continuing shift in the weight of college registration to the social and behavioral sciences and the humanities seems to me to constitute at least one external evidence of this development. Whether or not "Sputnik" and the enormous amounts of public and private funds being poured into the development of more and more effective means of destruction will manage to reverse this trend should show up shortly.

For the more shallow young person, the conscious or unconscious continuance of his earlier adolescent pattern of submerging himself safely in a group constitutes his major means for keeping his anxieties from getting completely out of hand. But for the student with greater personal depth, a surface conformity frequently serves as self-protective coloration, giving him the inner leeway he needs in order to work intensively on some very important personal questions. Such young people are studying man's past and man as a behaving being not for the purposes of escape from the present nor from themselves, but for the core reasons examination of history, comparative religion, ethics, philosophy, social anthropology, human behavior and development can play an indispensable role in every individual's growth towards humanity. Such examination can provide us with the conceptual tools and standards of judgment we must have in order for us to be able to look at the present with some degree of detachment, objectivity, and understanding. And it can provide us with an intellectually essential emotional "breather" from the smothering, omnipresent, often oppressively anxious "here and now."

Individuals who are able to see and to use their formal and informal studies in this way (and one of the characteristics of a good teacher is that he helps the learner of every age so to see and use them) are more likely than those who are not so able, to "return" to the physical and social present with the inner strength and understanding which permit them to act back on it intelligently and constructively. Those young people who are going through this inside-out process of retreat-re-examination-return today are going to make themselves felt tomorrow. I see them as a very important part of the group of emotionally and intellectually uncommitted "independents" to whom this book is specifically—and hopefully—addressed.

A new generation of public-spirited young people is beginning to assume participation in community and national affairs. Whether or not they will have a positive impact on the public welfare will largely depend on their capacity to update their picture of current social realities and their political goals. Their ability to go beyond the traditional American political concern over the power of the state to at least equivalent concern over the power of socially non-responsible big-business-getting-bigger will be one of the critical factors behind their social-contribution potential. The other will be their psychological emancipation from the touchstone fallacy—and with that emancipation, their refusal to continue to play the traditional American self-interested-group political game of applying pressure for an ever-bigger slice of the consumer-goods "pie" without *concomitant concern for the effect of that unilateral increase on the over-all quality of American life.*

Our most creatively gifted young people are traditionally drawn to New York City's concentration of outlets for creative expression. Madison Avenue's advertising industry and connected television opportunities have been added to Broadway's theaters as centers of attraction for this group. Not all these young people are having their creativity and personal integrity damaged beyond repair by their first-hand contact with the dominant philosophy of these two glittering streets— the credo which maintains not merely that the paying customer/ consumer is always right, but that the least esthetically and socially mature and sensitive consumer is *most* right because there are more of them. Rather, the direct experience of some of these gifted people with this credo is serving to immunize them thoroughly against it. One evidence of their reaction is the "off-Broadway movement," a trend towards experimental, serious theater which has had sufficient vitality to survive commercial success and to become "off-off-Broadway" (East Village) theater.

Three continuing factors are leading many middle-class women to react increasingly adaptively to their changed world. Their lesser degree of self-alienation as a group, as compared with their men; their own direct contacts with the world of work in which their husbands are functioning; and their awareness of their spouses' inner difficulties as they attempt to cope with the extreme competitive and status pressures on them, are combining in these perceptive and sensitive women in such a way that they are

freeing themselves of women's traditional emotional and intellectual incubus of belief in the superiority of the masculine social role;

becoming very much aware that something somewhere somehow in their society is very very wrong and needs correcting.

These reactions on the part of a slowly increasing number of women provide hope for the future. One effect is that they are approaching their own personal situations with a far higher degree of objectivity and adaptiveness than heretofore. These same reactions will eventually lead even the most conventional middle-class women to recognize that if they really want to be of assistance to their beleaguered husbands, sons, brothers, fathers, and friends, they must go beyond their traditional role of providing them with emotional support and reassurance. They must also

recognize that the middle class's picture of the male adult role imposes an unreasonably demanding set of expectations on the individual male adult;

help their menfolk (especially their sons) recognize this as well, as the individual male's starting point for assessing his individual situation more impersonally and objectively;

play an active role alongside their men in the creation of a far more human and humane middle-class adult male life-pattern;

participate towards this and other relevant ends in the public political arena when their family situations and personal predilections and competencies allow them to do so.

In this sensitive area of human relations, as in other such areas in our society, it is cooperation between mutually accepting adults, rather than competition between mutually threatened children, which needs to become the norm.

I believe that these diverse self-corrective developments will merge, in the not very distant future, into a series of new and positive worldwide philosophical trends. Eastern and Western thinkers will alike seek meaningful integrations of Western conceptions of social justice and of the dignity and importance of the individual, with traditional Eastern concern for the exploration and development of the inner world of self—*without* recourse to drugs. A general, apparently humanly and socially natural tendency towards self-correction must in any case be one of our major hopes for the future. The great risk here, however, is that destructive trends are accelerating so rapidly, they may well have already far out-distanced more slowly emerging self-corrective trends.

There was for a time a flicker of evidence here and there that the radio and T.V. networks were at long last beginning, in their approach to programming, at least to escape the narrow confines of the huckster's preconceptions about human nature, if not his motives. For a time it appeared that those who control these powerful educative—for better or for worse—media were taking these basic considerations into account in their programming approaches:

1. In a complex, diverse, stratified, and age-graded society like ours, there are a number of *limited publics* with different backgrounds of values, knowledge, tastes, readinesses to be catered to, cultivated, developed—rather than that meaningless abstraction, "*the* consumer public."

2. Listener and viewer preferences cannot be accurately judged at present because the majority of the listening and viewing public are not given any real choice of program. There is practically no range of alternatives available to them: their only genuine choice is to look and listen or *not* to look and listen. Since most habitual T.V. viewers keep their sets on primarily because in their eyes "there is nothing better to do," this medium has a "captive audience" in the fullest sense of the term. The only way viewers can express an unfavorable reaction is to go out of their way not to buy a nationally merchandised product, or to complain in writing to the program's sponsors, and most people just can't be bothered to make this much of an issue of the situation.

3. The great majority of Americans have not been brought up to be sufficiently self-perceptive, nor have they been exposed to a wide enough variety of self-enlarging experiences, actually to be consciously aware of what they like, are interested in, are challenged by. They are able to express their preferences only in a negative, passive way: they will follow along behind a new pied piper for at least a few blocks—until boredom sets in again. Unfortunately, in their driving need to escape from the tension and drabness of their daily living, they do not realize, and have not been helped to realize, that escape to a higher level of knowledge and understanding and feeling is a good deal more personally satisfying and individually and socially adaptive than repetitively sterile flights from self.

4. No single, simple "entertainment formula" can hope to keep the *sustained* interest of any one of the limited publics referred to in point 1 above, because any such simple formula ignores the strong natural tendency of all but the most psychologically crippled human beings to grow, learn, and change. Even the most susceptible child grows into the skeptical teen-ager; the overstimulated teen-ager becomes the surfeited adult; even not-too-bright adults (of whom there are fewer than the level of most "popular" entertainment assumes) become bored rather quickly with a shallow, static approach to reality and to the human personality.

5. It is not until program producers and other creative and talented employees and contributors are permitted

to create for the various limited publics that make up the American audience;

to meet the educational challenge of changing each such public from its current level of knowledge, taste and self-expressive maturity to a more personally fulfilling and emergent level of under-standing and expression (*i.e.,* to "complexify" rather than to simplify);

to work on a collaborative basis with equally well-trained *and creative* persons in those professions which make use of the be-havioral sciences in their approach to human communication— gifted teachers of children and adults, recreational group workers, group and individual psychotherapists,

that these creative people can hope to retain and even to advance some individual standards of craftsmanship.

Instead of growing into a bright and steady light, these few hopeful flickers have died out since the foregoing analysis was written. The networks seem not to realize that they have no alternative but to mend their ways: Americans are beginning to wake up to the knowledge that there is no law or section in the Constitution which says that commercial sponsors are indispensable to the operation of our mass broadcasting media.[5] The introduction of an additional, tax-supported national radio and TV network, offering programs of the type of the BBC's Third and Second programs, is no longer as shocking to middle-class sensibilities as it once was. Its provision of a real range of program choice to listeners and viewers, and its un-

---

[5] George Kirstein's essay in *The Nation* of June 1, 1964, was so delightfully apt an example of this "awakening," it is, with the kind permission of *The Nation,* being reprinted in its entirety as Appendix A.

doubted role of upgrading the caliber of commercial network programming constitute inviting reasons for its serious consideration.

Other signs of revolt against the corporate giants are now abroad in the land. Who could have predicted even a short while ago that the stone from a David's slingshot (51), while not striking the automobile-complex Goliath fatally on the forehead, would at least cause that heretofore unchallengeable giant to wince in pain? Measures against air and water pollution and even against "poverty" (where *were* all those poor people during the Eisenhower years?) are also being proposed and a few enforced. But the piecemeal, exposé-book-selling character of these efforts leave me skeptical both as to their persistence and their actual effectiveness: widespread awareness of the depth, breadth and scope of the changes needed in American society is still lacking among the great bulk of the middle class.

It is important to recognize that "concerned gropers" are present as individuals, and sometimes as highly influential leaders, among occupational groups which have been notorious for their high degree of social irresponsibility. I am thinking particularly of the public relations people and of management consultants. There is no doubt that such people are also present on the boards of directors of at least a few of our very large corporations.

Substantial numbers of both pure and applied scientists have been awakening to the realization that they have responsibilities that go beyond their paid-occupation function (the Society for Social Responsibility in Science is no longer as alone as it was in 1955!). This realization is so far being expressed along chiefly two lines: first, the necessity to take an active interest *as citizens,* at the least, in the ways in which science's findings are being applied; and second, the recognition that *the scientist has community-wide obligations in addition to those of his employer.* The former responsibility has been expressed in the setting up of organizational and publication avenues for systematic exploration of related issues (e.g., the Committee on Science and Human Welfare of the American Association for the Advancement of Science; the Federation of American Scientists; the Bulletin of the Atomic Scientists) and by addressing a protest *as scientists* in the winter of 1967 to the President concerning our techniques of warfare in VietNam. An example of the latter responsibility was the formation of the Scientists' Institute for Public Information in 1963; it publishes the journal *Scientist and Citizen* and the theme of its May '67 conference was "Crisis in the (Physical) Environment: the Scientists' Responsibility to the Public."

Last but not least, I want to list the circumstance that ethical and/or self-corrective trends are present in many professional groups, even among advertisers! A wide and continuing variety of effective advertising copy which does not depend on the exploitation of human weaknesses for its appeal clearly attests that the battle between producer and consumer can be won by the former without his recourse through his advertiser to such "below the belt" tactics.

Accredited representatives of a number of professional groups have begun both to express open concern about the drop in public esteem of many professions and professionals, and to attempt to analyze the reasons for this development. As this chapter's finale, let me present three excerpts from a perceptive address on the changing role of the health and welfare professions in American society (61):

My general thesis here is that along with the trend toward creative health we are due to see what we might call a democratization or secularization of the health and welfare professions. As people less frequently encounter life-and-death urgency in the area of health and when people possess more general knowledge about the problems they do encounter, there will be a reduced inclination to let professional people plant themselves on priestly pedestals or to play the role of magical fixers.

Already we can see many signs among the more educated segments of society (not only!—AUTHOR) of a hostility to the expert who plays his role directively. To my mind the future will bring increased pressure on teachers, lawyers, physicians, dentists, psychologists, engineers, to work out a somewhat revised professional role. The ignorant and dependent man with an urgent problem gives himself gladly, body and soul, into the hands of an expert who can solve his problem. And the more godlike the expert, the greater the comfort in the dependency. On the other hand, an informed and independent man with a nonemergency problem will not take gracefully to the magical fixer, whatever the label in the fixer's professional hat. Such a citizen—and his tribe will increase—wants to solve his own problems in his own way. He wants a highly competent expert to give him information rather than preformed answers. He wants facts and cues about alternative ways he can interpret them. He will be resistant to prefabricated solutions handed him on a ritualistic platter. He wants to make his own decisions about his own welfare. And once he makes his own decision he will be much more inclined to act on it than on decisions handed down "from above."

It seems to me that in the years ahead all the health and welfare professions will have to move along a road already being explored by public health. Down this road there will be more education and less priestly mandate, more advice and less control, more consultation and less prescription, more facts and fewer arcane pronouncements. . . .

There is an implicit thing that might well be called the principle of *habeas mentem*—the right of a man to his own mind. In our system of justice we have, by building the principle of *habeas corpus* into precept and precedent, protected the right of a man to his own body. In the coming years, in order to keep our experts from imposing their ideas and values on the not-so-expert, we may need to weave into all codes of professional conduct the principle of *habeas mentem*. . . .

Does all this have anything to do with health? . . . Probably not, if the concept of health needs to carry on its back the present related concepts of "patient," of the "doctor-patient relationships" and "total responsibility." These health concepts, so vitally necessary in an era of urgency, may have a strait-jacketing effect on our attempts to solve the problems of an era of creative behavioral health. Coming concerns and coming opportunities to advance welfare should not and cannot be avoided on the grounds that they do not fit into existing conceptual pigeon holes or into existing institutional niches. [6]

---

[6] These excerpts have turned out to be a personal memorial to a very fine human being and probably the best executive secretary the American Psychological Association has had: word of Fillmore Sanford's death at the age of 53 was received just before this edition of *The Failure of Success* went to press.

Chapter Seventeen

A Time for Choosing

THE CIRCUMSTANCE that the American middle class has within it many potential followers for a movement involving self and social re-evaluation and even active means-goals experimentation may well constitute the most positive indicator of all for the future. But perhaps the most negative aspect of the middle-class situation today is that we of this group have as yet practically no leadership for such an endeavor, intellectual *or* political. Our former leaders in ideas and in social action have lost us, because they, like the majority of the middle class, are continuing to live in the past: economic and social changes have been so rapid, most of our liberal editors, political leaders, educators, scholars, and socially sensitive business men have not realized that the plight of the culturally submerged, self-unaware and self-deluded—but politically potent—middle class is today's number one social-political problem; and that programs aimed at the poor and at problems ostensibly associated with poverty will have only minor and temporary effects so long as this fact of contemporary American life continues to be ignored.

There is another gap in addition to that in generations which is contributing to our leadership vacuum. Our new generation of social scientists, whose ability, training and skills make them highly suitable candidates for leading at least the "ideas attack" on this new problem-front, are not showing the same idealism and social responsibility in regard to it as an earlier generation of social scientists displayed in relation to the labor movement. The inauspicious national climate set by the McCarthy investigations and the more recent "we must stay ahead of the Russians in destructive and space-exploration capacity" obsession are of course underlying factors discouraging such activity. But it is too easy to use this circumstance as an excuse. More concrete factors are at work, many of which have already been discussed.

Perhaps the most immediately relevant reason for this group's default is that our social and behavioral scientists, as members of our most recently "socially arrived" scientific and professional disciplines, are especially ego-involved in their personal and professional groups' status struggles. Many are psychologically adept at using their research activity on socially relevant problems as an escape from direct social commitment and responsibility. The most typical reason members of these groups themselves give for not assuming a special responsibility for social speculation is the traditional value system of science which they have borrowed from the physical sciences at the very time when physical scientists are themselves in process of discarding it: "Values are unscientific and have no place in any social or behavioral science worthy of the name."

When those of us who have chosen the individual and collective behavior of human beings as our field of study take refuge behind what was merely intended to be a prescription for ensuring objectivity in *methods of study,* we are not merely committing a serious error in logic. We are showing that we have not fully grasped as professional groups the implications of our having chosen as our vocation, first, a science, and second, the study of a valuing form of life. As scientists, we are forced to espouse values about the society in which we live and to defend those values, even if we subscribe to no more than these two beliefs—beliefs which are implicit in the role of "knower":

> Knowledge is better than ignorance.
>
> Conditions which promote knowledge are better than conditions which promote ignorance.

And when we choose to study the individual and collective behavior of a symbolizing and valuing being, rather than the individual and collective behavior of atoms, microbes, ants—or rats!—we automatically assume a special social responsibility which extends beyond even that imposed on us by our role as knower. Beyond all other scientific groups we must be concerned about the social end-uses of our and others' scientific knowledges and skills. Our society will in any case not allow us to abdicate from this special responsibility.

The circumstance that some sociologists and economists have recently joined the technocratic game of future-planning and are urging that "quality of life" be added as an explicit variable to sheerly economic and technological considerations in such planning (5, 33) has not led me to modify the pessimistic tone of this earlier-edition reminder. Rather, since these apparently sincere social scientists expect to work within the prevailing American value-orientation, this reminder has become still more relevant: like the strategists of the RAND Corporation and the physicists and psychologists of the space-exploration program and the biochemists hard at work developing yet-further biological and chemical means of destruction and "control," they see themselves as also an informed-technical elite with *specialized skills to be merchandised.* As such, they appear to be more than eager to assist the big B-I-G team in its steadily expanding role of first, deciding what is best for the "consuming masses," and second, imposing it on them.

Still another reason for our leadership vacuum is indeed ironic. Those rare-enough persons who do have an awareness of the nature and dimensions of the problem and the readiness to lead in the attack on it are in most cases unable to assume effective leadership: their own upper-class or second-generation upper-middle-class background of life experiences is so different from that of the social groups they wish to influence, they do not know how to establish communication with them.

From whatever segments of the population our future leaders eventually emerge, it is clear that we of the middle classes are today standing at a major fork in the road to our own and our country's future —although most of us are not aware we are doing so. We do not realize it because each of the diverging pathways, which we can see only up to its first major curve, is so different from the other. One road is so obviously superior in its traveling conditions there seems to be no real choice. This superior road, although it has developed some bad cracks and potholes, goes reassuringly straight ahead up to the turn up ahead—a direct, easily followed continuation of the apparently secure pavement on which we have been traveling for many years. In contrast, the other road is crudely cleared and still unsurfaced, with many jolting ruts and wavering turns—hardly more than a wagon-track.

But there is a catch in this apparently cut and dried situation. The lack of real choice is only illusory, as this little book has tried to point out. The as-yet bearable cracks and holes in the straight broad highway increase rapidly until it becomes a crumbled waste, around the curve past which we cannot see. The other road, past the turn around which we cannot see, shows marked improvement. First it is a well-kept gravel road, then a two-lane pavement, and then a six-lane superhighway! (But, ironically enough, even this wonderful highway will lead some future generation to another fork in the road like the one we are at today.)

What is the nature of this new pathway, the clearing and following of which requires of us even more of the pioneer spirit than our forefathers had?

My answer is not the enunciation of yet another simple individual or social panacea: I do not believe there can ever be a single touch-stone, a simple formula, an easy "short-cut" for the emergent, lifelong and ages-long interrelated processes of realization of self and realization of a just society. Probably the very first thing we need to do is to accept the idea that the road to personal and social salvation is a road leading to receding horizons. To seek for absolutes, and to impose them after we think we have found the right ones, is invariably to incorporate human misery and revolution into our "ideal of ideals."

The most we can do at any period is to *maintain the desire to achieve such salvation,* and never to give up actively *trying to approximate the means for achieving it.* Perhaps here are the new, more individually and socially adaptive goals that we of the middle class must sooner than later adopt.

These two goals will require far more of us than may at first be apparent. The accomplishment of either or both requires that we "break through" as a group to entirely new levels of social and political behavior. We are today faced with the seeming paradox that in order for each of us to retain any degree of freedom and identity as individuals—to realize our inalienable rights to whose implementation our Constitution is dedicated—each of us must seek to become

> highly self-disciplined;
>
> dedicated to the general welfare;
>
> able to participate effectively in a wide variety of politically-oriented group situations.

We must learn, in short, to take an active and effective hand in the shaping of our own destiny.

To adopt these goals will require that we place major stress upon two complementary activities. We must seek to develop a constantly broadening understanding both of man as a unique form of life and of the nature of the interrelationships between man's development as an individual and the functioning of his social institutions. Perhaps then we shall at last start to make real headway towards solving the key "preventive mental health" problems of any complex society:

What are the most species-suited ways of rearing and educating children?

What types of economic and social institutions and community environments are most suited to human beings at every stage of their development? [1]

Until we have further explored and come to understand much better than we do now, the influence on the growing, behaving individual of these two foci of social experience, I cannot accept the old theological thesis that has recently been again gaining ground, as rapidly among disillusioned "liberal intellectuals" as among, coincidentally enough, professional apologists for the current economic-cultural status quo—that man is by his very nature sinful and unimprovable morally. Like orthodox Freudian theory and related psychiatric practice, this thesis turns us back to the old obsessions with our guilt as individuals, and away from a continuing, objective examination and evaluation of social and economic trends in our world and of the interrelationships between social and individual disorganization.

Coincident with the study of "man in his society," we must seek to build into the social-political-economic-educational organizations of our society, values and forms which make possible a continuing process of social-problem formulation and problem solution. Preparation for active and effective participation in this process should become a major function of the family, our schools and our youth organizations; and *the process itself must begin and be maintained at such basic group-units as family, neighborhood, school, work situation, clubs, adult education groups, community forums* (20).

Having been so foolhardy as to come right out and advocate so— we are being constantly told—"un-American" an individual-citizen responsibility as broadly conceived social planning, let me compound my "sin" by reviewing the basic steps I believe are involved in effective, flexible planning from the point of view of the participating citizen:

first, the constant re-examination and reformulation of our over-all social goals;

second, improvement of the attitudinal and intellectual tools we need to have in order to do relevant problem-raising and problem-solving;

third, the formulation and reformulation, with the assistance of appro-

---

[1] The author has addressed herself to at least some aspects of these questions in the closing chapters of a recently published theoretical monograph (48).

priate specialists, of problems, questions, alternatives, of fundamental
social and individual significance;

fourth, the seeking out of the best answers we can work out to these
questions, making use of the best past and present knowledge and
evidence available to us, again enlisting the skills of appropriate
specialists;

fifth, directing our political representatives and our governments at the
different levels to put the answers we arrive at into practice—knowing
full well that by the time they have been put into practice, they will
already be somewhat out of line with changed circumstances and new
knowledges, so that

sixth and first, we must begin the process of examination, problem formulation and problem solution all over again.

This has been an abstract formulation—intentionally so, since the
particular functioning forms which such problems-centered social
planning will take is a future development. There are, however, a
number of already existing forms and practices which may be pointing towards that future. I see such activity not as replacing our present
self-governing machinery, but as functioning in complementary fashion with it. The White House Conferences are an outstanding example of interlocking local-national problem-motivated group organization. But the initial widespread citizen participation at the local
level, a more representative method of selecting national delegates, and
the direct tie-in with the legislative and executive branches of government, which would convert such cooperative citizen-specialist thinking
and discussion into actual social planning, is as yet lacking. Also,
White House Conferences are called at far-apart intervals, whereas
I hope for a time when such participant-citizen problem-discussion is
as familiar and welcome an aspect of our daily living as the World
Series is today.

For the sake of further clarity, let me project two specific examples,
the first one involving a relatively simple, relatively non-controversial
and tangible land-use issue on which a good deal of pertinent, "con-
census" data is already at hand; and the other involving a whole
set of complicated, highly controversial issues with practically no objective and disinterested research-in-information now available.

Perhaps our most crucial national problem, not just of the present
but increasingly so of the near and distant future, is our continuing,
systematic destruction of the earth's cover through spreading subur-
banization and more and more six- and eight-lane super-highways.

Underlying these trends are the more fundamental facts of a burgeon-
ing population and American business' commitment to encouragement of population growth as an answer to the not-to-be questioned
imperative of an ever expanding economy, regardless of the social and
psychological side effects of such population growth. These interrelated problems are being aggravated, as are most of our problems,
by the circumstance that the major interests involved in and affected
by it are not in direct communication, and tend to work at self-
interested cross-purposes with regard to them.

According to the formulation here suggested, a "national planning
committee" would be organized at the request of the President, with
two major functions:

> (1) to correlate, and to receive the fruits of, the activities of local citi-
> zens' groups meeting to discuss the same problem;
>
> (2) to come up with a series of concrete recommendations based both
> on the thinking of the national committee and the thinking of the
> various citizens' groups, these recommendations to be transmitted to
> the appropriate political bodies—Congressional and state legislative
> committees, and federal and state executive departments.

Better still, the *sponsoring* by the national committee of an organized
series of local and national conferences devoted to the various interrelated facets of the earth-cover-destruction problem seems indicated.

The national committee should be small enough in number to work
together effectively, but large enough to include representatives nominated by every one of the major interests directly involved in and
affected by this problem. To a layman in this specialized area, these
interests appear to be: conservation organizations, the automobile
manufacturing industry, the highway construction industry, the truck
and trailer manufacturing industry, the trucking industry, large manufacturing corporations, residents of urbia and suburbia represented in
sufficient numbers to constitute the balance of power in the committee
(say one-third of the membership). And, as paid advisers to the committee, an independent air- and land- traffic consultant, a town-and-
country planner, a social psychologist specializing in the psychological
effects of the urban and suburban environment, official spokesmen
for the major shadings of related policy among the organized religions,
and an applied social scientist to expedite the committee's deliberations.

With the transmission of its recommendations to the appropriate
political bodies, such a national planning committee would disband,

but the local groups would be free either to continue to function as a political-pressure medium, or to disband and make use of other already existing avenues of organized citizen action, including political-party machinery.

My second problem-example pertains to scientific and technological research and application *priorities*—i.e., to the issues of (a) which areas of human endeavor or concern should first receive the largest servings of investigative talent, time and moneys, and which somewhat less; and (b) which areas of already available and authenticated knowledge should be applied in what priority-order. Because of the specialized-knowledge character of both these issues and because of the lack of communication among the various scientific disciplines that specialization has led to, the basic first step would be to set up machinery which would enable members of the various disciplines to talk directly to each other in small-group contexts. Only *after* investigators have discussed among themselves such prior issues as (1) what is the present actual (not idealized!) role in American society of the pure-research scientist, the applied-research scientist, the research-engineer, and (2) what *should* be the social role of each of these scientist-categories, would they then discuss issues (a) and (b) above. Thereafter, a national planning committee (NPC) would be appointed and the citizen-groups steps of the planning process would be undertaken, much as in the first example.

The over-all planning process on this complex dual-problem is summarized in the following chart; letters denote the various types of planning (P)-groups, while the numbers 1, 2, 3, 4 denote the time-succession of the meetings of the various P-groups: note that some of these meetings are concurrent.

Planning-Group Composition and its Basic Task	Time-Sequence of P-Group Meetings	
	At the Local &/or Regional Level (& added tasks)	At the National Level
A. Pure scientists of each specialized discipline; to discuss both related and central issues within own professional organizations.	1 (Elect/appoint delegates to P-groups G and H.)	1
B. Applied scientists in each specialized discipline; same charge as for P-group A.	1 (Same as P-group A)	1

C. Pure scientists of *related groupings* of disciplines (i.e., of the physical, biological, behavioral, social sciences); same charge as P-group A.

	2	2
	(Same as P-group A)	

D. Applied scientists of same related groupings as in P-group C; same charge as P-group A.

	2	2
	(Same as P-group A)	

E. National Planning Committee appointed after prior consultation with relevant professional organizations *and brilliant mavericks;* to be composed of one pure-scientist and one applied-scientist from each of the four major discipline-groupings (= 8); plus lay-members drawn from service and civic organizations, large and small business, educators, labor-unions, college-student organizations (= 9); plus non-voting conference-expediters. The NPC should have the same functions as indicated for the first problem example, listed on page 187).

F. Self-educating citizen-groups, who will draw as needed on pure and applied investigative personnel chosen from lists prepared by P-groups A, B, C, D.

	3
	(Elect delegates to P-groups G and H)

G. Citizen-pure scientist mixture; to make specific recommendations bearing on the first central issue to the NPC.

4	4
(Make suggestions for improving future conference procedures)	(NPC)

H. Citizen-applied scientist mixture; to make specific recommendations bearing on the second central issue to the NPC.

4	4
(Same as P-group G)	(NPC)

With the transmission of its recommendations to the appropriate political bodies, the national planning committee would disband but, as in the first example, the local citizen-groups would be free either to continue to function as a political-pressure medium, or to disband and make use of other, already existing avenues of organized citizen action, including political-party apparati. The planning-machinery for this problem-area should be reactivated every five or six years—which is about the length of time the process described in the chart above would probably take from initiation to completion.

The individual-social process of problem-formulation and problem-solution here envisaged should be as continuing and as widespread as the biological presence of the human species. With the possible exception of the golden age of Greece and the few great thinkers of each age, the formulation and reformulation of social goals, of basic social alternatives, of viable political and legal forms, have gone on in a haphazard manner, rather than as the result of conscious and informed effort on the part of broad segments of a society's population. With machines geared to our needs rather than the other way around, we are at long last on the threshold of an age when not just the privileged and the delegated few have the time for such activities, but every one of us who has the capacity for socially responsible behavior.

Here, certainly, is a far more human type of concern and activity than the incessant pursuit of a self-imposed delusion, a pursuit so accurately described in this classic passage (17):

> They thirst for novelty, for unkown delights, for nameless sensations, which nevertheless lose all their savor as soon as they are experienced. Then let the slightest reverse occur and men are powerless to bear it. The whole fever drops and people discover how futile the whole uproar was, and realize that any number of these novel experiences piled up indefinitely has not succeeded in accumulating a solid capital of happiness on which they could live in times of trial . . .
>
> The man who always expected everything from the future, who has lived with his eyes riveted on what is to come, has nothing in his past to fortify him against the tribulations of the present; for the past has been but a series of way-stations which he passed through impatiently. He was able to blind himself about his own condition precisely because he continually counted on finding around the next corner that happiness which he had not yet encountered. . . .
>
> And meanwhile, these tendencies have become so strongly entrenched that society itself has got itself used to regarding them as normal. People repeat endlessly that it is in the nature of man to be eternally discontented, to move ever forward without truce or rest toward an unknown destination. The passion for the infinite is presented every day as a mark of moral distinction, when in fact it can come into existence only in rule-less minds which elevate to the dignity of rule the very rulelessness of which they are the victims. The doctrine of progress at any cost and as rapidly as possible has become an article of faith.

This behavior, observed by Durkheim to be typical of the newly expanded middle classes of Western Europe at the end of the last century, has become typical of the expanded middle class of our own country half-a-century later. *Shall we in the next half-century also follow the*

*social and political paths that many European countries followed
between 1890 and 1940?*[2]

The always—and legitimately—raised question "What can I as one
individual do towards bringing about social change?" deserves a direct
and definite answer. I believe one person can do a great deal—but
not primarily in the form of exhorting others to mend their ways.
Rather, the most effective action an individual can take is, first, to
do a good deal of intensive thinking through and about his own values,
attitudes, aspirations. And second, to try to act consistently in accordance with the inner convictions so in process of development, in a
steadily increasing number of day-in and day-out life situations. This
sort of individual action has far more social effect than almost anything else we may do. Behind any change in social norms widespread
enough and definite enough to become evident is this circumstance:
the *basis* for the change was laid down *prior to* its actual occurrence.
*That which precedes visible social change is the development of an
inner readiness for such change on the part of the individuals involved.*

While there is just such an inner readiness present among a wide
range of socially aware and concerned sub-groups within the middle
class—cause-organization members, college students, professors and
teachers, civil-rights leaders and workers, business-persons, political
representatives, mass-media personnel—members of each such grouping are as yet talking only among themselves about how serious the
inter- or intra-national situation is and how badly one or another
fundamental change in American life or foreign policy is/are needed.
If and when such persons find each other, either through the medium
of the new discussion-group initiatives described in the previous chapter and/or through some other, explicitly politically oriented avenues,
then the first step towards the accomplishment of such changes will
have been taken.

In anticipation of such discussions-towards-change groups, I am
proposing an agenda for their consideration, in the shape of a series
of issues facing our time and our country: this listing is included as
Appendix B.

It has been said that a mass-production economy makes the current
trend to a mass culture and mass uniformity inevitable. The relation-

---

[2] If the reader is not already familiar with Ortega's *The Revolt of the Masses*,
he/she is urged to endure the mind-expanding jolt not only of reading it, but
after doing so, of noting its original place *and date* of publication (55).

ship is by no means a necessary one. So long as we allow our humanity to be subservient to that economy, so long as we make material possessions and occupation our major symbols of personal status, and so long as we bring up our children to value and to strive to achieve such external-to-self symbols no matter what the inner cost to themselves of such achievement, so long shall we have mass uniformity and conformity—at least for those who don't break down completely under the competitive strain.

But if we encourage our children from their earliest years to be attentive to their own and others' inner strivings, creativity, uniqueness —to place human values first—a mass-production economy can have a very different effect. Attentiveness to one's uniqueness and inner needs fosters discrimination and selectivity in how one lives, whom one associates with, what one wears, how one chooses to spend leisure time. Mass production can then serve to provide all of us with as wide a variety for selective choice as was formerly available only to the fortunate few. The relationship, under these circumstances, can become: a mass-production economy fosters individual difference and creativity.

It is possible to treat the American middle class's present state of subservience to the touchstone fallacy lightly. It can be seen as no more than the traditional—and passing—problem of the newly rich. Some social analysts have argued somewhat as follows: because the general upgrading of the economic hierarchy has pushed so many of us into the unaccustomed status of *nouveau riche,* comparatively, all at once and so soon after a devastating decade of depression, our entire national life has become dominated by the typically shallow values and taste of those who have acquired the means but who have not yet acquired either the wisdom or the personal standards for responsible individual and social use of those means. Only time is required for the self-conscious, tense and boorish "new rich" to become the cultured, serene and gracious "old rich."

I prefer to interpret our present subservience from a different perspective. We "little people" are being propelled all at once and ill prepared into the second—and crucial—phase of one of the greatest social experiments of the ages. We are standing at an historic roadfork. With machine slaves to do our menial and monotonous work, we are for the first time in any complex society gaining the leisure and the means to live at a *human* level. Whether we are aware of it or not, it is *up to ourselves* whether we use our physical emancipation towards increasing our personal and social emancipation, or towards spreading the newest—as well as the oldest—form of slavery: slavery to ourselves.

A dozen years later, I am not able to muster the degree of optimism implied in the original edition's closing paragraph:

> We still have some control over the eventual verdict of history. Shall future historians date the mid-twentieth century as the period when the decline and fall of the great American experiment first became clearly evident, as Walter Lippmann believes it has (39) or as the period when we of the American middle classes began to face up squarely to the necessity for developing fresh social, political, individual means for our continuing emergence towards human status?

Although the increased rate of societal feedback has contributed to a much greater and more widespread awareness of the cruciality of our predicament, the majority of both the older and the younger generations of the American middle classes have continued in the interim to escape from, rather than face up to, themselves and our steadily deteriorating situation.

This edition is being ended, much more pessimistically, with excerpts from statements by Archibald MacLeish and Tom Wicker, respectively:

> "History, like a badly constructed concert-hall, has occasional dead spots where the music can't be heard. Everything in the United States today—the boredom of the young, the numbness of the arts and the ineptitude of the politicians—indicates that we are caught in one of them. No matter how we crane our necks and cock our ears we seem unable to catch the tune.
>
> "The reason, I think, is fairly clear. We can't make out the tune of the time because we are still back behind it in the 1950s with the dilapidated bulk of 'anti-Communism' against our faces. . .
>
> "Once we recognize as a nation that 'anti-Communism,' like all the rest of the anti-isms, is not an effective policy or, indeed, a policy at all—once we recognize as a nation that *the only defense against the purposes of others is a better purpose of our own*—we may very possibly regain the freedom of action we have been progressively losing ever since VietNam began if not since Foster Dulles" (40).
>
> "VietNam and the racial question are the most dramatic and emotional issues in contemporary American life. They cause profound reactions among those concerned, and hone questions of personal responsibility to a far sharper point than most political or social situations. Therefore, the intellectuals anguished at the war and the Negroes who

have all but abandoned hope for white recognition of their humanity, have
only been forced more quickly than most others to the knowledge that
in the vast impersonality of the 20th century society and government,
it has become almost impossible for individuals to affect the grinding
course of things.

"*That* is the malaise beyond dissent—the fear that dissent does not
matter any more; that only action counts; but that no one really knows
what action to take. More and more, 20th century man crouches like
an old woman on her stoop, pointing her rusty shotgun at the oncoming
expressway, knowing all the time that in the end the bulldozers will go
through" (75).

References

1. ADLER, R., and ROSS, J.: You've Gotta Have Heart. Song from *Damnyankees*.
2. ADORNO, T.W., *et al.*: *The Prejudiced Personality*. Harper, 1950.
3. ALLEN, FRED: *Treadmill To Oblivion*. Little, Brown, 1954.
4. ARROWSMITH, WILLIAM: *The Future of Teaching*. Address at the opening general session of the American Council on Education 49th Annual Meeting, 1966.
5. BAUER, R.A. (ed.): *Social Indicators*. MIT Press, 1966.
6. BENEDICT, RUTH: *Patterns of Culture*. Penguin Books, 1934.
7. MILLER, D.T.: *Jacksonian Aristocracy: Class and Democracy in New York 1830-1860*. Oxford University Press, 1967.
8. BOGUE, D.J.: *The Population of the United States*. The Free Press, 1959.
9. BRONFENBRENNER, URI: The Changing American Child—A Speculative Analysis. *Journal of Social Issues, 17(1)*: 6-17, 1961.
10. BRONFENBRENNER, URI: Socialization and Social Class through Time and Space. *In* E.E. Maccoby *et al.* (eds.): *Readings in Social Psychology*, 3rd ed. Holt, 1958.
11. CLECKLEY, H.M.: *The Mask of Sanity*, 4th ed. C.V. Mosby Co., 1964.
12. COHEN, A.K.: *Delinquent Boys: The Culture of the Gang*. Free Press, 1955.
13. DAVIDSON, BILL: How to Think Your Way to the Top. *Collier's*, Feb'55.
14. DAVIS, ALLISON: American Status Systems and the Socialization of the Child. *Amer. Sociological Review, 6*:345-54, 1941.
15. DAVIS, A.: Socialization and Adolescent Personality. Chap. XI in the 43rd Yearbook of the Natl. Assn. for the Study of Education, part 1, *Adolescence*, 198-216, 1944.
16. DAVIS, A., and HAVIGHURST, R.J.: Social Class and Color Differences in Child-rearing. *Amer. Soc. Rev., 11*:698-710, 1946.
17. DURKHEIM, EMILE: On Anomie, pp. 272-8 of *Le Suicide, Etude de Sociologie*. Felix Alcan, 1897.
18. DUVALL, E. M.: Conceptions of Parenthood. *Amer. J. Sociol., 11*:193-203, 1946.
19. ERICSON, M.C.: Child Rearing and Social Status. *Amer. J. Sociol., 11*:190-2, 1946.
20. FOLLET, M.P.: *The New State*. Longman's, Green, 1918.
21. FOOTE, N.N., and HATT, P.K.: Social Mobility and Economic Advancement. *Amer. Econ. Rev., 43(2)*:364-378, 1953.
22. FRIEDAN, B.: *The Feminine Mystique*. Norton, 1963.
23. FRIEDENBERG, E.Z.: *Coming of Age in America, Growth and Acquiescence*. Random House, 1965.
24. FRIEDENBERG, E.Z.: *The Vanishing Adolescent*. Beacon Press, 1959.
25. FROMM, ERICH: *Escape from Freedom*. Rinehart, 1941.
26. GIBRAN, K.: *The Prophet*. A.A. Knopf, 1923, page 55.
27. GREEN, A.W.: The Middle-class Male Child and Neurosis. *Amer. Sociol. Rev., 11*:31-41, 1946.

28. HAZLEWOOD, LEE: The song *Sugartown.*
29. HERBERS, J.: Malaise in Congress. Item in *New York Times,* 3-20-67.
30. HORNEY, K.: *Neurotic Personality of Our Time.* Norton, 1937.
31. HUTCHINS, R.: The University and the Multiversity. *The Nation,* 15-17, April 1, 1967.
32. JACKSON, S.: *The Lottery.* Farrar, Straus, 1949.
33. KOPKIND, A.: The Future-Planners. *New Republic,* 19-23, Feb. 25, 1967.
34. KORZYBSKI, A.: *Time-Binding, the General Theory.* Inst. of General Semantics, 1949.
35. LEE, A. McL.: Institutional and Organizational Research in Sociology. *Amer. Sociol. Rev., 16(5)*:70107, 1951.
36. LERNER, P.: *The Nazi Elite.* Hoover Inst. Studies, Stanford University Press, 1951.
37. LEWIN, K.: Group Decision and Social Change. *In* T.M. Newcomb and E.L. Hartley (eds.) : *Readings in Social Psychology.* Holt, 1947, 330-344.
38. *Life,* Dec. 26, 1955.
39. LIPPMANN, W.: *Essays in the Public Philosophy.* Little, Brown, 1955.
40. MACLEISH, A.: The Seat Behind the Pillar. *New York Times* editorial page, Jan. 21, 1967.
41. MAUSNER, B., and J.: Study of the Anti-scientific Attitude. *Scientific American, 192(24)*:35-39, 1955.
42. MEAD, G.H.: *Mind, Self and Society.* University of Chicago Press, 1934.
43. MILLER, D.W., and SWANSON, G.E.: *The Changing American Family.* Wiley, 1958.
44. MILLER, H.P.: *Rich Man, Poor Man.* Crowell, 1964.
45. MILLER, W.: Old Man's Advice to Youth. *Life,* May 2, 1955.
46. MILLS, C.W.: *White Collar.* Oxford University Press, 1953.
47. MILNER, E.: A Species Theory of Anxiety. *Review of Existential Psychol. and Psychiat., 3(3)*:227-236, 1963.
48. MILNER, E.: *Human Neural and Behavioral Development: A Relational Inquiry,* with implications for personality. Thomas, 1967.
49. MILNER, E.: New Frontiers in Personality Theory. *J. Nat. Assn. Deans of Women, 17(3)*:105-119, 1954.
50. MURPHY, G.: Human Potentialities. *J. Soc. Issues,* 1953, Suppl. Series No. 7.
51. NADER, R.: *Unsafe At Any Speed.* Grossman, 1965.
52. *New York Sunday News,* photostory, Feb. 12, 1967.
53. *New York Times,* news item, March 1967.
54. NORDSTROM, C., FRIEDENBERG, E.Z., and GOLD, H.A.: *Society's Children:* A study of ressentiment in the secondary school. Random House, 1967.
55. ORTEGA, Y GASSET, J.: *The Revolt of the Masses.* Norton, 1932. (Spanish edition 1930.)
56. POHL, F., and KORNBLUTH, C.M.: *The Space Merchants.* Ballantine Books, 1953.
57. Presbyterian Lay Committee, advertisement in the *New York Times,* Dec. 27/66.
58. RIESMAN, D.: *The Lonely Crowd.* Yale University Press, 1950.
59. RIESMAN, D.: Some Observations on Changes in Leisure Attitudes. *Antioch Review,* 417-436, 1952-3.

60. ROGOFF, N.: Recent Trends in Urban Occupational Mobility. *In* P.K. Hatt and A.J. Riess, Jr. (eds.): *Reader in Urban Sociology.* Free Press, 1951, 406-420.

61. SANFORD, F.H.: (Then Executive Secretary of the American Psychological Assn.) Talk delivered to the 83rd annual meeting of the American Public Health Assn., 1955.

62. SEARS, R.R., *et al.*: *Patterns of Child Rearing.* Row, Peterson, 1957.

63. SELLTIZ, C., and WORMSER, M.H. (eds.): Community Self-Surveys: An Approach to Social Change. *J. Soc. Issues, 5(2):* 1949.

64. SROLE, L., *et al.*: *Mental Health in the Metropolis.* McGraw-Hill, 1962.

65. STRECKER, E.A.: *Their Mothers' Sons.* Lippincott, 1946.

66. TAWNEY, R. H.: *The Acquisitive Society.* Harcourt, Brace, 1920.

67. United States Dept. Of Labor, Women's Bureau, Leaflet 11, 1953.

68. WALLICH, H.C.: Column in *Newsweek* of Dec. 26, 1966.

69. WARNER, W.L., and LUNT, P.S.: *Social Life of a Modern Community.* Yale University Press, 1941.

70. WARNER, W.L., *et al.*: *Democracy in Jonesville.* Harper, 1949.

71. WARNER, W.L., *et al.*: *Social Class in America.* Science Research Assoc., 1949.

72. WEAVER, S.: Statement on radio program, *Youth Wants to Know*, WRCA, June 5, 1955.

73. WEBER, M.: *The Protestant Ethic and the Spirit of Capitalism.* Allen and Unwin, 1930.

74. WHITING, J.W.M., and CHILD, I.L.: *Child Training and Personality.* Yale University Press, 1953, chapter 4.

75. WICKER, TOM: The Malaise Beyond Dissent. Editorial page of *New York Times,* March 12, 1967.

76. WILLHELM, S.M., and POWELL, E.H.: Who Needs the Negro? *Trans-Action, 1(6):*3-6, 1964.

77. WILSON, C.: *The Outsider.* V. Gollancz, 1956.

78. WORTHY, W.: Interviewed by Charles Collingwood, WCBS, Dec. 14, 1955.

79. WOUK, H.: *The Caine Mutiny.* Doubleday, 1951.

80. MIEL, A.: *The Shortchanged Children of Suburbia.* Inst. of Human Relations Press, American Jewish Committee, 1967.

Appendix A

The Day the Ads Stopped [1]

GEORGE G. KIRSTEIN

THE DAY THE advertising stopped began just like any other day—the sun came up, the milk was delivered and people started for work. I noticed the first difference when I went out on the porch to pick up *The New York Times*. The news-dealer had advised me that the paper would now cost 50c a day so I was prepared for the new price beneath the weather forecast, but the paper was thinner than a Saturday edition in summer. I hefted it thoughtfully, and reflected that there really was no alternative to taking the *Times*. The *News* had suspended publication the day before the advertising stopped with a final gallant editorial blast at the Supreme Court which had declared the advertising prohibition constitutional. The *Herald Tribune* was continuing to publish, also at 50c, but almost no one was taking both papers and I preferred the *Times*.

As I glanced past the big headlines chronicling the foreign news, my eye was caught by a smaller bank:

1 KILLED, 1 INJURED IN
ELEVATOR ACCIDENT AT MACY'S.

The story was rather routine; a child had somehow gotten into the elevator pit and his mother had tried to rescue him. The elevator had descended, killing the woman, but fortunately had stopped before crushing the child. It was not so much the story as its locale that drew my attention. I realized that this was the first time in a full, rich life that I had ever read a newspaper account of an accident in a department store. I had suspected that these misfortunes befell stores, as they do all business institutions, but this was my first confirmation.

There were other noticeable changes in the *Times*. Accounts of traffic accidents now actually gave the manufacturers' names of the vehicles involved as, "A Cadillac driven by Harvey Gilmore demol-

---

[1] Reprinted in full from the June 1, 1964 issue of *The Nation*, with permission.

ished a Volkswagen operated by. . . ." The feature column on
"Advertising" which used to tell what agencies had lost what accounts
and what assistant vice president had been elevated was missing. As
a matter of fact, the whole newspaper, but particularly the Financial
Section, exhibited a dearth of "news" stories which could not possibly
interest anyone but the persons mentioned. Apparently, without major
expenditures for advertising, the promotion of Gimbels' stocking buyer
to assistant merchandise manager was not quite as "newsworthy" as
it had been only yesterday. Movies and plays were listed in their
familiar spot, as were descriptions of available apartments in what
used to be the classified section. The women's page was largely a
catalogue of special offerings in department and food stores, but no
comparative prices were given and all adjectives were omitted. One
could no longer discover from reading the *Times,* or any other paper,
who had been named Miss National Car Care Queen or who had
won the Miss Rheingold contest.

Driving to work, I observed workmen removing the billboards. The
grass and trees behind the wall of signs were beginning to reappear.
The ragged posters were being ripped from their familiar locations
on the walls of warehouses and stores, and the natural ugliness of
these structures was once more apparent without the augmenting
tawdriness of last year's political posters or last week's neighborhood
movie schedules.

I turned on the car radio to the subscription FM station to which I
had sent my $10 dues. The music came over the air without interrup-
tion, and after awhile a news announcer gave an uninterrupted version of current events and the weather outlook. No one yet knew
which radio stations would be able to continue broadcasting. It
depended on the loyalty with which their listeners continued to send
in their subscription dues. However, their prospects were better than
fair, for everyone realized that, since all merchandise which had previously been advertised would cost considerably less on the store
counter, people would have funds available to pay for the news they
read or the music or other programs they listened to. The absence of
the familiar commercials, the jingles, the songs and the endless repetition of the nonsense which had routinely offended our ears led me
to consider some of these savings. My wife's lipsticks would now cost
half as much as previously; the famous brand soaps were selling at
25 per cent below yesterday's prices; razor blades were 10 per cent
cheaper; and other appliances and merchandise which had previously
been nationally advertised were reduced by an average of 5 per cent.

The hallowed myth that retail prices did not reflect the additional cost of huge advertising campaigns was exploded once and for all. Certainly these savings should add up to enough for me to pay for what I listened to on my favorite radio station or read in the newspaper of my choice.

After parking my car, I passed the familiar newsstand between the garage and the office. "*Life* $1," the printed sign said. *Time* and *Newsweek,* 75c." Next to these announcements was a crayon-scrawled message: "*Consumer Reports* sold out. Bigger shipment next week." I stopped to chat with the newsie. "The mags like *Consumer Reports* that tell the truth about products are selling like crazy," he told me. "*Reader's Digest* is running a merchandise analysis section next month." I asked about the weekly journals of opinion. He said, "Well now they are half the price of the news magazines—*The Nation* and *The New Republic* prices have not gone up, you know, but I don't think that will help them much. After all, a lot of magazines are going to begin printing that exposé-type stuff. Besides, people are buying books now. Look!" He pointed across the street to the paperback bookstore where a crowd was milling around as though a fire sale were in progress.

I walked over to the bookstore and found no special event going on. But books represented much better value than magazines or newspapers, now that the latter were no longer subsidized by advertisements, and the public was snapping up the volumes.

Sitting in my office, I reviewed the events and the extraordinary political coalition that had been responsible for passing the advertising prohibition law through Congress by a close margin. The women, of course, had been the spearhead of the drive. Not since the Anti-Saloon-League days and the militant woman-suffrage movement at the beginning of the century had women organized so militantly or expended energy more tirelessly in pursuit of their objective. Their slogans were geared to two main themes which reflected their major grievances. The first slogan, "Stop making our kids killers," was geared mainly to the anti-television campaign. The sadism, killing and assorted violence which filled the TV screens over all channels from early morning to late at night had finally so outraged mothers' groups, PTAs and other organizations concerned with the country's youth that a massive parents' movement was mobilized.

The thrust of the women's drive was embodied in their effective two-word motto, "Stop lying." Women's organizations all over the country established committees to study all advertisements. For the first time in history, these common messages were analyzed in detail. The results were published in anti-advertising advertisements, by chain letter and by mouth. The results were devastating. No dog-food manufacturer could claim that pets loved his product without having the women demand, "How in the name of truth do you know? Did you interview the dogs?" No shampoo or cosmetic preparation could use the customary blandishments without having the women produce some witch who had used the particular product and who had lost her hair, developed acne or had her fingernails curl back.

Women led the attack, but the intellectuals soon joined them, and the clergy followed a little later. The intellectuals based their campaign largely on the argument that the English language was losing its usefulness, that word meanings were being so corrupted that it was almost impossible to teach youth to read to any purpose. One example commonly cited was the debasement of the superlative "greatest." The word had come to mean anything that didn't break down; viz., "the greatest lawn mower ever," interpreted realistically, was an instrument that, with luck, would cut grass for one summer. The clergy's campaign was geared simply to the proposition that it was impossible to teach people the virtues of truth when half-truths and lies were the commonly accepted fare of readers and viewers alike.

Opposition to the anti-advertising law was impressive, and at the beginning it looked as if all the big guns were arrayed against the women. Spokesmen for big business contended throughout the campaign that elimination of advertising meant elimination of jobs. The fallacy of this argument was soon exposed when all realized that it was not men's jobs but simply machine running time that was involved. By this decade of the century, the cybernetic revolution had developed to a point where very few men were involved in any of the production or distribution processes. No one could feel much sympathy for the poor machines and their companion computers because they would be running only four hours daily instead of six.

Some merchants tried to blunt the "stop lying" slogan by telling the absolute truth. One San Francisco store advertised:

2,000 overcoats — only $12. Let's face it — our buyer goofed! These coats are dogs or you couldn't possibly buy them at this price. We're losing our shirt on this sale and the buyer has been fired. But, at least, many of these coats will keep you warm.

The trouble with this technique was that it backfired in favor of the women. The few true ads, by contrast, drew attention to the vast volume of exaggeration, misrepresentation and outright lies that were printed as usual. The advertising industry published thirteen different editions of its "Advertisers Code" in the years preceding the law's passage, but few could detect any difference from the days when no code at all existed.

The press, of course, was the strongest opponent and loudest voice against the advertising prohibition. Its argument was largely legalistic, based on the First Amendment to the Constitution, for the publishers had decided at the outset of their defense not to emphasize the fact that if advertising stopped, readers would actually have to pay for what they read, rather than have America's largest corporations pay for the education and edification of the public. However, the words "Free Press" came to have a double meaning—both an unhampered press and a press that charged only a nominal fee for the publications.

The constitutional argument was really resolved in that final speech on the floor of the Senate before a gallery-packed audience by Senator Thorndike of Idaho. His memorable ovation, certainly among the greatest in the Senate's distinguished history, concluded:

And so, Mr. President, the opponents of this measure [the advertising prohibition] *claim that the founders of this republic, our glorious forefathers, in their august wisdom, forbade the Congress to interfere with the freedom of the press to conduct itself in any way it found profitable. But I say to you, that the framers of our Constitution intended to protect the public by permitting the press, without fear or favor, to examine all of the institutions of our democracy. Our forefathers planned a press free to criticize, free to analyze, free to dissent. They did not plan a subsidized press, a conformist press, a prostitute press.*

The applause was thunderous and the bill squeaked through the Senate by four votes. Three years later, the Supreme Court upheld Senator Thorndike's interpretation. That was two days ago, and today the advertising stopped.

All morning I worked in the office, and just before noon I went uptown for lunch. The subway cars were as drab as ever and seemed a little less bright because of the absence of the familiar posters. However, in one car the Camera Club of the Technical Trades High School had "hung" a show of New York City photographs chosen from student submissions. In another car, the posters on one side carried Session I of a course in Spanish for English-speaking riders, while the opposite side featured the same course in English for those speaking Spanish. This program was sponsored by the Board of

Education which had subcontracted the administration of it to the Berlitz School. A poster in both languages in the middle of the car explained that the lessons would proceed on a weekly basis and that by sending $1 to the Board of Education, review sheets and periodic tests would be available upon request.

On Madison Avenue, the shopping crowds were milling around as usual, but there was a noticeable absence of preoccupied and hatless young men hurrying along the street. The retirement plan that the advertising industry had worked out through the insurance companies was fairly generous, and the majority of key personnel that had been laid off when the agencies closed were relieved not to have to make the long trek from Westport or the nearer suburbs each day. Some of the copywriters who had been talking about it since their youth were now really going to write that novel.

Others had set up shop as public relations counselors, but the outlook for their craft was not bright. Without the club of advertising, city editors looked over mimeographed press releases with a new distaste, and it is even rumored that on some newspapers the orders had come down to throw out all such "handouts" without exception. On the magazines, the old struggle between the editorial staff and the advertising sales staff for dominance had finally been resolved by the elimination of the latter. There were even some skeptics who believed that public relations counseling would become a lost art, like hand basket-weaving. So most former advertising copywriters planned to potter about in their gardens, cure their ulcers and give up drinking. They were not so many. It was a surprise to most people to learn that the advertising industry, which had had such a profound effect on the country's habits and moral attitudes, directly employed fewer than 100,000 people.

Outside 383 Madison Avenue, moving vans were unloading scientific equipment and laboratory accessories into the space vacated by Batten, Barton, Durstine & Osborn. The ethical drug industry had evolved a plan, in the three-year interim between the passage of the advertising prohibition and the Supreme Court's validation of it, to test all new drugs at a central impartial laboratory. Computers and other of the latest information-gathering machinery were massed in the space vacated by this large advertising agency to correlate the results of drug tests which were being conducted in hospitals, clinics, laboratories and doctors' offices throughout the world.

The Ford Foundation had given one of its richest grants, nearly three-quarters of a billion dollars, to the establishment of this Central

Testing Bureau. The American Medical Association had finally agreed, under considerable public pressure, to take primary responsibility for its administration. It was pointed out to the doctors that when the drug companies could no longer make their individual claims through advertisements in the AMA bulletin or the medical society publications, a new and more reliable method of disseminating information would be required. At the outset, the AMA had joined the drug companies in fighting bitterly against the prohibition, but the doctors now took considerable pride in their centralized research and correlation facilities. The AMA bulletin, once swollen to the bulk of a small city's telephone directory, was now only as thick as a summer issue of *Newsweek*. Doctors no longer would find their mail boxes stuffed with throw-away material and sample pills; but they would receive the weekly scientific report from Central Testing Bureau as to the efficacy of and experience with all new preparations.

Late in the afternoon, I began to hear the first complaints about the way the new law worked. One of the men came in and picked up a folder of paper matches lying on my desk. "I'm swiping these; they're not giving them out any more, you know." Someone else who had been watching TV said that the two channels assigned to the government under a setup like that of the B.B.C., were boring. One channel showed the ball game, but the other had been limited to a short session of the Senate debating the farm bill, and a one-hour view of the UN Security Council taking up the latest African crisis. My informant told me the Yanks had won 8 to 0, and the Senate and the UN weren't worth watching. I reminded him that when the channel that was to be supervised by the American Academy of Arts and Sciences got on the air, as well as the one to be managed by a committee of the local universities, things might improve. "Cheer up," I told him, "At least it's better than the Westerns and the hair rinses."

Oh, there were some complaints, all right, and I suppose there were some unhappy people. But personally I thought the day the advertising stopped was the best day America had had since the last war ended.

Appendix B

Suggested Agenda for Discussion-Groups

IT IS BY NOW a cliché to say that we are living in a "period of transition." It is not as obvious, unfortunately, that we—decent American citizens—are either going to make a great many fundamental and difficult choices/decisions during the next five to ten years or *have them made for us.* Involved are decisions which will determine not only the direction and the shape of our society and of the individual life-career for generations to come, but even whether man and his social institutions are to survive in other-than-primitive forms. Not to enter actively into the making of these decisions itself constitutes a choice on our parts, since our default automatically permits a particular course of action to win out.

The crucial areas of choice, together with the alternative directions which may be taken with regard to them—as seen by this writer—are listed below (in a non-impartial manner!) :

1. In our increasingly complex, increasingly interdependent society, informed, coordinated social planning can no longer be postponed. Is it to be done by technical elites in big-government and big-industry and imposed from the top down, *or* should it be done through broadly based citizen-specialist collaboration, utilizing forms of communication, deliberation and representation yet to be, or in process of being, developed?

2. The present rate and scope of technological conversion to automated and cybernated production and distribution systems on a unilateral, solely profit-motivated basis allow one to describe the situation as the "second industrial revolution." We are all aware of the social and the individual impact—and still existing political effects—of the first, also unplanned and unilaterally imposed, industrial revolution. Is the second one also to be carried out without deliberative regard for its effects on society, on the individual life-career, on our physical environment—*or* is technology to be made subservient to man?

Fundamental to this complex and controversial area of choice are at least these societal and individual priority and/or value issues:

(a) Do human beings have social value only as consumers towards the end of advancing business and industry, or does business have value to the extent that it contributes to our advancement as growing human beings?

(b) Qualified analysts tell us that once the "second industrial revolution" is accomplished, there will be only three "classes" on the basis of occupation and employment status (in addition to a very small number of owners/employers) : a small group of professional and technical employed, a somewhat larger group of service and entertainment employed—and a great mass of unemployed. Should we simply sit back and let this pattern develop, so encouraging the emergence of a new feudalism with its attendant "nobodiness" for the masses, *or* should we begin *now* to counteract the social impact of this eventuality by instituting such measures as:
—broadening the definition of a service occupation and upgrading markedly such occupations' status and remuneration;
—introducing school curricula which will prepare everyone for constructive and creative use of leisure and for knowledgeable political participation;
—deciding how the profits earned by the work of the new machines are to be distributed?

(c) Should human beings be expected to adjust to whatever physical and social living and working conditions are available to them, or should our living/working environments be designed to meet the human needs of children, adolescents, mothers and fathers, families, adult men and women, older people?

(d) From the point of view of our society's occupational elite and the messages of our mass media, is the good life to continue to be considered/projected as a combination of individual competitive achievement of a constantly higher material standard of living and of power, economic and emotional, over others? Or is a comfortable physical standard of living for self and for everyone to be seen/projected primarily *as a pre-condition* for a more psychologically mature conception of the good life: as involving life-long striving for self-understanding and self-fulfillment, together with dedication—and service! — to ends higher than one's infantile-level appetites and finite existence?

(e) Concerning the social functions of pure and of applied science in these United States: Should the major efforts of research and theoretical scientists continue to be invested in currently acceptable problems—i.e., for which special-interest grants are readily available, *or* should the long-term-development needs of (1) our *and* world society and (2) their particular science, play much greater roles in the choice and formulation of problems investigated than they do at present? Should applied scientists/technologists continue to serve the special interest of whosoever pays their salaries and/or research grants *regardless of the social impact of the product/findings so sponsored,* or should they themselves, with the assistance of informed and responsible social-awareness analysts, have a direct voice in the making of decisions concerning the problems they are to investigate and the products they are to produce?

(f) As for public investment in basic and applied research and development, should the overwhelmingly major proportion of it continue to be deployed to support the discovery and/or continuing refinement of means of waging war *or* should such public investment be divided at least evenly between research on ideas and issues bearing on the control and prevention of war *and* research on means of destruction?

3. In our increasingly complex, fragmented and bewildered society, our eye and ear mass media can perform two functions of great integrative potentiality: they can put any group of persons anywhere in our country in immediate and direct communication with any other group anywhere else in our country or the world; and they can act as the best-informed and up-to-date private tutor ever available to man. Shall these media continue to be used towards the almost-exclusive ends of private profit and escapist entertainment *or* should they be treated as our most essential and precious *and powerful* public utility?

4. Concerning how our military power and our technological sophistication are to be used to forward our interests in the rest of the world, particularly in politically unstable, economically underdeveloped countries: Do we concur with the Executive Branch's (of

both Democratic and Republican administrations) unpublicized top-level policy-decision to support by CIA-arranged underground activity or by direct force of arms or both, any indigenous ruling-clique which is willing to cooperate with American business' desire for unabating, unregulated expansion, regardless of that clique's domestic representativeness—do we concur, that is, with a policy of active intervention to prevent the emergence to governmental control of regimes more popularly constituted but probably less accommodative to that desire? Or do we prefer to influence the politics and the way of life of other, developing countries less directly, primarily by exemplifying in the conduct of our own society the blessings of our economic system and of the American way of life, and secondarily by sharing our technological expertise, trained personnel and other surplus resources upon UN-channeled request—and to signal that decision to both major political parties in some unequivocal way?

5. Concerning the role and management of public education,
   (a) What should the *primary* goal of our public-school system be: to prepare technical and professional workers, either terminally, or through education for entry into colleges which serve the personnel-needs of industry at a higher level? Or should our lower schools' basic efforts be to educate towards creative leisure, informed and responsible parenthood, informed and responsible citizenship, broadly defined; and those of our higher-education institutions be for the full and creative use of the intellect and other uniquely human abilities and sensitivities?
   (b) A further, directly related choice-polarity bears on the qualifications we prefer in those whom we delegate to teach our children and on their role in the conduct of our schools and colleges. Should the dominant practiced criterion for retention of teachers of every school-level continue to be their unquestioning willingness to carry out the wishes of (politically appointed/elected) local school-boards and/or to fit smoothly into a mammoth bureaucracy—i.e., to be good civil-servants; *or* should those who teach be selected and retained for a combination of intellectual and professional excellence: creativity and independence of mind and positive personal impact on those whom they teach, and shall they share *equally and directly* with lay-citizens in the school-governing responsibility?

6. Most United States citizens—and most organized programs—approach the "population explosion" in sheerly economic and eco-

logical terms *and* as applying to Brazil and to India but not to these United States. The circumstance that increasing population also has major psychological and sociological—and political!—implications here at home is almost invariably overlooked, both in its present, still-exploding phase and if and when currently expanding efforts to slow it down hopefully succeed. These limitations of outlook prompt the posing of at least these three sets of alternatives:

(a) Shall each individual parental couple continue to see themselves as the sole arbiter of how many children they shall beget and rear—a right we want to deny to the poor and to persons in already-overcrowded lands? Or must we, as informed and responsible *citizens,* look ahead to the sociological and psychological and ecological and political effects of a completely urbanized North America?

(b) Let us suppose that efforts to convince all women everywhere to bear and rear no more than two or three children are eventually effective: how are most women to spend their lives after the age of 35 in these United States?

(c) As the population increases, more food and hard and soft goods will be produced/processed. Shall each particular company/industry continue to be the sole arbiter of its operations' impact on our common physical environment *or* is the long-term welfare of all of us to take precedence over short-term, special, interest?

7. Should the time and creative efforts of those in our healing professions—and of related research workers in the physiological and behavioral sciences—continue to be directed almost exclusively towards trying to repair the damage after it's been done? Or should far greater proportions of these persons' talent and time be channeled into preventive approaches; as, for example, coordinated, high-powered and creative interdisciplinary efforts to derive answers to such fundamental questions as:

What are the most species-suited ways of rearing and educating children? What types of social and economic and physical and community environments are most suited to human beings at each successive stage of their development?

8. (Issues of war and peace have been deliberately left to the last, in the belief that such issues represent a macroscopic level of analysis —that is, that such issues can be more meaningfully formulated *after* issues which bear on our tendency to be war-prone have been referred to.) Social and economic and national and international

political life in both the United States and the Union of Soviet Socialist Republics represents a direct or an indirect continuation of European patterns of believing and feeling and behaving and thinking—concepts and practices of the good life, of the nature of man, of the proper relationships between man and nature, man and man, man and woman, parent and child, government and citizen—which have made "western civilization" the most aggressive/destructive cultural tradition in the chronology of the human species. Shall we continue to follow in this tradition to the bloody end—a return to the caves of the few members of the human species who would survive a short nuclear war or a prolonged global convulsion? Or shall we begin actively to strive towards the development of a *post*-European version of man and of society, a version which will, hopefully, represent an emergence to higher levels of humanity?

Which of these choices do you take issue with, as formulated? Which additional choice-areas should have been included? Concerning each set of choices, how can we set about deciding which is the wiser choice? Or would some third, here-unenunciated alternative be the preferable one?

Once we do decide, how can we influence those who now hold economic and political power to see it our way?

Index

Selected Publications and Papers
By Esther Milner

BOOKS

The Failure of Success, The American Crisis in Values, First Ed. (M.s. written 1954-6) Exposition Press, 1959.

Human Neural and Behavioral Development: A Relational Inquiry, with implications for personality. Springfield, Thomas, 1967.

ARTICLES

Effects of sex-role and social status on the early-adolescent personality. *Genetic Psychology Monographs, 40:*231-325, 1949.

The role of anxiety in individual functioning. *Canadian Journal of Psychology, IV(3):*127-135, 1950.

A study of the relationship between reading readiness in Grade I schoolchildren and patterns of parent-child interaction. *Child Development, 22(2):*95-112, 1951. Since reprinted in whole or in part in:

F. DAMBROT *et al.* (eds.): *Readings for General Psychology* (for University of Akron closed-circuit TV course). Wm. C. Brown, 1965.

S.L. ELAM (ed.): *Readings in Child and Adolescent Psychology.* Selected Academic Readings, 1966.

Is it only readiness for reading that is involved? *The Reading Teacher, 6(2):* 9-17, 1952.

Some hypotheses concerning the influence of segregation on Negro personality development. *Psychiatry, 16(3):*291-7, 1953.

New frontiers in personality theory. *Journal of the National Association of Deans of Women, 17(3):*105-119, 1954.

Differing observational perspectives as a barrier to communication among behavioral scientists. *Review of Existential Psychology and Psychiatry, II(3),* 1962, 249-257.

A species theory of anxiety. *Review of Existential Psychology and Psychiatry, III(3):*227-236, 1963.

PAPERS

A Study of Student Preferences in Class Structuring and Teaching Method. Presented to the American Psychological Association 1948 annual conference.

A Species Theory of Anxiety. Presented to the XVth International Congress of Psychology, Brussels, 1957.

Social Irresponsibility among Those in Higher Status Occupations: A Social-psychological Analysis. Presented to the American Psychological Assoc. 1958 annual conference.

Differing Observational Perspectives as a Barrier to Communication among Behavioral Scientists. Presented to the XIVth International Conference of Applied Psychology, Copenhagen, 1961.

Psychological Implications of Increasing Population: Some Questions That Need Answering. Presented to the American Assoc. for the Advancement of Science 1962 annual conference.

Is the Current American Way of Life Making American Women and the Mothering Process Incompatible? Contribution to a multi-discipline panel on "The Mothering Process" presented to the American Psychiatric Assoc. 1963 conference.

Disarmament Planning: The Need for a Broader Frame of Reference. Presented to the Second International Arms Control and Disarmament Symposium, 1964.

Papers prepared and delivered to community groups under the auspices of the Dept. of Extra-mural Studies, Aberdeen University, Scotland, 1966: (1) *The Impact of the 'Second Industrial Revolution' on American Adolescents.* (2) *Resolved: That Women's Emerging Freedom of Choice Is a Good Thing for Society — and for Women.*

Cultural Impediments to Adequate Mothering. Presented to the Association of Workers for Maladjusted Children, Scottish Division, Edinburgh, 1966. Since reproduced in part in *Dialogue on Women,* Robert Theobald, ed., Bobbs-Merrill, 1967.